Breakthrough
Consulting

FINANCIAL TIMES
Prentice Hall

In an increasingly competitive world, it is quality
of thinking that gives an edge. An idea that opens new
doors, a technique that solves a problem, or an insight
that simply helps make sense of it all.

We work with leading authors in the fields of
management and finance to bring cutting-edge thinking
and best learning practice to a global market.

Under a range of leading imprints, including
Financial Times Prentice Hall, we create world-class
print publications and electronic products giving readers
knowledge and understanding which can then be
applied, whether studying or at work.

To find out more about our business and professional
products, you can visit us at www.business-minds.com

For other Pearson Education publications, visit
www.pearsoned-ema.com

Pearson
Education

Breakthrough Consulting

SO YOU WANT TO BE A CONSULTANT?
TURN YOUR EXPERTISE INTO A
SUCCESSFUL CONSULTING BUSINESS

Alex Dembitz and James Essinger

FINANCIAL TIMES
Prentice Hall

An imprint of Pearson Education

London · New York · San Francisco · Toronto · Sydney · Tokyo · Singapore
Hong Kong · Cape Town · Madrid · Amsterdam · Munich · Paris · Milan

PEARSON EDUCATION LIMITED

Head Office
Edinburgh Gate
Harlow CM20 2JE
Tel: +44 (0)1279 623623
Fax: +44 (0)1279 431059

London Office:
128 Long Acre
London WC2E 9AN
Tel: +44 (0)20 7447 2000
Fax: +44 (0)20 7240 5771
Website: www.business-minds.com

First published in Great Britain in 2000

© Pearson Education Limited 2000

The right of Alex Dembitz and James Essinger to be identified
as authors of this work has been asserted by them in accordance
with the Copyright, Designs and Patents Act 1988.

ISBN 0 273 63707 X

British Library Cataloguing in Publication Data
A CIP catalogue record for this book can be obtained from the British Library.

10 9 8 7 6 5 4 3 2 1

Typeset by Northern Phototypesetting Co. Ltd, Bolton
Printed and bound in Great Britain by Biddles Ltd, Guildford & King's Lynn

The Publishers' policy is to use paper manufactured from sustainable forests.

Contents

Acknowledgements

Our most fervent thanks go to our colleague Helen Wylie, who helped us greatly with text production and made many insightful and useful editorial suggestions. Helen really is one in a million.

We thank also our publishers, Pradeep Jethi and Richard Stagg, for suggesting to us that we might write this book, for bearing with us during delivery delays caused by pressure of consulting work, and for their extremely helpful editorial comments.

Finally, we thank all the consulting organizations that responded to our questionnaire and took time to provide illuminating and detailed responses. We are particularly grateful to Peter Robin of IBM for his hard work, his criteria for evaluating aspiring consultants that he kindly allowed us to reproduce as Appendix 2, and for drawing our attention to the passage in Exodus 18.

Getting to grips with consulting

Consulting: a phenomenon and an opportunity

Breakthrough Consulting is about the consulting business, a wonderfully interesting and exciting industry which is both a *phenomenon* and an *opportunity*.

Consulting – the phenomenon

The consulting industry is a *phenomenon* because over the past 20 years, and especially during the past five, it has enjoyed growth rates that are unprecedented and which show no signs of slowing in their momentum. Setting down financial figures here for the size of the consulting business would be futile: they would be out of date within a year or so. It is enough to say that consulting is a major multi-billion dollar industry in the United States and around the world.

Consulting – the opportunity

The consulting industry is also an *opportunity* because of the prodigious possibilities for career development and very substantial income which it offers to those who have the skill, intelligence and determination to take advantage of them.

Consulting is, in fact, one of the few professions in the world that makes a significant proportion of its practitioners rich, and many of its practitioners very rich indeed.

What this book will do for you

Breakthrough Consulting tells you everything you need to know about the consulting industry to make a great success of it specifically if you are about to enter it for the first time. Our aim has been to produce a book that provides comprehensive provocation for the mind, practical advice, solid theory, and generally expresses our personal philosophy of consulting: that like love, it is more about giving than taking.

This is not to say that *Breakthrough Consulting* applies trendy modern theories of nebulous emotional matters to the extremely hard-headed business of consulting. But we stick by our guns in how we see the essence of what consulting is all about.

At a more subtle level, consulting *must* be more about giving than taking because ultimately it works only if the consultant has a service to offer – one consisting, typically, of elements such as strategic advice, practical skills, contacts and general inspiration – whose value exceeds what the user is paying for it. Above all, you will enjoy the true pleasure of being a consultant only if you are aware that what you are doing for your clients is of greater value than what they are paying for.

Why another book about consulting?

There are many books about consulting on the market, so why do we believe there is a need for another one?

It has been said that writers write because they cannot find the book they most want to read. This is certainly true of us. We have written *Breakthrough Consulting* because we cannot find in the marketplace (not even on the vast shelves of business books at our regular haunts of John F. Kennedy and Heathrow airports) the consulting book we most want to read.

What kind of book is that exactly? It is not only a book that is full of useful, hands-on practical advice but one that is also intensely human and respects and accommodates the fact that it is personality that wins business for consultants as much as technical skills. It is a book that is stimulating yet fun to read, not full of management jargon or so stuffed with flow charts and diagrams that it looks more like a school textbook than something to be enjoyed by adults. It is a book that does not regard clients as pitiable dupes to be fleeced of their cash with maximum haste but rather sees them as collaborators or partners with whom great and successful initiatives can be shared.

There is, quite simply, no other way to work with clients because if the work consultants undertake for them is not a true collaboration or a real partnership, it cannot possibly be of value.

All great consultancies – and we mean great here in the sense that they are great to work with, that the people who work in them are great to be with, and that the consultancies delight their clients – need to be customer-care consultancies. Their very essence must be about looking after their clients and helping them to resolve their problems and grow.

Why have we called it *Breakthrough Consulting*? Because our overriding aim is to help you break through any barriers which may inhibit you from fulfilling the outer limits of your potential as far as your enjoyment of consulting is concerned and the income you derive from it. We see our job, then, as to write not only the consulting book *we* most want to read but also the one *you* most want to read – a book that helps you to break through and build a successful career in consulting.

Who are we?

Before we start on our journey with you, we ought to say something about ourselves. As you will see from the front cover and the title pages, *Breakthrough Consulting* is a kind of authorial joint venture. It seems to us self-evident that there is no justification for an authorial collaboration if the resulting book is not going to be better than anything which either author could have produced working alone. In the case of *Breakthrough Consulting*, we have welded our minds together for the simple reason that we believe we can best produce this consulting book by working in collaboration. Our experience to date is radically different, and each of us has set ourselves the objective of bringing the best of himself to this book.

One of us (Alex Dembitz) is the founder of the international consultancy IDOM SA, which during the late 1980s and the 1990s played a major role in bringing Western standards of business administration and software to industries in Central Europe which were managing the difficult transition from centrally planned to market economies. The IDOM Group grew at an unprecedented rate. Within six years of its foundation, it had a presence in 13 countries and employed 300 consultants.

In 1993, Alex realized that the best needs of his clients would be served by IDOM becoming part of a larger organization, and so he merged the IDOM Group with the international professional services organization Deloitte & Touche. Alex now acts as a consultant in a private capacity to many fast-growing organizations. He has a particular interest in helping start-ups with ambitious expansion plans, and he also lectures on business in leading business schools.

The other (James Essinger) is a prolific writer who has published more than 25 business books. He has published a short book about consulting, designed for readers entering the consulting business for the first time, but that book, *Starting a High-income Consultancy* (first published in 1994 by Pitman Publishing, now Pearson Education), is superseded by *Breakthrough Consulting*.

The material we aim to cover

Business books need to be written in an interesting way, but they are not literary works. The purpose of a business book is to be thought-provoking and interesting, and to communicate useful information which the reader can apply to his or her career.

In *Breakthrough Consulting*, we aim to cover the following – in our view – essential points: why consulting has become a major global industry; how, if you are not a consultant already, you can decide whether you will make a good one, and if necessary how you can change your attitude towards certain aspects of yourself and business in order to be a better consultant; how, if you *are* a consultant already, you can become a better one; how to start and run a successful consultancy or consulting division; how to minimize the financial risk of operating a consulting business; how to make your clients think you are wonderful; how to put into practice our guiding principle that being a consultant is more about giving than taking; how to work out what you should charge; how to write stunning proposals and reports; how to promote yourself and your consultancy; how to decide when you should expand your consultancy and how to go about it.

> For full information about *Breakthrough Consulting* and for further help with turning your expertise into a successful consulting career, go to www.breakthroughconsulting.co.uk

CHAPTER ONE

Consulting talk

Why has consulting become a major global industry?

Consulting can attribute most of its success as an industry or profession to certain important political and economic changes during the past 20 years. In developed countries, the business world of today has changed out of recognition compared to that of 30, or even 20 years ago.

There are many reasons for the sweeping changes in the nature of the business world. The main ones are as follows.

Political stability

Since the 1970s the developed world has enjoyed considerable political stability, especially since the collapse of communism in East/Central Europe and Russia.

The impact of information technology

Computers have given organizations of all kinds unprecedented levels of control over the information needed to make a business successful. Information relating to production, productivity, financial management and general management is available today at the push of a button. From a business standpoint, technology is a highly democratizing force: software packages which embody all types of hard-won business skills can give even the smallest organization access to state-of-the-art management techniques. Technology consequently tends to increase competitiveness throughout industry and commerce, bestowing the particular benefits of efficiency, quality of customer service, and speed to market of innovations, and tending to place a special premium on know-how generally.

The impact of the Internet: the new economy

New communications technology such as computerized data communications and the Internet have created a true global communications village in which a business's physical location can often be irrelevant. The growing importance of e-business (the entirety of business activity conducted over the World Wide Web) and e-commerce (specifically, buying and selling via the Web) are such that almost every organization of any size has little choice but to seek to exploit the possibilities this technology offers.

Technical sophistication of business

There is a marked tendency for the activities of commercial organizations to become generally more complex and technically more demanding. This happens for similar reasons to why it happens in disciplines such as the physical sciences and medicine: as time goes by these sciences and disciplines simply accumulate more and more knowledge. A specialist in almost any field needs to know more about his chosen subject than his predecessor did even 20 or 30 years ago. A modern hospital doctor, for example, needs to know vastly more than a hospital doctor of the 1950s, simply because there is more knowledge available.

This accumulation of expertise is enhanced by the commercial fact that organizations tend to maximize profitability when they specialize in what they do best. This point has been the focus of much discussion by business thinkers in recent years. The general consensus is that for most organizations, what they do best will form the true basis of the 'mandate' their customers give them, and the organizations will tend to maximize their sales revenue if they focus on what customers really want. The importance of this concept has been emphasized by business writers such as Charles Handy. It goes a long way to explaining why outsourcing – paying others to operate functions which are not part of one's core activities – is enjoying an unprecedented popularity that shows no signs of diminishing. In any event, it is incontestable that an increasing number of organizations depend for their leading edge development (such development is often, not entirely facetiously, called 'bleeding-edge development') on technical specialists. Frequently, for reasons that are discussed in greater detail below, an organization will choose to gain access to such specialists' expertise by hiring them as consultants.

Increasingly homogeneous national markets

All these developments have conspired to create increasingly homogeneous global markets, with local differences between the types of demand in specific national markets becoming superficial, and sometimes irrelevant. This has led to a situation where the rewards for an organization adopting a global perspective are potentially enormous. Conversely, organizations can no longer expect to be protected from foreign competition by a successful tradition of market penetration at home; increasingly these domestic markets are open to aggressive competitors from abroad which have the requisite know-how and financial muscle to put it into practice. Generally, the rewards for excellence, true entrepreneurial flair, efficiency in internal operation, speed to market of new products, competitiveness in export sales and general competitive excellence have never been greater than they are today.

Increases in customer expectations

There has been an enormous surge in consumers' knowledge of what is available in the marketplace, and a corresponding decrease in customer loyalty. Today, more than ever, organizations need to have a thorough and deep understanding of their markets, to be absolutely certain about the type of benefit they offer their customers, and to do their utmost to keep on refining and developing their customer value proposition (CVP).

Deregulation

In recent years governments have tended to recognize the importance of maximizing the efficiency of the business sector by dismantling legislation which has in the past limited competitiveness. Such legislation has often made it difficult for newcomers to enter industrial and commercial sectors. As a result of deregulation, competition and competitiveness have exploded in many industries, with inefficient organizations either being forced to increase their competitive power or be eliminated.

A prime implication of these developments is that the demand for external advisers is huge – organizations of all kinds will want people who provide the specialized expertise which helps them to realize their potential in the enormously exciting business world of today. Enterprising, intelligent, articulate and success-driven people who have the talent, commitment and specialized skill will find that consulting can offer a career where the sky really is the limit. Incidentally, you will find it difficult to practise successfully as a consultant unless you *do* have a specialized skill to offer – general consulting advice is only occasionally required and in any case tends to be supplied by consultants who specialize in some area.

The appeal of consulting

What about money? Many successful consultants enjoy an annual income well into six figures, and some earn a good deal more. It is increasingly possible for an independent consultant, who is billable for 80 per cent of his time, to aim realistically for an annual income in the vicinity of $200 000. Many do better even than that. Furthermore, those consultants who set up their own consulting organization which, if it has delivered client satisfaction and won loyalty from major clients, may become an extremely valuable property which the founder can sell, thereby achieving considerable personal wealth. Ironically, in our experience, many consultants who become millionaires in this way nevertheless continue to work as con-sultants, in spite of their financial security. Make no mistake, consulting can be a delight, and the more successful you are at it, the more of a delight it is. Once the consulting bug bites you, you tend to stay bitten.

Quite apart from the financial considerations, however, the great appeal of consulting to many people – especially those who are intellectually gifted – is that being a consultant is, or should be, extremely *interesting*. Almost by definition, a new day in the life of a consultant will present a variety of new challenges, even if some of these are new versions of challenges that have been faced before. The variety stems to some extent from the fact that consulting remains an interpersonal business. Consultants are not (or should not be) robots who supply a stock response to a situation. They tend to be well educated, and genuinely interested in meeting their clients' needs. They need to have the general quality of intellect and cultural background that makes them interesting people on whom a client is proud and pleased to rely. And because by its very nature consulting work tends to be leading-edge from a knowledge and know-how point of view, it should never become boring or repetitive: if it does, the consultant can be pretty certain that he (we stick to *he* from now on, but note that many fine consultants are women) is doing a bad job. Consulting is not something a person of the calibre to become a star consultant is ever likely to find dull.

Definitions

According to the *Oxford English Dictionary*, the first use of the word 'consult' in the sense of 'ask advice of, seek counsel from; to have recourse to for instruction or professional advice' dates back surprisingly far, to 1635. The first recorded use of the word 'consultant' in English occurred in 1697, but then it meant the opposite of what it means today. People in the 18th century thought of a consultant as someone who consults something, such as an oracle. It was not until 1878 that the modern meaning appeared as someone *who is consulted*. By then, it was increasingly common to refer to a professional such as a consulting physician or consulting engineer as a 'consultant', and in medicine the term is still used to denote a doctor who is an expert on a particular type of ailment or part of the body.

And here we have the point: a consultant has to be an expert *at* something. It is difficult, though not impossible, for someone to practise as a consultant unless they have some proven expertise in a particular discipline. Some experts do need to acquire officially recognized qualifications – in medicine, engineering and some areas of the financial sector, for example. But generally all you need to do is convince a prospective client of your skill.

We make this point early on because it explains why there are many more bad consultants than good ones. Sadly, bad consultants make life difficult for the good ones who are genuinely committed to providing value for money and looking after their clients. Because personality and charisma are so important in the winning of business for consultants, there is always a danger that somebody whose expertise consists *only* of personality and charisma will win business even if he does not have the skill to back it up.

Happily, the increasing complexity and competitive demands of both the private and public sectors make clients much more selective when it comes to appointing consultants. A successful track record is immensely important, and consultants who are not able to carry out assignments properly are finding themselves without clients. Yet despite the high standards many consultants achieve, there is still a perception among some clients that consultants can be a waste of money, and that too many consultants, in effect, do little more than borrow your watch and tell you the time, then expect to be paid for doing so.

As a practising or would-be consultant who is (we hope) committed to giving his best to his clients, you need to be prepared for clients to start off by having a comparatively low expectation of what you might be able to do for them. It is perfectly possible for this attitude to co-exist with a desperate need on their part for your help. Perhaps the client will have had a disastrous experience with consultants in the past. Faced with this situation, it hardly needs adding that you will not only be engaging on the client's project, you will also be aiming to redeem your client's view of consultants.

In order to emphasize our belief that a consultant needs to take a pride in providing a service which will meet, and indeed exceed, expectations, we propose our own definition of 'consultant' for the purposes of *Breakthrough Consulting*. Our definition is:

A person who makes a living from providing professional advice to a client that the client is unable to provide for itself, or which it is not economic for the client to provide for itself.

The principle enshrined in this definition is essential to the work of the best consultants. They have a knowledge of the subject, an ability to communicate that knowledge, and the skill to put those recommendations into place, perhaps by heading an implementation team.

But a *really* good consultant is much more even than that. A consultant in the best sense of the word can galvanize an organization into attaining triumphs which are well beyond what the organization ever imagined to be possible. That is the kind of consultant we want you to aspire to, if you aren't already.

The origins of consulting

Consulting is not just a job, it is a profession. Even more than that, it is a vocation. Star consultants are special people: leaders of society, thinkers, innovators, people who make things happen, who make businesses more efficient and more effective, who, generally, make society – and the world – a better place.

It is not difficult to imagine how prehistoric human communities would have attributed status to knowledgeable elders who understood matters which the tribe regarded as extremely important. The secrets of producing fire on demand, the expertise to carve or chip effective weapons, or advise on which plants and fungi were edible and which would kill – knowledge such as this would surely have won status and rewards for those who possessed it.

The societies of Ancient Rome and Greece offer many examples of the importance of thinkers and practitioners in different disciplines. These people may be seen as the Classical equivalent of consultants – consider for example, the nature of the Socratic dialogue, in which the young knowledge seeker adopts a deliberately humble role when asking advice of the philosopher.

All human cultures prize the wisdom of an elder or some person in authority whose advice is regarded as so valuable that it is seen as close to divine, or actually so, in origin. In Jewish culture, for example, the rabbi (the word means 'teacher') is not only someone to be consulted on religious matters but also a person to provide moral and practical guidance. A remarkable passage in Exodus 18 vs 13–27 has Jethro – Moses' father-in-law – advising Moses to stop trying to be the only person who gives the people advice because this is too exhausting for Moses and means that the people are kept waiting many hours. Instead, Jethro counsels Moses to select capable men from the people and appoint them as officials who can decide all simple cases, with Moses himself only deciding the most difficult cases. Was Jethro the world's first management consultant? Possibly.

The importance of the wise elder is shown in a more frivolous way in the song which the milkman Tevye sings in the musical *Fiddler on the Roof*, the plot of which is based closely on stories that have been part of Jewish folklore for centuries.

In the song 'If I Were a Rich Man', Tevye tells of his yearning to be rich and successful, and how if he were, he would be revered by his community:

'The most important men in town would come to fawn on me.
They'd ask me to advise them, like King Solomon the wise …
And it wouldn't make one bit of difference if I answer right or wrong
When you're rich, they think you really know!'

What the song is saying is relevant to consulting today. Tevye is in effect reminding us that much of the status of an adviser, elder, shaman, rabbi, guru or whatever depends on him being perceived as *really knowing*: in other words, that as a consultant he enjoys a reverence among those who seek knowledge.

From a psychological perspective, this reverence is of great importance, for two reasons. First, the fact that we do respect the advice makes us more likely to take it seriously and to put it into practice, which is necessary if it is going to do us any good. Second, the status of the guru or teacher gives us the psychological comfort of knowing there is somebody who will help us or advise in a moment of difficulty or crisis. Incidentally, Tevye's dream reference to himself as rich and, consequently, someone people consult, is more subtle than it seems: earlier in the song, he has emphasized that wealth would free him from his daily drudgery and enable him to devote time to study which would, in turn, help to make him someone who could be consulted.

Tevye's song also emphasizes the power of the rich man/elder/teacher in people's lives. However, a consultant needs to have the moral fibre and courage to admit when he does *not* know something, or knows an insufficient amount about the matter in hand. This can be a difficult thing to confess, especially if you have been hired at a high rate to provide advice. There is nothing wrong with confessing to a gap in your knowledge. Doing so will not make you look stupid; indeed, your client will usually respect you for your honesty. But there is a way of doing it. The best procedure is to say, 'I don't know this, but I will find it out', and give yourself a tight deadline for doing so. You should certainly have enough contacts and resources to turn to – any consultant worth his salt should be able to find out any important fact within 24 hours of being set the task.

The notion of mutual co-operation

It is common practice for all types of closed societies to cultivate a mystique and aura of exclusiveness so that their members retain the status they need if their advice is to be followed. One big drawback to such a culture of the 'exclusiveness of the expert' is that what is deemed to be important are the privileges of the expert rather than the job they need to do. In fact, economic and social progress has frequently been shown to depend not on the creation of barriers to the dissemination of know-how but on mutual co-operation and assistance.

Ideas emphasizing the importance of such mutual co-operation and assistance usually receive bad press in highly competitive market economies, but this does not dilute their importance. With this in mind, it is relevant to regard as one of the intellectual ancestors of modern consulting the somewhat unlikely figure of Russian revolutionary Peter Kropotkin (1842–1921), the foremost theorist of the anarchist movement.

An almost forgotten social theory today, anarchism was maligned by its detractors (and there were plenty of them) who saw it as the advocacy of mere lawlessness. Kropotkin was anything but a saint – he advocated violence in the pursuit of his aims, and he hated his enemies with a vengeance – but he deserves credit for pointing out the importance of the cultural and economic principle of co-operation. In his book *Mutual Aid*, which made a considerable impact internationally when it came out in 1902, Kropotkin argued that despite the Darwinist concept of the 'survival of the fittest', the chief factor in the evolution of species was in fact not conflict but co-operation. Providing numerous examples, he showed that co-operation is a dominant aspect at every level of the animal world.

Among humans, too, he found that mutual aid had been the rule rather than the exception. Kropotkin traced the evolution of voluntary co-operation from the primitive tribe, peasant village, and medieval commune to a variety of modern associations – trade unions, learned societies, the Red Cross – which he saw as having continued to practise mutual support despite the rise of the coercive bureaucratic state. The trend of modern history, Kropotkin believed, was pointing back towards decentralized, non-political, co-operative societies in which people could develop their creative faculties without interference from rulers, priests or soldiers.

Kropotkin's identification of the significance of such bodies as trade unions and learned societies in providing mutual support (he did not mention medieval trade guilds, but no doubt he would have seen them in a similar light) is evidence that his perspective on human society was uncannily close to the new attitudes that underline a perception of the importance of organizations sourcing expertise from external service providers. Even more to the point, he emphasized the principle of mutual aid and support in co-operation. In much the same way, the most successful consulting relationships between client and consultant are creative, long-term, mutually supportive collaborations based on achieving essentially shared goals; a partnership in which both parties benefit, rather than a constant battle to get the better of each other.

Ideally, a consultant should not only have that type of collaboration in mind as the ideal goal but should also be prepared to show commitment to it. Consulting is either creative and collaborative or it is nothing.

Types of consulting activity

There are as many different types of consulting as there are clients needing advice. In consulting, there is a very real sense in which every client needs – and should receive – a tailor-made service which may in fact involve several different types of consulting advice or guidance. In practice, though, it is necessary for consultants to operate under specific categories of consulting.

Management consulting – the provision of a range of consulting services to the management of organizations – is the most widespread type of commercial consulting, but it is a mistake to assume that other types of consulting activity are unimportant. Management consulting typically involves advising organizations on one or more of the following activities:

○ business process re-engineering (BPR) – this is a somewhat pompous term meaning 'doing the same or new things more efficiently than you did them before';

○ commercial strategy;

○ competitive effectiveness;

○ dealing with new regulations;

○ improving all aspects of customer service;

○ managing change;

○ rethinking the nature of core activity;

○ using outsourcing as a tool to enable greater focus to be placed on core activity.

Some areas of management consulting have become so specialized that they are now usually regarded as individual types of consulting in their own right (see below). The usual clients of management consulting are for-profit and non-profit organizations that want to make a concerted effort to maximize their success.

Breakthrough Consulting is geared towards helping you make a success of working as a management consultant, but our thinking applies to *all* types of consulting. Examples of other popular types of consulting are as follows:

○ *Financial management consulting:* advising clients on any aspect of their organization's financial management, and setting up accounting and financial management systems;

○ *Human resources consulting:* advising on the use of human resources. This often includes providing related services such as outplacement, executive search and selection, head-hunting and compensation planning;

○ *Information technology consulting:* advising on the use of information technology, such as the selection of hardware and software and systems integration;

○ *Marketing consulting:* advising clients on any aspect of marketing, such as advertising, sales promotion and public relations and sales training.

In practice, once a consultant has established a good relationship with a client, they will often move on to advising clients about other activities beyond their initial remit. For example, it is fairly common for an IT consultant to get involved with such areas as BPR and strategic consulting. However, it remains useful to categorize different types of consulting because there is, in fact, a distinct trend today towards specialization of the consulting function.

Types of client

A consultant's clients may be any of the following:

○ individuals;

○ small informal groups of people with common interests;

○ charities;

○ pension funds;

○ other types of organization set up to benefit others;

○ public bodies employing many thousands of people;

○ commercial organizations such as partnerships, private companies or public companies.

Note, however, that whatever the nature of the organization, a consultant tends to report to a specific individual at the client organization, even though he may interface in his work with many people there. Furthermore, the decision on whether to hire the consultant is often taken by just one person. These two points are extremely important from the perspective of how a consultant develops his activities and is given full consideration in the next chapter.

Note also that there is an increasing tendency among public bodies to seek the same standards of excellence and customer service to which commercial organizations aspire. This trend has been initiated by governments which have grown tired of the wastefulness of many public bodies and the often low levels of service they provide. Public bodies nowadays are expected to perform to the highest standards and will have specific performance targets which they are required to attain.

Types of consultancy involvement

Just as there are different types of consultant and client there are different types of consultancy involvement. The most important of these are:

○ the amount of time the consultancy devotes to the client;

○ the difficulty of the project;

○ the additional resources that the consultant brings to the project;

○ the importance of the project to the client;

○ whether the consultant works on the project at his own premises or at the client's premises;

○ the revenue the project brings to the consultancy.

Typical frameworks for consultant involvement are listed in ascending order of 'intensity' of involvement.

○ *Provision of remote strategic advice:* here, the consultant is both geographically and culturally at a distance and is usually asked to provide advice based on reading documentation. This type of consulting is increasingly rare in today's hands-on environment.

○ *Provision of strategic advice based on on-site research:* this takes the first type of intervention a stage further. The consultant visits the client and will typically hold several meetings with client staff members. However, the consultant will usually write the report at his own premises and may or may not implement his recommendations himself. There is a definite trend towards consultants implementing advice they provide rather than merely writing a report. The only type of consulting where it is usual for the client to carry out the implementation is strategic consulting, where the consultant provides strategic advice which the client will then consider and act on as it thinks fit.

○ *The consultant spends part of his working week at the client's premises:* here, the consultant starts to become a definite part of the organization's resources.

○ *The consultant works full-time at the client's premises:* this is self-explanatory. The consultant remains an independent external resource but for reasons of convenience works full-time at the client's premises. Typically, however, he will not become a salaried member of staff but will be paid on a project basis or a time/materials basis. Working full-time at a client's premises for a defined period is particularly common among IT consultants, who are usually needed to implement a system they have specified or designed. For example, IDOM's consultants often worked full-time at a particular client's premises, sometimes for several months on end. However, they remained consultants and were paid by IDOM, not directly by the client. IT consulting is particularly likely to be a hands-on form of consulting, with many IT consultants spending much of their time writing code (i.e. software) for their clients, and also engaged on specific activity to build or otherwise implement a system.

Good and bad consultants

There is little point doing anything in life if you are not going to excel at it, and consulting is no exception. Equally to the point, only a good consultant is likely to do well, and only an extremely good consultant is likely to do very well.

In consulting, as with so many other areas of human activity, quality is everything. Just as the difference between an Oscar-winning acting performance and a mediocre amateur treading the boards in a village hall is essentially merely a difference in quality, there is a whole world of difference between the expertise and personal inspiration offered by a superb, committed, knowledgeable and dedicated consultant and one who has no real concept of the responsibilities of consulting and even less real expertise in the area in which he is supposed to be offering advice.

There are three clearly identifiable elements to the quality of a consultant:

○ the quality of the expertise offered;
○ the quality of the consultant's commitment and desire to help the client;
○ the ability to relate to a client's culture.

These are of such importance that each deserves to be looked at in detail.

The quality of the expertise offered

Any good consultant needs to offer state-of-the-art advice. This means that he needs to have leading edge knowledge of his specialization, and he needs to be competent to deliver that knowledge to his client. It follows that this involves a professional duty to keep up to date with the latest developments in his field.

Obviously, this aspect of a consultant's expertise is limited to the leading edge of development of the field. The medical consultants of the 19th century were treated much like royalty in the hospitals where they worked, but they did not really know very much about medicine, though this is more a reflection of the lamentably undeveloped science of medicine in those days than of their abilities. Confronted with a case of, say, typhoid fever they could do little apart from wait for the fever to reach a crisis and hope the patient would survive, but this did not necessarily mean they were bad consultants. Many of them were dedicated medical men, a fact highlighted by their willingness to work with patients whose diseases posed almost as much danger to the consultants as to the patients themselves. Nevertheless, anybody unfortunate enough to suffer from typhoid fever in a 19th-century hospital surely might have preferred to be seen by an indifferent and even impolite consultant if that consultant had had access to antibiotics.

Clearly, then, technical expertise can be a substitute for interpersonal skills to some extent, but it is important to remember that much of the effectiveness of technical advice depends on how it is communicated, especially if, as is likely to be the case, the advice needs to be implemented or followed up by the client. So a consultant who makes a poor impression, or who has a presentation style that fails to inspire confidence, may ultimately find his usefulness limited, despite the quality of his technical knowledge.

The consultant's duty to keep up to date with developments in his specialization means that he should make every effort, to ensure that his knowledge remains at the leading edge of what is going on. Many consultants obtain and disseminate this knowledge by reading and writing articles and books, and many post their work on the Internet (incidentally, never forget that the Internet is an enormously important research tool for both consultants and their clients).

We firmly believe that a consultant should take pride in participating in the intellectual discourse of his specialization by publishing relevant material, posting it on the Internet, and by speaking at relevant seminars and conferences when time permits. Furthermore, as our section on marketing oneself shows, bringing one's thoughts and expertise to the attention of a wider public can be a useful, and entirely effective, way of winning new business.

The quality of the consultant's commitment and desire to help the client

One characteristic all star consultants have in common is a strong belief in the principle that consulting should be about caring for clients' needs and developing an empathy with the problems with which clients are faced. They are absolutely right to adhere to this belief. The consultant is nothing if he does not believe that mutual co-operation is what really matters in business. Some consultants take this even further: 'We are here to help each other' they like to say.

At one level these views may seem slightly absurd, at least to anybody who has set up a consulting business and undergone all the problems and stress (and sometimes, in the early days, threat of insolvency) that the process entails. Surely the business world is a jungle, a battle where no mercy is given?

Yes, in a sense it is. But the truth is that a real and dedicated commitment to helping clients, and a sincere belief that this is something that truly matters, is not some wishy-washy personal philosophy but an extremely important precept for you to follow. Even more, you must set out to amaze your client with the quality of your work. Merely turning in a competent performance is never going to be good enough.

One of the reasons why IDOM enjoyed such spectacular success was that the consultancy was based on the philosophy that in Central Europe, one day of a consultant's time (in the early 1990s this cost about $1500) would cost a client about 20 times what it would typically cost to employ a senior manager for one day. Looked at another way, one day was equivalent to a month's salary for a senior manager (as there are 20 working days in a month). IDOM set its consultants the task of 'being seen to be at least 20 times as good as the client' and consultants were expected to live up to this maxim.

Today, the maxim still holds good, although the precise multiple will vary depending on the sector the client is in, and the level at which the consultant is operating. Despite the importance of the maxim, money is *not*, in the end, what consulting is all about, any more than a dedicated musician who loves his music thinks only of the money at the end of a hugely successful concert when he sees his ecstatic audience cheering and clapping. Money is a by-product of success, not the heart of it.

The ability to relate to a client's culture

Consulting, like life itself, does not and should not take place in a vacuum. All businesses are run by people, and people are different; it therefore follows that businesses are different. The ability to relate to, and ideally empathize with, a client's culture is central to the success of any consulting initiative.

This means that the solution must be proposed, delivered and followed up in a way that is appropriate to the particular needs of each client.

An ability to relate to and empathize with a client's culture is a rare skill, but it is one that the founder of a consulting firm must have if the business is to stand any chance of success.

The first steps in achieving good client relations

Unfortunately, making your clients so happy that they are stamping their feet and cheering at you while you stand on your consulting pedestal, exhausted after your hard work, is an infrequent scenario. For many clients, the visit to the 'consulting concert' turns out to be an evening to forget rather than one to remember. Clients often end up voicing the following complaints:

○ 'we were overcharged';

- ○ 'the advice we were given was nothing like as useful as the consultant had led us to believe it would be';
- ○ 'the consultant wasted too much time – time for which we were paying – learning about our business';
- ○ 'the consultant was pompous, pretentious and lazy';
- ○ 'the consultant didn't keep us informed of his progress';
- ○ 'the consultant's written reports were wordy and vague';
- ○ 'the consultant did not want to find out about the peculiarities of our business'.

Experienced consultants reading this may well at this point be thinking: 'I hope these two guys aren't going on to say that the above problems are always the fault of the consultant. Everybody with any experience of consulting knows that clients are as much to blame as consultants when things go wrong.'

Sorry, but we don't agree.

The great literary figure Dr Johnson was right, as ever, when he remarked in the 18th century that it was entirely legitimate for you to comment adversely on the bad workmanship of a poorly made chair, even if you do not make chairs yourself. 'Making chairs is not your business,' he said. Which is precisely the point. By extension, it is entirely reasonable for you to condemn a bad book, a bad movie, a bad airline service, a bad anything, even if you are not yourself an author, a film director, running an airline or whatever else. The fact that you could not necessarily do better yourself is not the point.

What *is* the point is that you are a customer, and as a customer you are paying for what should be a superb product or service and you are therefore entitled to complain if the product or service is not satisfactory.

Taking this one stage further and applying it to the consulting industry, there is an essential point that you need to keep in mind at all times. A major part of a consultant's professionalism needs to be the management of the relationship with the client. It is no good the consultant blaming the client for being unreasonable or for being disappointed.

Therefore, as a consultant, you need to make an effort to reveal as much of the real nature of what you have to offer as you can before you start working with the client.

The need for an ultra-clear written agreement

By agreeing everything in writing up front you will minimize the likelihood that your clients will be disappointed. In particular, you need to make the following points absolutely clear to your clients before starting to work with any of them, even on the smallest, most humble project. *This is extremely important.* Whether you and your consultancy are going to be engaged for a morning's or for a millennium's worth of man-hours, do not start working unless all the following points are agreed, and in writing:

- precisely what you will be doing for them;
- precisely what benefits they can expect from your work;
- when you will be starting to work for them;
- when you will be stopping working for them;
- how much time in aggregate you will be spending on their behalf and when you will be charging for this;
- how much money you will be charging as expenses and what the basis is for a cost qualifying as a rechargeable expense;
- when you will be sending invoices, and how much the invoices will be for;
- when you expect your invoices to be paid;
- when the client can expect a written report and how long this is likely to be;
- any other key issues relating to your work for the client;
- the resources the client needs to make available to you, including access to people, systems and premises.

Even though this is an introductory chapter, the above advice for preventing client disappointment by giving your client all the crucial information they need up front needs to be outlined here. Giving your client this information *before* you start work is enormously important, indeed it is essential.

No excuses, please. No saying, 'but how can we possibly tell the client in advance what we will be charging them? We don't know how much work we'll be doing for them!'

One of the biggest sources of contention between consultants and clients is the failure of consultants to inform their clients in advance of when invoices will be sent and how much the invoices will be for.

You have no business sending clients invoices which they are not expecting, and which they have not agreed to pay. The work you undertake on behalf of your clients must be covered by a signed agreement (it can be a well-written letter that is signed by both parties: it does not need to be a formal legal contract) that specifies exactly how much time you will be devoting to the client, how much you will be charging for this time, what expenses you will be charging, when invoices will be sent, and when they need to be paid.

We look at the mechanics of drawing up this agreement in Chapter Four. In the meantime, the point to make is that if you *do* base your consulting activity around the strict policy of working to a written agreement that specifies key points, you will immediately remove an enormous area of potential difficulty with clients.

If you are working on a project where it is not genuinely clear in advance how much time you will be required to work, the simple solution is to agree in advance a certain amount of time (typically a fixed number of hours or consulting days) which you will work and stipulate that additional time will be agreed in advance by your client, ideally in writing. You must also agree in advance with the client what expenses you are likely to incur and what the basis is for defining what rechargeable expenses are allowed. Putting a fixed ceiling on expenses you incur on the client's behalf does not work in practice: unpredictable things always happen in business and you need a framework which will accommodate unforeseen changes. What you must never do is work additional time or charge additional expenses which your client is not expecting. It is the certain route to disaster.

By agreeing all the above crucial points in advance, you basically ensure that your consulting work is copper-bottomed, meaning that you are proceeding as your client wants you to proceed.

Setting everything down in a solid and clear written agreement does not mean you will necessarily make a success of the mandate, but it will help you to keep your objectives firmly in mind at all times, and it will also show to your client from the outset that you are efficient. Generally speaking, the more time and effort you invest in getting the up-front agreement right for both parties, the fewer unpleasant surprises either side will encounter. As long as you complement this professionalism with hard work and commitment, and as long as you do not pretend an expertise which you do not possess, your consulting activity has every chance of being a success.

Dealing with unreasonable clients

This ultra-professional and ultra-businesslike approach is extremely important because it ensures that when clients *are* unreasonable, you are operating from a position of strength. There is no doubt that clients can sometimes be unreasonable. Even if you have clearly agreed all crucial elements of your work and charges in advance, there will always be clients who try to claim that they did not know they had signed a legally binding contract.

As long as you have written your letter/contract clearly and intelligently, an unreasonable client should not be able to use that argument with any success. And as long as the financial aspects of what you will be doing for your client are clear and set out in writing, it is difficult for the client to claim that an invoice should not be paid if the work has evidently been done. Also, you should always make sure that prior to being sent to the client, any letter/contract is seen by a lawyer located in the country where the work will be carried out, in order to avoid the danger that the letter/contract contravenes the laws of the country in question. This is especially important when you undertake mandates abroad.

A more troublesome – and common – type of unreasonableness from clients occurs when a key person you were reporting to in the client organization changes jobs, or leaves the organization. As today's business world tends to make many senior management jobs essentially project-based activities, such changes of key personnel are frequent occurrences; indeed, the majority of consulting projects lasting more than about six months are likely to be affected by such change.

The problem is that when a new person takes over from a manager who was friendly to you, this person will have a different perception of you, at least to start with. This comes down to human psychology; it has little to do with the quality of your work (we are assuming that the quality of your work has not fallen off). People in new appointments are usually keen to make an impact. Research has proven that managers are under particularly intense pressure to perform in the first three months of their appointment.

Often, one of the first things a new manager does is to look around at his suppliers and decide who can be replaced. Unfortunately, this sometimes means that he replaces suppliers who were doing a perfectly good job.

If your contract is coming to an end at about the time the new manager is appointed, there is not much you can do, although if he tries to claim on some spurious grounds that your contract should be cancelled, you should pass the matter to your legal adviser. It is usually best to make a firm but courteous stand against a hostile new manager. That way, you have a good chance of convincing him that your real commitment is to the client organization.

Another problem here is that the new manager will often have his own consultant contacts and may be keen to bring them in. The usual reason he provides for this is that 'he wants to work with people with whom he has had experience in the past', which is sometimes a euphemistic way of saying, 'I want to work with people I know already and who aren't likely to tax my abilities too much'. Again, there is not much you can do apart from expecting the client to honour the signed contract and then finding new clients who will appreciate your talents more.

Summing up, we would say that your professionalism as a consultant needs to include the management of the client relationship, and often this boils down to cultivating a business friendship. The client is entitled to know what you will be doing for his organization, when you will be doing it, and how much you will be charging. Conversely, as a professional, you are entitled to be treated ethically and with respect, and if clients suddenly decide that they do not wish to treat you in this way, you should not allow them to renege on signed promises without paying for the privilege.

Having addressed this difficult issue, let us move on to a matter that most definitely belongs in this introductory chapter: the reasons why clients want to use consultants at all.

Why consultants can be so useful

In the previous section, we looked at some of the more negative potential aspects of the client/consultant relationship and suggested how these could be dealt with and, ideally, avoided. We will now consider factors that explain not only why clients may want to use consultants but also why the client/consultant relationship can be so successful.

The medieval Scholastics – Catholic philosophers who took the existence of the Catholic God for granted and spent their lives writing about religious issues – believed there were watertight arguments that proved conclusively the existence of God. Today, especially in the light of the widespread acceptance of the theory of evolution, some of the scholars' arguments are starting to look more than a little threadbare. There are similar, though less divine, arguments in favour of using consultants, arguments that, fortunately, the passage of time seems to reinforce rather than erode.

These arguments are as follows.

A disinterested observer often sees things that are not clear to those on the inside. As a consultant, you should be impartial when you view a situation or dynamic connected with the area in which you are consulting. Being disinterested means having no personal axe to grind in relation to the matter on which you have been asked to focus your attention – in other words, that you can be impartial because you are cut off from the political aspects of the decision. It does not mean that you are *uninterested* in the matter because of course you will not be much use as a consultant if you do not find your work interesting.

The reason why a disinterested observer usually has a better perspective on matters than people on the inside is not hard to work out: those on the inside are often distracted by their emotional and political concerns. It never ceases to surprise us how *un*objective many highly intelligent people can be when caught up in complex issues in the organization where they work. Sometimes, the simple fact that the consultant is an outsider who is *interested* in the matter at hand *but not emotionally involved in it* gives the consultant a wonderfully privileged position that allows him to see what exactly needs to be done.

The movie *Titanic* drew much of its effect and power from the fact that it was shot to give the audience the sensation of being on the doomed ship. The audience became, in effect, time travellers who had a comprehensive perspective of what was happening on the ship without any fear of drowning or freezing to death themselves.

There is a sense in which all consultants are, or should be, like the audience of *Titanic*: passionately interested in what is going on, yet operating at a crucial remove from the desperation and confusion and consequently able to gain the clearest perspective on events.

An outsider is not afraid of saying what he thinks. However much a corporate body tries to convince its employees – and itself – that it is an extremely reasonably-minded organization which is primarily concerned with the personal development of its staff, the fact remains that the main aim of any commercial organization is to make a profit, and woe betide any employee who, even for an instant, gets in the way of that all-important objective.

The trouble with this prime directive is that it can prevent salaried employees from taking considered risks. This lamentable situation often means that underlings are reluctant to criticize their boss, even when the boss has made decisions which any outsider would regard as utterly foolish. An external consultant, on the other hand, has no such fear of being sacked and should not be afraid to say what he thinks.

The consultant has the opportunity – indeed, has the duty – to be completely objective in the advice he bestows. And if one consequence of providing that advice means that one or more of the client's directors are relieved of their positions, then so be it.

Of course, the objection might be raised here: 'Well, that sounds all right in practice, but what consultant would dare suggest that one or more of the client's directors were behaving in such an irresponsible way that they should be dismissed?' While we freely concede that the proportion of cases in which a consultant would need to advise a client to dismiss directors or senior managers is relatively small, no consultant should balk from this task if it is necessary. And no client who was worth having as a client would dispense with the services of a consultant, or refuse to pay a consultant's fee, merely because *after careful and thoughtful deliberation* the consultant concluded that the best interests of the organization would be served by dismissing certain directors or senior managers.

Unfortunately, there are occasionally clients who are foolish enough to believe that the main reason for using a consultant is to obtain an authoritative third-party recommendation for doing something the client badly wants to do. When, as often happens, the consultant's advice is the opposite (or at very least differs greatly) to what the client hoped, the client will sometimes become irritable and start throwing all sorts of irrational accusations at the consultant. Since it is rarely possible to be absolutely certain that a client will not behave in this manner, the only way for a consultant to protect himself is to ensure that one single client does not constitute too large a part of his business. Remember that if you allow yourself to lose your objectivity as a consultant, you can no longer describe yourself as a consultant in anything other than name.

One of the most essential things to remember when working as a consultant is that those of your clients who are worth having as clients will respect you only if you strive to tell them what, after due consideration, you really think, not what you think they want to hear.

It may be impossible for the client to gain access to a specific advanced level of skill other than by using the services of a consultant. When someone has acquired a high level of expertise, they will – unless they have a particularly charitable frame of mind – wish to sell that expertise for the highest price they can get. In most cases it is likely that they will be able to make far more money from that expertise by offering themselves as consultants than by working on a salaried basis. Furthermore, many such experts relish the job diversity of the consulting profession. For this reason, many clients have to face the fact that they will have to go to a consultant or consultancy to get these high levels of expertise.

It is often more cost-effective for a client to use an outsider to provide a skill which is only infrequently required by the client. For many clients, this rationale constitutes the economic basis for using the services of a consultant. Quite apart from the benefits discussed above of unwillingness to speak one's mind and access to advanced skills, there can be a fundamental financial benefit in using a consultant. In view of the high expense an organization will inevitably incur when it sets up an in-house management function, it makes sense to use the services of an outsider if the new management function is required only on an occasional basis.

Sometimes a large organization will get around this problem by offering the services of the department to other organizations on a commercial basis, but it cannot escape the fact that it is uneconomic to create an in-house department for which there is not enough specialist work to keep it fully employed.

For example, an organization that wants to increase the coverage it receives in newspapers and journals read by its existing and potential customers may decide to set up an in-house public relations function. The following costs would be incurred:

○ cost of recruiting and/or retraining staff;

○ staff salaries (including related payments such as pension contributions and government insurance contributions);

○ cost of office space (note that even if existing office space is being used, there will still be the opportunity cost of not being able to devote this space to another function);

○ cost of office equipment;

○ ongoing expenses incurred in running the new department (e.g. cost of stationery, postage, telephone calls, fax transmissions, etc.);

○ additional insurance costs.

These fixed and ongoing costs can be so high that it rarely makes sense for an organization to set up an in-house department to provide a function that is not essential to the organization's operation.

On the other hand, using a consultant to undertake this function gives the organization a high level of flexibility as it can decide exactly how much it wants to use the consultant. Likewise, the cost of the consultant's input can be rigidly controlled, whether the consultant is working on an *ad hoc* (i.e. project) basis or on a regular (i.e. retainer) basis. When using the consultant, the cost of undertaking the function will simply be the consultant's fee, plus any out-of-pocket expenses that are agreed beforehand. Unless the organization completely mismanages its use of the service, the cost of delegating the occasionally-required function to the consultant will be much lower than the cost of setting up and running an in-house department – a course of action that will also be extremely wasteful if the function is indeed required only occasionally.

Similarly, where an organization wants to test out a particular new aspect of functionality, or wants to initiate a pilot scheme, it is almost invariably much cheaper to use consultants rather than recruit salaried staff. This is because it is usually far less expensive to 'pull the plug' on consultants than on salaried staff if the organization decides not to proceed with the experiment. Abruptly firing salaried staff can cause ethical problems which are not trivial in this age when corporate organizations take considerable trouble over how they present themselves to the public.

There is, in any case, a tendency for employment within organizations of all kinds to move towards being based around specific projects. This trend tends to make organizations more familiar with the idea of taking on consultants, rather than salaried employees, to handle a specific project. Increasingly, former salaried employees are being rehired to work on a contractual basis. This is particularly common under an outsourcing arrangement whereby the organization sources a particular service from an external service provider that employs, or is run by, former employees.

The rise of the hands-on consultant

Consulting has become very much a hands-on task, and indeed, there is widespread cynicism (often deserved) about consultants who write lengthy advisory reports but either make no effort to implement their recommendations or have no interest in doing so.

When IDOM was in its heyday, its consultants thronged the offices of nascent Central European market economies. IDOM consultants had a reputation for being deeply culturally rooted in the countries where they were operating. A common joke during dinner table conversation in cities such as Budapest, Prague and Warsaw was to call those Western consultants who fondly imagined they could jet over to a Central European city for a few days, write an expensive report and then fly back, 'seagull' consultants. This was because they dropped their reports from a great height and flew off!

Those days are over. The successful consultant of today must be a hands-on consultant – he must either be able to undertake the actual implementation of his recommended action, or he must have people (the consultancy's employees, most likely) who will implement his recommendations with him.

A principal reason for the rise in demand for consultants who make recommendations *and* implement those recommendations once the client has accepted them is that the business world has become more hard-headed, informal and results-orientated than it was before. One result of this is that client organizations are often impatient with consulting advice that does not come with an option to implement the advice.

Having said that, there is no hard and fast rule here – a few consultants continue to provide purely strategic advice and do very well from this.

Certainly, if you want to put into practice the beliefs and principles we set down in this book, you need to face the fact that you will probably reduce the chances of making your consulting a success if you do not offer a hands-on service as well as advisory guidance.

Moving ahead

In this chapter we have provided a general introduction to the nature of consulting activity, the benefits clients can hope to gain from consultants, and we have emphasized the need for the consultant to adhere to the highest standards of expertise, know-how, sincerity and professionalism. It is time to move on to specifics, and the first specific we need to look at is what matters most of all: *you.*

CHAPTER TWO

It's personality that wins business

Introduction

If there is one lesson practising consultants learn over and over again through their experience of marketing themselves, it is the one which we have chosen as the title for this chapter. In consulting, it's personality, above all, that wins business.

Why should this be so? In order to explain, we need to delve into the nature of the psychology at work when a client decides to hire a consultant.

The most important preliminary point to make is that consultants are always hired by a person, not by an organization. It is true that at the procurement stage it may appear to the consultant that they are being approached by the organization in a corporate sense, but there will always have been somebody at the organization who has decided that a consultant needs to be hired. Even if the consultant will be reporting to a committee, there will always be a chairman of the committee who, ultimately, makes the formal decision, or casts the decisive vote for or against the consultant's appointment. Furthermore, in the vast majority of cases a committee will need to report to someone higher up and that person will be responsible for the committee's activities and the work of any consultant who has been appointed.

So the point is made. Consultants are appointed by people. And it follows that what you need to understand here is not so much corporate psychology as personal psychology.

The real reasons why people appoint consultants

People who work in organizations – it does not matter for the purposes of this argument what kind of industry the organization is in, and whether it is a profit-orientated business or a public body, or even a charitable concern – tend to have two basic objectives:

- to bolster their position in the organization and where possible to win promotion and a higher salary;

● to be seen to do their job more effectively. The 'to be seen to' is significant: it really is important to them that their work is noticed. For many of them this will actually be more important than the process of working more effectively.

People entering the consulting industry – and even some consultants with a fair amount of experience – often fail to understand that a consultant is typically hired as much to meet the second objective as the first.

We are not being cynical here, we are merely stating a fact. Of course, consultants will need to do a good job, but their ability to do that good job is far from being the only reason why they are appointed. In fact, people usually appoint consultants as much for political reasons (that is, reasons relating to bolstering the reputation of the person doing the appointing in the corporate hierarchy) as for the practical reason that a particular job needs to be done.

The political reasons are often surprisingly complex, and certainly, as an external consultant, you are unlikely to know precisely what is going through a person's mind in their efforts to improve their position within the organization and to win promotion. You can, however, be certain of four other points, that lead on naturally from the two observations above:

○ people appoint consultants because they feel that doing so shows colleagues that they themselves are of a sufficient stature within the corporate hierarchy to appoint consultants. Yes, we know this sounds like a kind of psychotic Catch-22, but it is often central to the psychology of anybody within an organization who appoints consultants;

○ if somebody appoints an intelligent, hard-working, charismatic, committed and dedicated consultant who gets results and delivers value for money, that person's own stature as a corporate animal will increase. He will, in effect, bask in the reflected glory of the consultant's skill and charisma;

○ people want to enjoy their work, and believe that hiring – and working with – an intelligent, able and committed consultant will indeed make their work more enjoyable. (Of course, it usually will.);

○ consultants are often appointed because it is politically expedient for the client to appoint them. An example is where a regional or national office of the client organization appoints the same consulting firm that has been appointed by the head office. Managers of the regional or national office may do this to please their more senior colleagues at head office level, even if no specific directive has been issued by the head office. On another tack, many consulting firms are appointed because of personal friendships between a member of the client organization and a senior consultant.

The implications of these additional points to consultants are momentous. The following important conclusions can be drawn from them:

○ people want to hire consultants who do a good job, and ideally who do a *great* job;

○ people want to hire consultants who give real value for money;

○ people want to hire consultants who are stimulating and fascinating company;

○ people want to hire consultants who are an inspiration to work with;

○ people want to hire consultants whose appointment will increase the status, from a political perspective, of the person doing the appointing.

You might regard the last three conclusions as incidental and less important than the first two. They are not. They apply just as much as the first two, and in many situations are even more important. The reason for this is obvious. There are far more consultants in the market who will do a good job and give real value for money, but who are ordinary and uninspiring people, than there are good, value-for-money, consultants who are also stimulating, fascinating and an inspiration to be with.

Fortunately, there is plenty of consulting work available for people who are 'merely' good at their job and who offer real value for money. Consultants like that are unlikely to spend much time without work. But by the same token, they are not likely to achieve their full potential as consultants. They are unlikely to break through their apparent limits and achieve consulting stardom and the income that goes with it.

Have you got what it takes to be a star consultant?

If you want to be the kind of star consultant that we want you to be, you need to be more than simply good at your profession, and you need to do more than offer value for money. You also need to be *the* person everybody wants to work with.

Maybe you are that kind of person already. If that is so, congratulations and good luck to you. On the other hand, maybe you are more realistic about your abilities and know just what you need to do to make yourself more inspirational and more the kind of person who can break through their own, inevitably limited, perception of how good you really can be. Maybe you are, in any case, intrigued by our views of what a great consulting personality really is.

Whichever of these is most on your mind, this chapter is most definitely for you. In it, we invite you to make an audit of your own personality, then offer some comments on the conclusions you may have come to. We end the chapter with some straight-talking advice about how you can boost yourself into being an outstanding consultant, with a personality to match.

The only other preliminary point to make here concerns the question of whether you are planning to be a star consultant in your own consulting business (which you may not even have set up yet) or whether you are happy to be a star consultant within an existing consulting organization.

Among the following questions, there are obviously some that are geared towards entrepreneurial consultants who are keen to start their own consultancy or have already done so. However, we do not provide separate sections for entrepreneurial consultants, first because there is a real sense in which *all* consultants are entrepreneurial, and second because most consultants will probably become involved with start-up consultancies or consulting divisions at some point in their careers.

How you use the following personal audit is obviously up to you. You might prefer simply to read the questions and then consider our comments on possible responses to them. You will probably find it useful to jot down answers to questions on a separate piece of paper before moving on to our suggested answers. That way, you will be able to make what should be a useful comparison between your own answers and our comments.

There are, of course, no 'right' or 'wrong' answers: the purpose of the exercise is to consider whether you are, on balance, likely to have the right kind of personality either to make a success of being a consultant or – if you are already a consultant – are likely to rise to the top of your profession. As we believe personality to be such an important element in the success of a consultant, we offer suggestions about the kind of attitudes and approaches to life that are likely to form part of a successful 'consultant personality'.

Our comments and suggestions are based on our own experience, and you should take them for what they are: just one viewpoint. It is true that, between us, we have about 40 years of experience as consultants, experience that has ranged over many different types of consulting projects in different countries, but ultimately we cannot claim to have all the answers relating to the personality factor in consultants. Far from it. Nor do we set out to be highly prescriptive in what we say about the link between success as a consultant and personality traits.

The different personality of every client

Every client has a different personality, just as every client has a different set of fingerprints. There is, consequently, no one, set-in-stone type of appropriate personality that all consultants should have. After all, social relationships in business are only a subset of social relationships in life generally. You would no doubt think, for example, that it was pretty stupid if someone published a book that recommended that in order for a man to be successful with women he should adopt a certain kind of personality designed to be a kind of 'catch-all' that all women would adore.

Similarly, your clients will have a wide range of preferences for the kind of people they like to deal with. While there is a difference between projecting your personality in order to be regarded as a highly professional consultant and doing so in order to be regarded as a suitor, there is less difference between the two activities than some might imagine. The point is that in both cases you are setting out to be charming and interesting. You simply cannot know in advance what type of personality is likely to appeal to your client, and so in many respects the overriding need is for a consultant to have a personality that is able to adapt *with total sincerity* to different clients.

The lesson of the weaver bird

Learn a lesson from the weaver bird, a small finch-like bird found in Africa. The male weaver woos its mate by making a little nest, then hanging upside down from it and calling and fluttering its wings. Sounds stupid but actually it isn't. The weaver doesn't tighten the little stems that go to make the structure until he has successfully persuaded a female to live there with him. If he fails, his caution enables him to loosen the stems and build the nest in a different way, then try the same female again or target another. Consultants who want to break through to higher and higher levels of success could learn a great deal from the weaver bird's trick.

This is why those training seminars designed to teach people to be strong, assertive and dynamic sales men and sales women are so patently ridiculous. Every trainee is taught to adopt a kind of 'dynamic' personality in which he or she is supposed to regard customers' objections as mere obstacles to be jumped over or, ideally, knocked down. The idea is that you take on the kind of extrovert, energetic and basically annoying 'personality' that may appeal to some weak-minded and feeble-spirited customers but which most customers are likely to regard as extremely irritating.

The truth is that the only generalization you can offer to somebody who wants to learn how to sell is to urge them to *listen* to what the customer wants and to *shut up* until the customer has said everything he or she wants to say. If you want to see an entertaining demolition of the whole idea that sales people succeed by being smooth-talking cynics, rent the movie *Glengarry Glen Ross* and see how *not* to sell.

There is simply no such thing as a standard 'good consultant personality'.

The personality audit – questions

There are two types of personal question that need to be considered in the person-ality audit. First, there are 'big questions' which we feel are so important for indicating whether consulting is the right profession for you that they deserve a section to themselves. Second, there are 'other key questions' which are also important but less critical.

In our discussion of possible responses which follows the questions you will see that we analyze possible responses to the big questions with more dogmatism than we apply to responses to the other questions.

The big questions

We believe that if you are to get the most out of *Breakthrough Consulting* and, by extension, make the most of your potential as a consultant, your responses to the following questions are particularly vital.

○ Do you fear boredom more than worry?

○ Do you sincerely want to succeed in your profession?

○ Are you deeply interested in your particular professional skill?

○ Are you prepared to work whatever hours you need to work to become successful?

○ Are you genuinely able to learn from your mistakes?

○ Do you have a university degree, and ideally also a professional qualification?

○ Do you make efforts to develop your mind along lateral lines?

○ Are you a good listener?

Other key questions

These cover a variety of topics and are presented under their respective sub-headings.

Ambition

○ Do you feel completely fulfilled?

○ Do you sincerely want to be rich?

○ Have you set out clear and concrete plans on how you are going to achieve your ambitions?

○ Do you want to be thought of as a nice person more than as a successful person?

○ Do you consider yourself able to concentrate on a given task?

○ Do you consider yourself good at facing reality?

○ Are you prepared to work as long as it takes to get something done properly?

○ Do you regard your personal life as an essential support to your ambitions?

○ Do you feel you live in an age of exciting opportunity?

○ Are you able to face – and deal with – the possibility that you might sometimes be wrong about something?

○ Are you sincerely ready to learn new skills?

○ Are you prepared to listen to advice about your personal presentation and appearance?

Money

○ Are you being paid what you think you deserve?

○ Is your personal financial situation an important element of your happiness?

○ Do you get a real buzz out of making money?

○ Are you prepared to make money if it means someone else will lose out?

Family and personal life

○ Do you feel responsible for giving your family a better standard of living?

○ Is your spouse or partner supportive of your work?

○ Are you happy with the amount of time you spend with your family?

Society

○ Do you consider you have a duty to contribute to the well-being of your society by means of your personal success?

○ Do you play any role in your trade association or professional association?

○ Do you ever write letters to the editors of newspapers on issues you feel strongly about?

○ Do you read the daily and specialized press?

Your attitude to new ideas

○ Are you constantly on the look-out for new ideas?

○ Do you try to find ways of applying great new ideas you hear about to your own consulting activity?

○ Are you enthusiastic about technology?

Your customers

○ What do you really think of your customers?

Criticism

○ How well do you handle criticism?

○ If you are already in a corporate position, do you ever actively seek constructive criticism from those above you?

○ Do you ever seek constructive criticism from those below you?

And finally ...

○ Why did you buy this book?

The personality audit – comment

We now set down our comments on your possible answers. These comments are not set in stone – you can take them or leave them – but we have drawn on all our experience as consultants in preparing them, and we believe that if you follow the advice we provide here, it will help make you successful or, if you are successful already, even more so.

The big questions

Do you fear boredom more than worry?

If you are going to make a success of being a consultant, you certainly do need to fear boredom more than you fear worry. Of course, ideally we would not want you to experience either boredom or worry in your working life. However, in reality you are probably going to have to choose a working life that is sometimes either boring or worrying. All we are saying is that somebody who is going to make a success of a career as a consultant needs to be more a foe of boredom than of worry.

Boredom should be your real enemy. If it is, this means you instinctively know that boredom affects you only when your learning curve has flattened out, or when you no longer find your job interesting – which generally amount to the same thing. Not finding your job interesting is one of the great tragedies in life, one that needs to be avoided at any cost. After all, you are going to be spending more time working than you do anything else. If you do not enjoy what you do, you are accepting an enormous, and in our view unnecessary, compromise in the quality of your life.

But the most important reasons why consultants of any calibre need to be more comfortable with worry than boredom are, first, bored people are very rarely effective, and second, a certain amount of worry about your clients' needs and challenges goes hand in hand with success as a consultant.

Don't get us wrong. We do not think there is anything inherently good about worry. Beyond a modest extent, worry will not only be a damaging force for your business effectiveness but also bad for your health. But a certain amount of worry – or perhaps we should call it concern – about your clients and about your professional activities is good news because it means you care and it means you find your job interesting. We have never met a really good consultant who does not thrive on modest levels of worry or concern. For them, it comes with the territory.

Do you sincerely want to succeed in your profession?

There is no room for compromise here: if you do not sincerely want to succeed in your profession, you are not going to be a star consultant, or much of a consultant of any kind, and had better stick with some undemanding occupation where your indifference to success will not affect your performance.

Organizations always need unambitious people who are happy to waste their life – this glorious opportunity to live and fulfil oneself in between two eternities of oblivion. If you want to be one of those unambitious nobodies, then good luck to you, but you have wasted your money on this book too.

At this point we should add that neither of us was born to success or prosperity: we had to make our own way in the world. If we had not done the occasional menial and desperately dull job along the way, we would not feel so passionately now about wanting to succeed in doing what we love.

Are you deeply interested in your particular professional skill?

With the occasional exception of consultants who are able to find clients to pay them handsomely for providing very general but nonetheless useful advice, the vast majority of consultants have got to consult *in* something. It is difficult to see how you can possibly be a successful consultant, let alone a star consultant, if you do not love the professional skill or discipline in which you specialize. Ideally, you need to take pride in your mastery of it, too.

Are you prepared to work whatever hours you need to work to become successful?

The question of how willing you should be to work long hours is more difficult than it seems. On the one hand, many star consultants take it for granted that they need to work long hours, and many of them will attribute their success – especially when they look back on their early years – to working extremely hard. On the other hand, many successful business people whose opinions and perspectives on business, and the world generally, we greatly respect have often told us that they think it a mistake to work exceptionally long hours.

Certainly, there is no inherent virtue in working long hours for the sake of it. Apart from anything else, it depends what you do. It is necessary to make the point that what matters is not the duration of your working effort but what you do with the time.

In his highly entertaining book *Down and Out in Paris and London*, George Orwell tells the story of his life working in various menial jobs in Paris in the 1930s. The other semi-slaves in the hotels and restaurants where he worked, spent most of their lives in toil, sometimes having only three or four hours' sleep a night. It wrecked their health, and they achieved nothing. All they managed to do was earn enough to eat and drink to stay alive, just about.

Today, sadly, many millions of people, particularly in developing countries, work similarly tortuous hours and gain little from it. That is deeply unfortunate, and any self-respecting consultant who has the opportunity to help improve this state of affairs will want to do so. One of the reasons why running IDOM was so satisfying was that the consultancy made a real contribution to bringing technology to the new market economies of Central Europe and, by definition, helped to remove much of the drudgery associated with work in those countries, especially in the banking and manufacturing industries.

As part of our research for the appendix of this book, we asked a number of successful consultancies a range of questions about their attitude to the consulting profession. One of the questions related to the 'long hours' culture of the business. CEDAR International, the UK human resources consultancy, said:

> *'We do not uphold a "long hours" culture. It's sometimes necessary to work long hours to meet client demands, but that is the exception rather than the rule. We prefer to focus our culture around doing a really good job.'*

This is a sensible and sane viewpoint. There is no doubt, say, that five hours a day of quality work is infinitely better than 12 hours of exhausted, muddled thinking. This connects to our central point here, which is that working long hours is of itself irrelevant and not necessarily going to get you anywhere. What you need to do is work hard *and* work smart, and ideally ensure you have the right 'wicket' to work on: one that will give you a chance to fulfil yourself and make your dreams come true. After all, even the best batsmen in the world will come unstuck if they are batting on a wicket six inches deep in mud.

Given all the above, it still remains the case that the consulting business does usually require its exponents – and especially its stars – to work long hours. For one thing, your remuneration will usually be directly linked to the number of hours you work (most consultants, as we show later, need to submit detailed time sheets when they invoice for jobs). But even when you are charging by the day and have already done your eight hours, you will want to devote all the time necessary to getting crucial jobs done for your client and ensuring that milestones (specific contractual points of achievement during the project) are met. Furthermore, you will also need to find time to fit in the mechanics of running your consultancy, if you are a senior manager of a consultancy or a consulting division.

Make no mistake, consultants work long hours, and if you have set up your own consultancy and want to make it successful, you probably are not going to see much of your family for the first couple of years. Incidentally, this is one good argument for being based at home in the early days, at least as long as you are able to commandeer a room as your office. If you are based at home, you will at least be able to see your family when you are there and not at your clients' premises.

In any event, you need to focus with great intensity on your profession. Leisure activities will have to become of secondary importance and sometimes put on hold. This is not the time to take on a major role with your local operatic society, to become the champion of your golf, bridge or chess club, or to write that novel you always thought you had in you. There will be time to do these other things, but become a star consultant first.

Are you genuinely able to learn from your mistakes?

It is a myth that people are 'born' with a particular expertise. Think about it: how many babies would develop into experts in *anything* if they were not properly educated, given the training they need and the opportunity to make mistakes? The answer is: none. The myth that people are born with a certain expertise was invented by lazy people who want to console themselves for their failure.

We *all* have to learn, and nobody can learn without making mistakes. 'Ah,' you might say, 'but surely these guys aren't going to say that a consultant charging goodness knows what per day for their time should be making mistakes while working for his client?' Of course we aren't saying that. There are obviously different levels of mistakes. While you are learning your trade in the particular skill in which you will be consulting, you are going to make different kinds of mistake – more significant mistakes, in fact – than those you will make when you are actually practising as a consultant. When you reach the stage of being a consultant, you need to be so good at what you do that the 'mistakes' you make are really matters of fine-tuning your skills to meet the clients' needs, or else are deficiencies in your knowledge that you sort out *before* they cause any problems to your clients.

Think of this as being like a space rocket launching from Earth to dock with a space station. The really big decisions, the really big potential dangers, come on the launch pad. When the rocket approaches the space station at a safe, slow speed, it may need to fine-tune its approach in order to dock precisely and thereby give the space station exactly what it needs to make the docking complete, but it will not be in a state where there is a danger of it shooting off at 5000 mph. The rocket has reached where it wants to be, and is precise about what is happening and what it is doing.

Do you have a university degree, and ideally also a professional qualification?

There are many great consultants who do not have a university degree. Some of these people are truly talented individuals who have worked hard to overcome initial educational disadvantages. Most of them are probably reaching the apex of their careers by now and may well already have done so. On the whole, they tend to belong to the older generation.

In today's highly competitive consulting world, you really do need a degree if you are going to be a player. It does not necessarily matter what subject your degree is in: many top-flight consultants hold degrees in exotic subjects such as obscure languages, archaeology, philosophy and so on. Your degree signifies, above all, that you are a well-educated person who is used to applying his mind to solve complex problems. If you do not have a degree but want to make a success of consulting, we urge you to explore opportunities for gaining a degree, and possibly doing so part-time if you are working full-time.

Of course, your degree is only a beginning. If you are not deeply embarrassed by reading your university essays ten years after you wrote them, you should worry. The human mind goes on developing – or should do – throughout an individual's life: you don't reach a plateau when you get your degree. This being so, most good consultants also have some kind of professional qualification. An increasingly popular one is the Master in Business Administration (MBA) which can be a superb training for business and for all types of rigorous analysis.

Do you make efforts to develop your mind along lateral lines?

Your mind is your most precious possession. It can make or mar you, it can turn you into a multi-millionaire, a multi-billionaire, or it can lead you to a park bench and several daily cans of strong cider. You have a duty to expand and train your mind as much as you can.

The complexity of the modern world means that specialization of professional skills is more and more important. Today, for example, it is unthinkable for someone to be an expert in everything to do with computers: they are only going to be able to be an expert in certain narrow (but extremely significant) aspects of computing – systems integration, for example, programming in certain languages, computer security, networking and so on. This specialization has arisen from the fact that the technical complexity of our world requires experts to devote many years of their lives to mastering one niche. There simply is not time to master everything, any more than there is time for someone, say, to learn to be a surgeon on any part of the human body. You have to specialize.

Unfortunately, one of the consequences of specialization is that far too many experts are ignorant of just about everything *except* their specialization. Sometimes such ignorance is actually regarded as praiseworthy in the business press. During the 1980s there was an article in a business magazine that profiled a successful City of London foreign exchange (forex) dealer and actually praised his admission that he wasn't in the least interested in *anything* apart from forex. Would you really like to become like that forex dealer? If you are content to devote all your energies to making money on the forex market, perhaps being like that is all right, at least as long as you do not want to be a human being, too. But if you are going to be a star consultant, it won't do.

Why? *Because consultants must be as interested in their clients' activities as the clients are themselves.* By definition, a successful consultant is going to have many clients, either simultaneously or over a number of years, and he needs to be genuinely interested in all of them, and in everything they are doing. Furthermore, you need to be interested in your clients as *people*. Being in business is not a matter of delivering a technical skill that meets the needs of an organization; it is about delivering a skill that meets the needs of people. How can you really know about people's needs if you are not interested in them? And how can you know about people if you do not have a well-rounded knowledge of the world?

Nobody can teach you to think laterally – meaning to make unobvious horizontal connections between apparently unrelated matters. Nobody can teach you to think for yourself in a creative way. There are, however, things you can do to improve your powers of lateral thinking.

For one thing, you need to read. What should you be reading? There are some excellent business books that set out to train the reader to think about business from a creative standpoint, Charles Handy's books being a good example. Some quality magazines contain remarkably good articles about business from a wider perspective. *The Economist*, for example, often contains jewels of exploration of what business really means.

Are you a good listener?

If you are a consultant, the whole point of your activities is that you listen to your clients and help them solve their problems. Consultants must be great listeners! After all, how can you help people if you don't listen? And not only listen when you first meet them, but keep on listening throughout the time you are working with them.

Listening is not simply a matter of absorbing the literal meaning of what your clients or would-be clients are saying. Frequently, people have a subtext when they speak. You need the skill of a psychologist, and a sympathetic one at that, to unravel it. Furthermore, you need to have a knowledge of the human personality to know when what someone tells you is either deliberately misleading, or is being said because they have an agenda that is not being otherwise revealed to you.

You also need to remember that in many cases, you will be meeting people who are talking to you not because they *want* to do so but because they have been *told to do so* by their superior. They may be resentful of having to talk to you at all, they may be bored, or they may fear that ultimately your recommendations will lead to them losing their job, which, if they continue to be more protective of their position than they are of doing their job properly. They may well do.

In any event, the point is clear. Not taking the time or effort to listen is an irritating and self-defeating trait. If you do not listen to what people want to say to you, you are not going to be switched on to their agendas, or to what is going on around you in a more general sense.

Other key questions

Do you feel completely fulfilled?

No truly successful or dynamic person ever feels completely fulfilled. There are always new challenges they want to overcome, new opportunities to exploit – but that does not mean that on the way there are not going to be plenty of opportunities to enjoy a high level of self-fulfilment.

Do you sincerely want to be rich?

Whether you do or not, if you put the principles of this book into action, you can hardly fail to become richer than you are already. If you do sincerely want to be rich, that suggests you have the motivation to make the most of your talents and abilities.

Have you set out clear and concrete plans on how you are going to achieve your ambitions?

If you do not have some clear, definite ideas of what you want to achieve in your working life, you cannot know what you want to do. Take the time now to plan your long-term goals and what you are actively going to do to achieve them.

Do you want to be thought of as a nice person more than as a successful person?

This is a tricky one. We have already emphasized that a star consultant needs to be someone who ideally has a personality and charisma that makes people relish the opportunity to work with him. They should find him so energetic, full of ideas, willing to listen, thoughtful and good company that they are proud to act on his advice. In that sense, a consultant has to be a 'nice person' in that being with him is a pleasant experience.

On the other hand, a consultant can never afford to be *so* nice that he is afraid of disrupting his client's organization, causing dramatic change, even turning over the entire organization. Consultants must above all be faithful to their perception of the truth of what needs to be done. This must ultimately be even more important than keeping the client happy. If you are going to remain true to your perception of how things need to be at the organization, there is no way you can be nice all the time. Sometimes, you are going to have to be anything but nice.

Even today, when competitive pressure and governmental rules force many non-profit organizations to be as efficient and competitive as for-profit organizations, too many organizations of all kinds have dead wood in them. This may consist of employees who do not pull their weight or who, despite their talents and hard work, are no longer necessary. It may consist of divisions that are unprofitable and have no future. It may consist of information technology systems that belong in a science museum rather than in a modern, success-hungry organization.

As a consultant, your job – no, your duty – will often be to recommend that this dead wood be chucked into the river, and you may even be asked to do the chucking.

The message is clear: try to be *too* nice, and you become ineffective. Try to be *too* pleasant, and there is a danger your advice will cease to have teeth. Sometimes, inevitably, you will be confronting people who are interested only in protecting their livelihoods and not in the long-term health of the organization they work for. It may not even occur to them that they would be happier and better paid in another job: all they will think is that you are out to get them.

In the end, if you want to be a star consultant, you have to develop a special kind of thick skin – special, because it needs to allow you to listen to people, absorb their needs, and be sensitive to everything going on in their organization. In other words, your thick skin needs to incorporate a sort of biological valve. But your skin must be thick enough to allow you to get on with what you want to do in order to fulfil your obligations under your contract. You cannot afford to be too preoccupied with what people think of you. To get things done you sometimes need to be tough and aggressive, albeit in a courteous way. You should aim to develop positive, trusting relationships so that people will want to do things to help you.

As a final point, you might like to consider that almost all people who really do something with their lives and achieve success are disliked by somebody, somewhere. The reason is that the majority of people never achieve what they want to achieve and never gain self-fulfilment.

If you try too hard to be nice, you might end up like that majority who often find their prime consolation is the envy of successful people.

Do you consider yourself able to concentrate on a given task?

Concentration is a key criterion in achieving the breakthrough to stardom as a consultant. If you do not consider it to be one of your strong points, make a conscious effort to eliminate sources of distraction from your working life. Also, try to get into the habit of completing a task, or an important part of a task, before you get up for that cup of tea, that chat or that visit to the bathroom.

Do you consider yourself good at facing reality?

It is human nature to see things as we want to see them rather than as they actually are. Be aware of this general failing and try to train yourself to make a habit of accepting reality. Horror stories about those who have refused to face reality are all around us. You will certainly know of examples from your own experience of business. Keep them in mind, and learn from the mistakes that others have made.

Are you prepared to work as long as it takes to get something done properly?

If not, why are you in business? This should be something you take for granted in your business career.

Do you regard your personal life as an essential support to your ambitions?

Too many business books assume that their reader isn't really a human being but a curriculum vitae with money-making ambitions.

We do not make that mistake. We know that you *are* a human being, and that as well as having career ambitions you will want to be happy in your personal life. We also know that an unhappy consultant is unlikely to be a good one, partly because his concentration is likely to wander, but – more subtly – because if he is not happy himself, he is unlikely to be able to listen with sympathy and sensitivity to other people telling him about their problems. That communication process is at the heart of what consulting is.

There is no doubt that maintaining the right balance between career and personal life is inherently a difficult task for consultants. The fact that you usually need to work long hours and may also be obliged to spend several (or many) nights away from home every month does not always make it easy for you to make a success of your personal life.

Admittedly, if you are single, you may find the lifestyle of a consultant suits your needs. You will probably have plenty of money (at least you will if you do your job properly) and the prospect of travel and meeting different people may appeal to you. In our experience, though, consultants who make it to the top tend to have stable personal lives. Even more to the point, they place immense significance on that stability. One of their main motivations for achieving success and financial security is to do so for their families.

It is not too difficult to work out why success as a consultant often goes hand in hand with a stable personal life. The great French writer Gustave Flaubert once wrote:

> *'Be regular and orderly in your life, so that you may be violent and original in your work.'*

This is great advice. At a minor level, it explains why consultants want to run a tidy ship back at their office and operate efficient and meticulous filing systems. But it has a more profound meaning relating to the need for a successful consultant (or any other type of business person) to aim for a stable personal life. By having a 'regular and orderly' emotional life, you can free your inner spirit for being adventurous and original in your work. You can fulfil yourself professionally and take considered risks, while knowing that back home you have stability and people on whom you can rely. What greater blessing can a consultant have, apart from good health? And doesn't this make it clear why a star consultant should aim to have an ordered and happy personal life?

Do you feel you live in an age of exciting opportunity?

During your lifetime, or during the decade or so before you were born, men have walked on the moon, the majority of serious infectious diseases have been stamped out or controlled in the developed world (and in large parts of the developing world), most people in developed countries have got into the habit of eating a balanced diet, rockets have been sent to Mars and even beyond the solar system, and enjoying a holiday abroad has become the norm for much of the world's population. International travel is quick and easy, and for the first time in history, the world's leading nations are mainly collaborating over developing productive friendships and economic relations rather than thinking up new ways of destroying one another.

This isn't to say that there aren't many things that cannot be improved in our world. Still, only the most pessimistic person would refuse to agree that we live in an extremely exciting age. Very possibly, life has never had the potential to be as interesting and happy as it can be today.

If you do not feel you live in an age of exciting opportunity, maybe you are not as knowledgeable about the world you live in as you ought to be, or not sufficiently in touch with it.

Are you able to face – and deal with – the possibility that you might sometimes be wrong about something?

If you think you are always right, you are probably going to be wrong much of the time. Making mistakes is a big part of life. You cannot avoid them. The secret is to learn from your mistakes, and not to make them again.

As the Victorian reformer Samuel Smiles once remarked: 'He who never made a mistake never made a discovery.' We might add another: the person who never made a mistake never made *anything*.

In business, it is always difficult to strike a balance between your need to feel confident in what you do and the equally pressing requirement that you must not close your mind to new ideas, including the one that you might be wrong. Having the guts to face up to being wrong is the first step; the next is to do something about it, and soon.

Incidentally, remember that sometimes you might start out by being right but might wind up being wrong due to an important development that affects you and your activities. This often happens as a result of some significant technological change. If you do not take the change on board, you are going to become outdated very quickly. For example, organizations that were manufacturing typewriters in the 1960s were right to do so, but they would have been wrong to have done so in the 1980s, by which point typewriters had been largely replaced by word processors. The great steel and railway magnate Andrew Carnegie was famous for keeping the machinery in his foundry absolutely up to date with state-of-the-art developments. He would sometimes rip out a machine only a few months after it had been installed, if that machine had been superseded by some new type of device. Carnegie saw that even a small technological improvement could transform him from being right about what he was installing to being completely wrong.

Are you sincerely ready to learn new skills?

The learning curve of a successful consultant – and any other successful business person – is continuous and you should relish the opportunity to learn. If you are continually acquiring new skills you will never get bored. You will also radically improve your career prospects.

Are you prepared to listen to advice about your personal presentation and appearance?

Many people fail to advance in their career because they do not make a positive first impression on other people. We live in a highly visual age where appearance matters a great deal. Most of us are introduced to new people almost every day. Like it or not, first impressions count.

In medieval times, a villager would usually meet only about 70 people in his entire lifetime. Today the average business person will meet many thousands, even tens of thousands. There usually is not time to get to know the person behind the appearance. That person might be a wonderfully interesting and fascinating character, but if their appearance puts you off them, you may well never want to get to know them at all. The reason why people do judge by first impressions is because frequently it is the only thing they have to go on. Besides, many of your best business contacts will be people you talk to mainly on the telephone and rarely meet, so you have to make a good impression every time you do meet them.

How do you make a good impression? Above all, by accepting that attending to your personal presentation and appearance is something that really matters. You need to be well groomed, clean, with a sensible haircut and smart clothes. Your shoes need to shine and when you smile at your clients, they want to see white teeth, not cavernous gaps. Be careful about body odour. One way of preventing problems here is to avoid wearing shirts (and, even more importantly, socks) made of synthetic fabrics that do not allow the skin to breathe properly and tend to trap odours. You need to use deodorant every day, and if you are working into the evening, it makes sense to try to find time to shower. Many large organizations have shower facilities for this very reason. You should also take a toothbrush and tooth-paste to work and use it at least once during the day.

This may all seem pretty obvious (and perhaps tasteless) advice but some people have lower standards of personal presentation and grooming than they ought to have and their career suffers as a consequence. If you work in a team, it is your professional duty to inform any of your colleagues if any aspect of their personal hygiene has fallen below the standard that can be realistically expected. Nobody can have much respect for someone who has body odour or bad breath, or practises any other social solecism. If someone suffering from any of these problems is in your team, your team will always be downgraded in your clients' estimation.

Professional women, being more inherently conscious of the need for care in personal grooming, hardly ever suffer from these embarrassing problems. The challenge that faces them relates more to dress and other aspects of their appearance. Advising women consultants over presentation matters is something beyond our experience. So we turned to the human resources consultancy CEDAR International for expert advice. Helen Pitcher, managing director, and Julie Weiss, business development director, provide their thoughts on the matter.

Helen and Julie suggested that every woman wishing to be taken seriously in business should see a colour and style consultant who will advise her about the colours and style which are right for her. It is extremely important that colours are well co-ordinated and match one another. They emphasised that many clothes designers provide matching outfits in order to meet this need.

'*Ultimately, every woman's clothing, perfume, jewellery and shoes should be chosen according to her personality and personal factors such as skin and hair colour: you really do need professional advice here if you are to make the most of yourself.*'

We also asked Helen and Julie to what extent a woman should plan her dress according to the type of client she is about to meet, and whether they would advise a woman to dress differently to meet the board of, say, a conservative New York investment bank than when they were meeting, say, the billionaire head of a Silicon Valley computer corporation who is widely known to prefer casual outfits. They said:

'*Yes, you do need to be extremely sensitive about this. There are no hard and fast rules: it depends on circumstances, but we would certainly recommend wearing a smart business outfit for a meeting, for example, at an investment bank. The female consultant's preferred dress here should incorporate a skirt that is not too short. Dark colours are most appropriate.*

'*On the other hand, if you are meeting somebody who is both successful and famous for being casual, you may give the wrong impression if you dress too formally. Unless you know that they prefer consultants to be dressed in this way, you might consider wearing less formal clothes, such as a trouser suit. Sometimes you may even find it necessary to wear extremely informal clothes, but you should do this only if you know for certain that your client will appreciate it.*'

Are you being paid what you think you deserve?

One of the joys of being a consultant is that once you establish a successful business you should be able to earn a great deal more than if you were working for a salary. This is why many consultants prefer to work in comparatively small consultancies that they often have helped to set up: in such a situation, they can maximize their earnings. Obviously, if you are working for an average of, say, 15 billable days per month at $2500 per day, you can reasonably expect to have a large part of that revenue yourself if you are working in a relatively small organization with minimum overheads. On the other hand, if you are working for a big organization, overheads may eat up a large proportion of that.

As a consultant, there should be no reason for you to complain about what you are being paid. If you are not being paid enough, that is either because you are not earning enough for yourself or for the consultancy, or because you have not got yourself the best deal you can. Consulting is a form of entrepreneurship, and just as an entrepreneur has only himself (or his choice of activity) to blame if he winds up a pauper rather than a millionaire, a consultant who is not earning enough has no grounds for complaining to anyone but himself.

Is your personal financial situation an important element in your happiness?

It is not for us to make you into a materialistic person. Many people have enjoyable and fulfilling lives and regard the money they make from their jobs purely as something that gives them the resources to meet their basic needs.

That said, by purchasing this book you have shown that you are keen to become excellent from a competitive standpoint. There is no doubt that people who regard money as an important measure of their business performance tend to do better in business than those who don't.

How about seeing whether you can make more money than you are doing at present? Maybe you will find that quest fun in itself, and also enjoy its fruits.

Do you get a real buzz out of making money?

If you do, you are already highly motivated to excel from a competitive standpoint and the chances are you will get a great deal from this book. If you don't, are you sure it is not because of a general lack of confidence? Why not try to overcome that lack of confidence? After all, what have the rich got that you haven't? If you say 'nothing, except for more money', then you might be on the way to joining them.

Are you prepared to make money if it means someone else will lose out?

Another tricky one. Good business activity should ideally be creative: everybody should win because something new and exciting is being brought to market.

This is certainly true of people such as writers and artists, and it is also true of pioneers in technological innovation, and of thousands of other trades where some tangible object is being created. The trouble is that it is not true of thousands of industrial and commercial activities which are highly competitive, or where what is being provided is an important but fairly intangible service. In all these cases, you can only win a real edge in the market by depriving other market participants of their share.

Good consultants are always in demand; indeed, the main complaint a good consultant is likely to have is that he is overworked. There are more projects crying out for good consultants than there are good consultants: it is as simple as that. On the other hand, there is always going to be competition among consultancies, and the more lucrative and exciting the market in which the consultancy operates, the more intense the competition will be.

If you are going to run a successful consultancy, or play a key role in a successful consulting division (and all star consultants will be doing one or the other), you have little choice but to be merciless towards your competition. After all, if they are pitching for a job that you sincerely believe you could do better, you will want to try to produce an even better pitch. There are no prizes or moral bonus points for retiring gracefully from the competition (at least as long as you believe the client will have the money to pay you). Business is business, and capitalism is based on efficiency being generated by competition putting a premium on quality. After all, if you were running, say, an airline, you would want to win passengers who might otherwise go to your competitors, so why should running a consultancy be any different?

Therefore you really don't have much choice but to be prepared to make money even if it means someone else will lose out. Fortunately, in the developed world, losing out on a competitive business pitch does not usually mean that you lose the ability to feed yourself and your family. In any case, the loser may be obliged to review why they did not win, and may become a better player or consultant as a result.

Generally, there is no avoiding the basic competitive fact that in any finite market you can succeed only at the expense of others. Don't let it worry you, though. After all, *you* didn't make the world.

Do you feel responsible for giving your family a better standard of living?

Presumably you will, and if you don't, maybe you ought to think about developing that responsibility. There is nothing like the sense that really important things – such as your family's standard of living – are at stake for making you perform at your best.

Is your spouse or partner supportive of your work?

If they are, congratulations, you are lucky to have an ally in your efforts. If they are not, you will not be able to change their mind overnight, but you should let them know on a fairly regular basis that you really would appreciate their support.

When Alex was making plans to set up IDOM, he and his wife, Kati, spent many hours discussing the risk that would inevitably be involved. Alex had spent 17 years working for Midland Bank (now part of HSBC) and setting up IDOM meant not only leaving a well-paid job but also taking a financial risk. What if not enough clients were forthcoming? What if the first client (which had already been won) turned out to be the last?

With hindsight, all success looks inevitable, but at the time it hardly ever does, and it certainly didn't in IDOM's case. Today, Alex attributes much of IDOM's success to his wife's understanding and support, which ultimately provided a bedrock whereby her work as a doctor would have supported the family if IDOM had not succeeded.

Are you happy with the amount of time you spend with your family?

In both the book and film versions of *The Godfather*, the hugely successful Don Corleone – who is presented sympathetically throughout the book as a caring, sincere and genuine man – is always telling ambitious people who seek his advice that they should spend more time with their families if they want happiness and success.

We can't prove it, but we think it likely that many people who work extremely long hours in search of career success would do better if they reduced their hours somewhat, devoted more time to making those hours truly productive, and then went home to spend time with their family.

Yes, you do need to work hard to be truly successful, but you also need to be a rounded and fulfilled person in every sense. Neglecting your family is the way to losing their affection and, as tragically sometimes happens, losing them completely.

Do you consider you have a duty to contribute to the well-being of your society by means of your personal success?

This is probably not something you have thought about very much, and at an early stage of your career it perhaps is not very important. However, developing a sense of social responsibility as you progress in your career is likely to be a fruitful experience that will ultimately contribute to your success and to your vision of yourself and your organization. Many successful business people get a great deal of enjoyment and general spiritual enrichment out of helping others, whether through participating in local government, being involved in charities and other interest groups, or by volunteering for some useful social programme.

Ideally, as we have seen, consulting should be about giving, and because all star consultants are, by definition, givers, they find that if time permits, they want to give in other ways, too.

Do you play any role in your trade association or professional association?

This can be an excellent way to find out what your competitors are doing and what the 'buzz' concepts are in your chosen sector. You might also find it a useful source of new business.

Do you ever write letters to the editors of newspapers on issues you feel strongly about?

If not, why not start? A regular published letter to an editor on an issue you want to help influence can, if you are careful to include your job title and the name of your organization, get your consultancy useful – and gratis – public relations exposure. But if you are doing this, and you are not in charge of the consultancy, make sure your press office clears your initiative first or it may backfire.

Do you read the daily and specialized press?

If you don't, you should do. Consultants need to be people of broad knowledge and culture, who have a detailed knowledge of what is going on in the world at a national and international level, and also of what is going on in different industrial and commercial sectors.

Are you constantly on the look-out for new ideas?

Almost by definition, consultants are expected to generate ideas with the same regularity and reliability that a power station is expected to generate electricity. After all, while your ability to cast a disinterested perspective on a problem is one of the reasons why you are being hired as a consultant, you are also usually expected to find solutions, and many solutions are arrived at only after intense and creative thinking.

Consultants *need* to be genuinely creative thinkers, particularly in the context of creativity as the ability to develop original models or structures using only a knowledge of more simple and unoriginal models or structures. In other words, if, as a consultant, you are not constantly looking out for new ideas and, ideally, producing them, you are not really a consultant at all.

Do you try to find ways of applying great new ideas you hear about to your own consultancy?

Injections of new ideas and improvements are essential for any business's vitality. If you are the boss of a consultancy or playing a key role in one, make your consultancy flexible enough so that improvements and good ideas can be taken on board with the minimum upheaval. If you work for a consultancy in a more subordinate capacity, try to win yourself a reputation for making good and constructive suggestions.

Are you enthusiastic about technology?

In the end, most modern consulting activity is related to technology to a greater or lesser extent. This is not surprising: technology is the most exciting radical business tool available to consultants today and, properly applied, can transform a business's operations. You need to be interested in it and enthusiastic about it, but you should never be enthusiastic about technology for its own sake. *What matters is not how state-of-the-art a technology is, but what it can do for your clients.*

What do you really think of your customers?

First, call them 'clients'. Shopkeepers have customers, consultants have clients. The different terminology is not a matter of snobbery: it is due to the fact that the notion of a 'client' implies a more interactive relationship with a customer than simply selling them some retail product.

Clients are the lifeblood of any consultancy. If you are not motivated and enthusiastic, your clients will not need a radar to detect your lack of interest. There will always be plenty of competitors around to lure your unhappy clients away.

Within your consultancy, cultivate an awareness that clients are an integral part of your business activity, not a separate entity. Concentrate on their needs. As self-improvement guru Dale Carnegie once tellingly remarked: 'You can make more friends in two months by becoming more interested in other people than you can in two years by trying to get people interested in you.'

How well do you handle criticism?

Constructive criticism is just that: a constructive tool that you can learn from. Your work will benefit if you start to see criticism as a helpful pointer that steers you in the right direction rather than as a personal affront.

Of course, there are always 'professional complainers' out there for whom nothing you do can be right and who are never happy. Professional complainers rarely change their ways – accept them for what they are and minimize your exposure to them.

If you are already in a corporate position, do you ever actively seek constructive criticism from those above you?

You should do this as a matter of course. If you do not actively seek it, you are going to find that they give it to you anyway.

Do you ever seek constructive criticism from those below you?

Never allow yourself to become so arrogant that you do not believe you have anything to learn from people below you in the corporate hierarchy. Remember that many junior people, and many secretaries and administrative assistants, are likely to be as well educated as you (or even more so). More to the point, they do not intend to stay where they are for ever. In particular, the days when women were prepared to be secretaries all their working lives are, fortunately, over. Respect your subordinates and seek their advice. Apart from anything else, you need to take on board the fact that your subordinates may become your peers, your clients or even your superiors.

Why did you buy this book?

We hope for all of the following reasons:

○   to be entertained;

○ to be stimulated;

○ to become a better consultant.

Let's hope that by the end of the book, you will feel that we have done *our* job properly.

CHAPTER THREE

Starting out

Introduction

This chapter is essential reading for people who are on the verge of setting up their own consultancy or are about to start playing a key role in running their own consulting division.

However, it isn't only for them. We have designed it to be relevant to anybody planning to be a star consultant.

An essential element of stardom from a consulting perspective is being quite clear in your mind about how your consultancy is better than others. Helping you to understand this is, above all, what this chapter is about. Naturally, this is a particularly important issue for start-ups, but it is obviously a major issue for all consultants, no matter how long they have been working.

If you think about it, you are going to make a success of any kind of new business, whether it is a consultancy, a butcher's shop, an airline, a global computer company or even a hot-dog stall, only if you are entirely clear – and we mean entirely clear, not partially clear, not almost clear – about why the world needs your business and, if there are already other businesses doing similar things to what your business will be doing, why your business is special.

What applies to all kinds of businesses applies particularly to consultancies. Why? Because there are so many consultancies about already. *Too many*, a cynic might say, and the cynic would be right. There are too many consultancies that do not give value for money, too many that do not take the trouble to listen to their clients, too many that apply a standardized, formulaic solution to a client's problems without having the sense to realize that there are as many different client problems as there are different clients. In short, there are too many consultancies that aren't up to the job.

Why are there so many consultancies about? The main reasons are:

○ it does not (and should not) cost very much to set up a consultancy, and the relatively low overheads mean that, at least for one-man bands or smaller consultancies, most of the fees earned can go straight into the consultant's pocket;

○ many experienced senior people who become unemployed later in their careers often find it difficult or impossible to find another job. For them, consultancy is an extremely attractive option (incidentally, many of these people make superb consultants);

○ for all the reasons we outlined in the Introduction, consulting is a growing business, and ambitious people who want to earn high salaries are naturally attracted to it;

○ another point we made in the Introduction – that there is an increasing tendency for employment within organizations of all kinds to be project-based – naturally cuts both ways. As well as helping to explain why organizations are often prepared to use consultants rather than hire salaried staff to do the same job, it also tends to create a project-based labour market in which people are often encouraged to consider operating as consultants rather than simply seeking another job;

○ the income that can be earned from consulting is usually substantial. Many experienced consultants – even one-man bands – can charge at least $1500 per day for their work and often as much as $5000 or more;

○ there are no barriers to entry for most types of consulting: anybody can do it and there are no stipulated professional qualifications needed. Even in industries where many consultants belong to official bodies such as professional institutes and trade associations, membership is not usually necessary in order to practise as a consultant.

Why you need to demonstrate that you are special

All these reasons add up to a situation where there are almost certainly going to be many other consultants and consultancies out there in the field in which you specialize. You will only have any chance of succeeding if you are quite clear in your mind – and can express this clarity in your marketing literature and general marketing efforts – not only *why* clients would want to hire a consultant in the first place, but also why they would want to hire *you*.

Why should they be interested in using your services at all when there are so many other consultancies and consultants practising? Indeed, this question is so important that you should not proceed with creating your consultancy or consulting division, or with continuing to practise as a consultant in the way you have practised in the past, unless you have a very good, robust answer to it.

The question of your unique selling proposition (USP) – an extremely important marketing term meaning what makes you special compared with your rivals – is so fundamental to your activities as a consultant that it is the very next question you need to ask yourself after addressing the first two questions of the planning process: 'What kind of consulting services will I be offering?' and 'Is there a significant demand for these services in the marketplace?'

In a moment, we look at these, and other, extremely important questions in detail. Finding answers to them is the most vital task in the process of planning your consulting activity, whether or not you are a start-up. Before we consider them, though, let us set down some points about the importance of the planning stage.

Why preparatory planning is so important

Starting out as a consultant, or starting a new consultancy or consulting division, is an adventure and can be extremely exciting, even thrilling, but that does not give you an excuse to start behaving impulsively and erratically, any more than being impulsive and erratic will help you if you are involved in *any* adventure.

Try to climb Everest for fun wearing trainers and trendy casual clothes and you aren't going to come back (or, more realistically, we hope you will have the sense to give up your adventure long before you even reach the foot of the mountain). But climb another dozen or so smaller mountains by way of rehearsal, do your planning carefully and thoughtfully, train obsessively to get fit, check weather conditions, wear the right clothes and equipment, and go as part of an expedition run by someone with the sense to turn back if it gets risky up there, and you might, just might, succeed.

Starting a consultancy or consulting division is not as physically dangerous as climbing Mount Everest, but if you fail – if you do not do it properly, if you end up losing money and have to make an ignominious return to the world of the salaried employee (and the monotonous Japanese word for this, *sarariman*, sums up perfectly the obscurity and ordinariness of that status) – the harm to your career could be overwhelming.

Besides, who is to say that career damage is not as serious a form of damage to you as getting frostbite at 25 000ft? The loss of self-esteem and the depression that career failure causes can be extremely damaging (and in rare cases can lead to suicide). Such damage to your ego (and finances) can affect your whole personality. So get it right. Do the job properly, and make things work as they ought to work. Read our advice, and follow it.

Later in *Breakthrough Consulting*, we introduce you to the notion of the self-fuelling consultancy (SFC), which is a start-up consulting model that allows you to minimize your financial and career risk. Your financial commitment grows only as your income from the consultancy grows, and basically it is difficult for the SFC to go wrong as long as you face reality all the time and keep your feet on the ground. The SFC, viewed as a model of how a new consultancy should grow, is also immensely useful for anybody who is setting up a new division within an existing consulting organization, and the lessons deriving from the SFC business model are highly relevant to all consultants, everywhere.

Starting a new consultancy, like starting any other business, is a profoundly creative enterprise and as such requires careful preliminary planning. Successful new consultancies do not suddenly spring, fully formed, into life any more than successful novels, films or plays do. New consultancies, like works of art, like anything that is to be created, require thoughtful planning and preparation.

The five questions you have to ask

So how *do* you plan your consulting? The process is not as daunting as it may at first seem. What you have to do – assuming you have decided that your life will not be complete unless you start your own consultancy (and if you do *not* feel this, you may not be sufficiently motivated) – is address the following five questions with great intensity of thought and concentration.

❍ What kind of consulting services will I be offering?

❍ Is there a significant demand for these services in the marketplace?

❍ Can I bring something special to the marketplace that existing consultants in this field are not already offering?

❍ Do I have a genuine ability to sell by identifying client needs?

❍ Do I have my first client in place?

You should proceed with your start-up consultancy or consulting division only if you are *absolutely* convinced that your answers to these five questions are such that your start-up cannot do anything but succeed!

Note how we phrased that. We did not say that your answers must be so convincing that your start-up has a good chance of success, we said that *they must be such that your start-up really cannot do anything but succeed.* Your knowledge of what you are doing, and of the marketplace in which you will be operating, really does need to be as deep and comprehensive as that.

We now look at these questions in detail.

What kind of consulting services will I be offering?

The answer to this question should arise naturally and easily out of your existing professional or vocational experience. The only situation in which you might need to give some protracted thought to what type of services you would be offering would be where you had detailed expertise in two or more areas but were not sure in which one you should specialize. For example, somebody with extensive experience in marketing may have to decide whether to set up as a marketing consultant, public relations consultant or advertising agent.

However, since it is likely that the two (or more) areas in which you have specialized to date will be related, it may be advisable for you to solve this problem by offering both (or all) types of service. It will, after all, usually be acceptable to your marketplace for you to offer them under the umbrella of a particular kind of consulting description.

How extensive an experience of a particular specialization is sufficient to give you the level of ability and knowledge that you will need in your life as a consultant? There cannot be a hard and fast rule about this; after all, people assimilate information at widely varying speeds, and what one person can master in a year, another person may need several years to absorb properly. However, it is doubtful that you will have sufficient expertise and confidence to offer consulting services in your specialization unless you have at least five years of experience in practising that specialization. There may be exceptions to this rule, such as if you are one of the few people in your country who knows about a particularly specialized field of expertise, but generally the five-year rule holds.

Quite apart from the fact that you cannot expect clients to pay for your specialized and hard-won advice if your experience is *not* specialized and hard-won, it obviously makes sense for you to make as many business mistakes as you can at other people's expense, i.e. at the expense of people who employ you during those five or more years. There are quite enough mistakes that can be made after you set up your consultancy for you to have every reason to want to make fundamental business mistakes while you are still an employee.

Is there a significant demand for these services in the marketplace?

There are two aspects to this question: the notion of a demand existing for your service, and a *significant* demand existing. Ultimately, only you can decide, using your knowledge of the industry in which you will be operating, what exactly constitutes a *significant* demand. We cannot attach any precise quantities to that because it is a function not of the overall level of demand but of the overall level of demand in relation to the supply of consultants able to meet it.

We once knew an enormously successful international consultant who was essentially the only specialist in his field globally in dealing with a particular aspect of corrosion that affects oil rigs. Even though there are only a small number of oil companies in the world and this particular type of corrosion was comparatively rare, this consultant was still phenomenally busy and could charge several thousand dollars per day for his services.

Whether you are offering a service that is clearly in demand in the marketplace by virtue of the fact that many existing consultancies offer it, or whether you are a specialist in oil rig corrosion, you need to know your market so well that you can be certain that you will be busy, and busy all the year round. If you have a specialization that is in demand only during, say, the summer months, you obviously are not going to be able to work full-time as a consultant throughout the year. You need to apply your common sense to every aspect of this planning process.

Remember, too, that in economic terms *demand* is not the same as *want*. Want is human need without money to get the want satisfied. Sadly, the developing countries are frequently overburdened with want, but it is not demand because the money does not exist to pay for meeting the want. Similarly, you need to be realistic about the ability of your prospective market to pay you. For example, if you have experience in helping charities manage their financial planning, you need to be certain that they will be prepared to pay you for providing this advice, otherwise you will be phenomenally busy, but also phenomenally impoverished.

Answering this second question is very much your job rather than ours. We cannot know what area you are consulting in; but what we do know is that if you are not familiar enough with your prospective marketplace to know whether there is going to be enough of a demand for your services to enable you to make a good living (which is as good a definition of 'significant demand' as any), you need to become more familiar with your market before you even thinking of launching into it as a consultant.

Can I bring something special to the marketplace that existing consultants in this field are not already offering?

Let us again make it quite clear: you must have a good answer – and ideally several answers – to this question before taking the plunge and setting up your own consultancy. This is no time for dishonesty or self-delusion; indeed, when you are thinking of setting up a high-income consultancy there is never any time for dishonesty or self-delusion. You have simply got to ensure, before you take the plunge, that *you can offer the market something it does not have already*.

What we mean here is that you need to find yourself a significant incremental advantage that will allow you to stand out from your rivals. You need to identify, establish and maintain a competitive advantage that is sufficiently significant that you can attract clients because they perceive you as special.

In essence, it is the idea which provides this competitive advantage that justifies the creation of your consultancy. It will almost certainly only be an incremental advantage: that is, it will operate at the margin of what an existing market wants rather than be something so radical and enormous that you in effect create a completely new market of your own.

Unless you are exceptionally gifted, or very lucky, you will probably not be able to find an entirely new type of consulting service to offer. But don't despair. There are several types of incremental advantage that you can establish over your rivals. We will examine some of these in a moment. For the time being, keep firmly in your mind the unpleasant but incontestable fact that there are consultancies being set up in the business world all the time, and far too few of the consultants who run those consultancies have ever bothered to try to work out what they can offer that the competition cannot. If you *do* do this, you have an edge over them.

The principal reason why so many new consultancies do not survive more than a few weeks or months is that they have failed to identify the precise nature of the competitive advantages they can offer.

What you really need to do here is to list your USPs and keep them in mind at all times. If you can't think of any, there are only two things you can do:

○ work like crazy to develop some, and soon;
○ abandon the idea of starting a new consultancy or consulting division.

The matter really is as simple as that. Face reality *now*, do not put it off until six months or a year into trying to start up a consultancy that nobody wants, when the consequences of facing reality will be much less pleasant, and even extremely *unpleasant*.

So what types of incremental advantages, or USPs, could a start-up consultancy offer? We suggest the following, but please do *not* regard this list as necessarily inclusive of all possibilities. It isn't. If you believe you are able to establish a type of incremental advantage that we have not mentioned here, and have solid evidence for this belief, you may be right.

A better knowledge of the market

If you genuinely have a better knowledge of the market than your rivals, or a better knowledge of a niche sector in the market in which you are operating, you should be well on your way to establishing an important incremental advantage over your rivals.

Alex was able to get IDOM off to a flying start by utilizing his extensive knowledge of Hungarian business and the fact that Hungarian is his mother tongue. Alex was able to use this knowledge to sell his consultancy's rigorous and results-orientated information technology consulting services to Hungarian banks. These banks were keen to modify their operational structures and technology bases to make these suitable for trading within the market economies that started to prevail in Hungary and other Eastern European countries after 1989.

Alex secured his first clients in Hungary, and having learned exactly how he could help Hungarian banks to achieve their goals, took the logical step of developing his business to its utmost in Hungary while establishing offices in other Central European countries. The consultancy enjoyed spectacular success. When Alex sold it, he guaranteed financial security for himself and his family, and was able to launch a new career as an international entrepreneur.

An ability to provide better proposals and reports

Writing proposals and reports – that is, making recommendations to your clients for action that you advise them to take, and subsequently reporting back to them on what action you did take and what the results of it were – is an essential part of the consulting business. (We explore this vital subject in Chapter Seven.)

The quality of writing that goes into many proposals consultants provide to their clients can be horribly low. In particular, proposals are usually much too long. Even highly experienced consultants all too frequently believe it is better to use a long word in a report when a short one will do, and also that the more words you use, the more profound or clever you are being. Both these ideas are, of course, nonsense. William Shakespeare, the greatest writer of all, wrote: 'Shall I compare thee to a summer's day?', not, 'Would it be in my interest to effect a comparison between you and any unspecified 24-hour period that occurs at or around the summer solstice?' What is good enough for Shakespeare should be good enough for you. Chapter Seven gives you the low-down on writing great reports and proposals, but in the meantime the following rules for good business writing need to become an immediate part of your fundamental expertise as a consultant.

○ Never use a long word or phrase when a short one will do. 'Begin' is always better than 'commence', just as 'wordy nonsense' is always better than 'excessive verbosity that hinders the communications process'.

○ Remember, as Shakespeare had Polonius say in *Hamlet*, that 'brevity is the soul of wit'. In other words, the fewer words you can use to say what you want to say, the better.

○ Avoid repeating words on the same page if you can. The only exceptions are those short, familiar words such as 'and', 'a', 'the', 'is', 'are' and so on, that you can hardly avoid using fairly frequently. However, even with these you should try to avoid excessive repetition.

○ When you have finished the first draft of a report or any writing you are doing for your business, always get a print-out of the document and revise it before inputting your revisions to produce a final draft. This is a far more effective method of revision than staring at the document on a screen. And ideally, allow at least one day to elapse between writing your draft and revising it.

Being able to offer a more cost-effective service

Generally speaking, if you can undercut your rival consultancies on price and provide an equivalent or even better level of service, you should be able to get a foothold in whatever market you choose. Although there are always clients who insist on believing that the more their consultants charge them, the better the consultant is, most clients have enough sense to realize that if they can get what they want from a consultant at a lower price, that consultant is worth using.

A moment's thought should show you that this particular possibility for incremental advantage should be very much in your favour, as someone setting up an independent consultancy. Whether or not you decide to begin as a one-person band or to start your consultancy with one or more assistants or associates, you should have little difficulty in undercutting larger consultancies with higher overheads and numerous staff. We look at pricing in detail in the next chapter, but for the moment you should bear in mind that many large consultancies charge about $5000 or even much more per day for the services of a senior consultant, with junior consultants (who may be only a year or so out of college or university) being charged out at around $1000 per day.

Of course, clients realize perfectly well that if they want to hire a consultant from one of the world's largest management firms they will need in effect to pay not only the consultant's salary but also a substantial contribution towards the consultancy's overheads, the salaries of administrative staff and the firm's profit margin.

Yet clients are fed up with receiving huge bills from large consultancies and are highly motivated to obtain their consulting advice at a lower price if they can. It is for this reason that a chance of winning business exists for someone who is setting up a new consultancy. As evidence of this, even large consultancies are having to look at ways of giving clients better value for money.

If you are planning on making price advantage one of your incremental advantages – and we suspect it is more than likely that you *will be* doing this – never describe yourself, whether face-to-face with a business prospect or in your corporate literature, as 'cheap'. Nobody wants to use a consultant who is cheap. We do not like the phrase 'competitively priced' either; it is pompous and meaningless. Instead, say you offer 'value for money' or are 'cost-effective'.

Remember, too, that being cost-effective is not just a matter of the level of your pricing. It is also about maximizing the tangible benefits your clients receive from using you. These tangible benefits will depend on many things but primarily on your expertise, know-how, sincerity and experience. This partly explains why it helps if you are a relatively senior heavyweight in the industry. You do not need to be older than 40, with 20 years' experience in your field, to be an outstanding consultant, but it certainly helps if you are.

Displaying a willingness to make part of your remuneration dependent on the results you achieve for your clients

It is becoming a growing trend for consultants to woo clients by being prepared to make at least part of their remuneration dependent on the results they achieve. Payment by results is already a major feature of the legal industry in the United States and is becoming a feature of legal industries in many other countries, including Britain.

The logic of consultants following suit in this respect is that it gives them an opportunity to put their money where their mouth is. And after all, if they are hands-on consultants, who are actually carrying out the recommendations they set down, it is not surprising that clients may expect them to make part of their payment dependent on results.

Of course, doing this is only a good idea where the success of the enterprise is clearly dependent on you. Sometimes, this is not really the case. For example, if you are a public relations consultant, there is every reason for the client to expect you to take responsibility for the amount of editorial coverage you generate. However, you cannot possibly have any influence over the level of sales the client receives from that coverage – this is beyond your control and it is pointless for your payment to depend on the sales the client generates from that coverage. In any case, it is virtually impossible for a client to be certain which particular strand of their marketing led to a particular sale.

On the other hand, if you have specified a new front-office trading analysis system for a Wall Street derivatives trader, you may well find it in your interest to make some of your remuneration dependent on the amount of money the new system makes for the trader in, say, the first year of operation. After all, the amount of money it makes will be a function of its quality as a system. This kind of arrangement is becoming increasingly common.

Strategic consultants, too, are prepared to make part of their remuneration dependent on, say, the cost savings their recommendations achieve for a client during the first year after their implementation. Generally, if you are prepared to do this, it may add up to a significant incremental competitive advantage for you in your field, at least if no one else is doing it. Even if they are, you may be able to devise a type of payment-by-results arrangement which particularly appeals to prospective clients.

Offering a more hands-on service

Your practical experience of the industry in which you are going to be consulting is always going to be an essential element of your business proposition as a consultant. This aspect of your sales proposition often gives a particular advantage to small, start-up consultancies. Why? Because these tend to be started by people who already have extensive, hands-on experience of the industry where they want to consult, whereas many large consulting firms are staffed by consultants who went to university and probably then to business school before joining a large consulting firm. They may be highly intelligent, they may be great at listening, they may have the capacity to empathize with clients and help them, but their careers have shown a disconcerting lack of real experience in the firing line of making a business work, and their effectiveness may be limited as a result.

Alex founded IDOM only after spending 17 years working in banking. Many of the world's best consultants consult only when they have had many years' experience in a particular industrial sector. Charteris, a highly successful UK management consultancy (profiled in detail in the appendix) only hires consultants who have specific, hands-on experience of deriving true business benefits from technology in management positions. It does not hire people straight out of business school – to join Charteris you need to prove yourself first in your career as a hands-on manager.

Offering a more sincere, personal service

We emphasized at the start of the last chapter that in the consulting business it is ultimately personality that wins accounts. Even where clients are dealing with a consultancy which is large enough or has been established for long enough to have acquired a corporate identity, clients will always regard themselves as dealing with a particular person or group of people at the organization. The term 'a people business' is used too widely in the modern business world, but it is certainly true of the consulting business.

If you choose, as we think you should, to start your consultancy small and let it grow organically through fuelling its own success (we will look at this further in Chapter Five), you will set out with an in-built advantage in terms of giving your clients a sincere, personal service – as long as you can back up your sincerity and ability to deliver a personal service with real expertise and experience in the field in which you are consulting. When your clients deal with your consultancy they will be dealing with *you*, or perhaps you and one or two associates, but you will be the linchpin of the service that is offered to the client and you can make that service personal and sincere.

Clients who deal with large consultancies frequently complain that they have to deal with different consultants at different times. This, as you can imagine, is particularly annoying for clients who have found one consultant within the large consultancy who understands their needs and seems intelligent and helpful. Another frequent complaint levelled at large consultancies – and often not without justification, it has to be said – is that the team of people who *win* the business is rarely the same as the team of people who *handle* the business. Most large consultancies have specialized 'new business' teams whose task it is to seek out and win new business for the consultancy and who often include, for obvious reasons, the most talented and dynamic people who work for the consultancy – a kind of bait, you might say. Unfortunately for the client, in a large consultancy the new business team rarely actually works on the new business it has won, often leaving it to be carried out by a lower calibre of person.

Clearly, for a start-up consultancy, the people who win the business will also be those who work on it. This makes for client goodwill, since the consultant will have been familiar with the client's business from the outset and will know exactly what the client is aiming to do. Of course, this inherent advantage will apply only if you can win enough trust and respect from your prospective clients to make them want to use your service in the first place.

Offering a more thoughtful service

Small, independent consultancies are often able to offer a service that the client perceives as (and that may in fact be) more thoughtful than that offered by rival consultancies, and particularly by larger rivals. The main reason for this is that the client is likely to perceive the small, independent consultancy as comprised of 'chiefs' rather than 'Indians'. Furthermore, a client will often be amenable to the idea that a small consultancy can provide a specialized service in a niche market, although if you want your client to believe this you will need to provide evidence of your abilities in this niche market.

We should hardly need to point out that even if the existing or prospective client does believe these things about your consultancy, this will only be the case until you do something stupid that convinces the client you are not terribly thoughtful after all. Don't give the client the opportunity to think anything other than that you and your associates are exceptional and gifted people with whom the client should feel privileged to work.

Offering a service backed by more specialized expertise

Closely related to the last point is the principle that a small independent consultancy will usually be able to orientate itself around a niche specialization (i.e. a specialization 'within a specialization'). Given that there is a demand for the niche specialization, providing that service – which is of course possible only if you have the requisite expertise – can provide an important competitive edge.

Displaying a willingness to take infinite pains

The writer and wit Oscar Wilde once wrote: 'Talent is the capacity for taking infinite pains.' Being seen as someone who will stop at nothing to look after your clients is without doubt a way to establish an extremely important incremental competitive advantage. Ultimately, however, you will only be able to take infinite pains on your clients' behalf if you are truly devoted to them and if you love what you do. You can pretend for a while, but not for long. Now back to the other main questions relating to preliminary planning.

Do I have a genuine ability to sell by identifying client needs?

This is a rarer skill than might be imagined. Even if you are a good listener, you need to be able to convince prospective clients that their needs/problems/challenges can be addressed by hiring your consulting firm. Even more important, you have to be able to show clients that they may have needs/problems/challenges *that they are not even aware of* and that you can address these, too.

Do I have my first client in place?

Every new consultancy or new consulting wing of an existing organization needs to have its first client in place before it can get started. There should, in effect, be a transition phase between you doing what you were doing in the past (e.g. working as a salaried employee) and changing to being a consultant. During that transition phase you need to use whatever of your existing contacts and relationships are appropriate in order to get your first client.

The first client may be an organization you are already involved with professionally; one that you know will engage you as a consultant. Your first client may come to you via a friend, a business contact, or whatever: what matters is your skill at relationship selling, which enables you to turn that relationship into a genuine first client, a client who will, ideally, eventually give you a glowing reference that you can use to build up your business.

The importance of proceeding with your plan to create a consultancy only when you have got that client cannot be overstated. *Finding that first client is your first real job as a consultant*, not forming your consultancy idea into a corporation or obtaining office premises or advertising for a secretarial assistant. Forget all those things. Your priority is to get your first client.

Do not imagine that a consulting business consists of its premises, its logo, its stationery and its bank account. It doesn't. A business is, and always has been, a relationship between a seller and a buyer. It is true that when a business grows and develops, the nature of the relationship between seller and buyer becomes, to some extent, standardized – sometimes by the product that is sold being made into a 'branded' product – but what constitutes a business is the buyer and seller relationship at the heart of it.

This is true for all businesses, but in many businesses involve the buying and selling of a product, the relationship between seller and buyer becomes formalized, with the personalities of individual buyers becoming unimportant. McDonald's, the fast-food chain, would no doubt prefer you to eat regularly at its restaurants, but if you decided tomorrow you would never visit a McDonald's restaurant again, nobody at McDonald's would lose any sleep over it.

When you start up a consultancy you revert to the purest form of business: the personal relationship between seller and buyer. That being the case, isn't it slightly absurd to begin a consultancy without at least one such relationship to get you started?

By getting your first client before you start your consultancy in any formal sense you will gain the following benefits:

❍ having won one client, you will enjoy the essential, all-important confidence that you will be able to win additional clients;

❍ the nature of the service you are providing to your first client will help to clarify in your mind precisely what kind of service you will need to offer as a consultant;

❍ you will have at least some income for the inevitably difficult first months when you have no salary coming in;

❍ you may, if you do a good job for your first client (as you must, if you want to survive), wind up with a client who is prepared to recommend you to other potential clients, or who at the very least should be prepared to give you a reference;

❍ when you meet prospective clients, it will be greatly in your favour if you are able to talk (in terms which, for reasons of client confidentiality, should be general rather than too specific) about a current assignment or assignments on which you are working. Obviously you have got to start somewhere, and there will be that 'first client' who really is your first client, but it is never a good idea to let prospective clients suspect, even for an instant, that you are currently 'resting'. People think an actor can 'rest' and still be good, but they do not look at consultants in the same way. Consultants without anything to do are regarded – not entirely unfairly, perhaps – as bad ones.

There is, unfortunately, no easy answer to how to get your first client. It is, however, most likely to stem from an existing relationship. IDOM's first client was the Hungarian Foreign Trade Bank, which Alex had got to know while working at Midland Bank. That one client provided IDOM with a glowing reference, and in a sense all IDOM's success stemmed from that.

Generally, if you are the kind of person who has the aptitude to make a success of starting a consultancy, and if you have completed the minimum five years of experience in your chosen field which, as we have already stated, we believe you need if you are going to consult for a living, you should already have numerous business contacts, any one of which may turn into your first client. You need to bear in mind that if you are already working (or have been working) in a service business, you may need to abide by contractual arrangements that prevent you from working for one of your employer's existing clients for a certain period. Law courts tend to take those contracts seriously, so you will have to be careful not to break the terms of your agreement, or not to break them openly. However, you are also likely to have potentially useful business contacts from jobs other than your current (or last) job.

With any luck you should be able to identify at least half a dozen business contacts whom you believe could become your first client. Go and see all of them – in your own time, not in your employer's time – and confide your plans to them. Even if they do not become a client, they will appreciate your having confided in them and they may well help you out by telling their contacts about your plans and about who you are.

In Chapter Six we look at the all-important task of winning new business, but it needs to be said here that most consultants get the vast majority of their new business from personal recommendation and word of mouth, and by existing clients asking the consultant to do something else. There are other methods of obtaining new business, and these can be very useful, but personal recommendation and word of mouth are by far the most important ways to win business, whether you are starting out or after you have been a consultant for ten years.

So now you have your first client, or even your first and second clients. Try to negotiate a deal with them that gives you at the very least enough revenue to meet your basic needs for six months, or a year if you can get it. That way, you will have some leeway while you work on their business and also build up your consultancy. But before we move on to look at the specific practicalities of setting up your consultancy or consulting division, you need to think hard about something that is going to be an extremely important issue for you in your work, and life, as a star consultant – money.

CHAPTER FOUR

Money

Introduction

Perchik: *Money is the curse of the world.*
Tevye: *May God smite me with it.*

from *Fiddler on the Roof*

This chapter is all about money. Some may see money as a distasteful subject for an entire chapter of what is designed at least in part to be an inspirational book. We don't agree.

You cannot pursue the goal of being a star consultant with all your energy and concentration unless you have sorted out in your mind what money means to you. Indeed, you cannot be certain of your motivation for even *wanting* to be a star consultant unless you know where you stand as far as money is concerned.

In this chapter, we look at money in more detail than you might expect to see in a business book. We start our discussion with a consideration of the attitudes held in Western culture and consider how these might underlie your conscious or unconscious thinking about money. We then move on to consider what money should mean to anybody wishing to be a consultant of any kind, and especially a star consultant.

Why do we start by looking at attitudes to money in Western culture? Because these attitudes are bound to underpin your attitude to money, and if you are to be a successful consultant there must be nothing confused or equivocal about how you see money. It is an important, and fascinating, subject, and it needs some hard thinking applied to it. You need to get your attitude to money absolutely clear in your mind. After all, if you don't know exactly what money means to you, why would you want to work to make it?

Attitudes to money

Money – the ultimate taboo

Everybody knows the radio talkshow host – and quintessential 'shock-jock' – Howard Stern. This irreverent, highly intelligent, extremely hard-working and creative man (who likes to be known, with becoming modesty, as the 'King of All Media') has catapulted himself to the height of the ferociously competitive US media industry – and to a secure, if controversial, niche in American culture – by virtue of his talent. He has written one extremely good book about his life and starred (showing remarkable acting ability) in a witty and insightful film of the book. More than 20 million Americans regularly tune in to his morning radio programme.

A few years ago, Stern made a bid to become mayor of New York. He probably started his campaign more as a publicity stunt than for any serious reason, but it quickly gathered momentum, and as it did, Stern took his bid more seriously. The possibility that he might become mayor became increasingly real.

Then, when many polls were in his favour, he suddenly quit. Why? Because he had been forced to accept that, in order to qualify as a mayoral candidate, he had to make public disclosure of his income and details of his personal wealth. He refused to do this, and as a result was obliged to withdraw from the race.

What was this? Howard Stern was regarding his finances as taboo? A man who had achieved much of his fame through his highly entertaining and often extremely witty refusal to kow-tow to conventional taboos relating to matters such as sex and personal hygiene, and who specialized in the public humiliation of celebrities? Yes, when it came to the crunch, it was clear that Howard Stern regarded money – his money – as a taboo he was not prepared to discuss in public. He earns millions from his show and has other showbiz interests, and he considered this to be nobody else's business.

We are not saying he was wrong or hypocritical to make money his personal taboo. He has often said that he is essentially a very private person and that his show and other work is just entertainment. Even so, it is undeniable, and remarkable, that a man who has no respect for sexual taboos (his radio show is famous for being so sexually arousing that it forces some motorists into a lay-by while they cool down), and who hires a chronically stammering interviewer to ask celebrities embarrassing questions – which, because the interviewer stutters so badly, they feel obliged to answer – is prepared so unashamedly to accept that his own money is an insurmountable taboo.

Has money become a bigger taboo in America than sex? Possibly. But this example illustrates what is evident in modern America and other developed countries: people are terribly confused about what to make of money.

The paradox of Western attitudes

So why the problem? Why the 'confusion' about attitudes towards money? Surely everything is simple? People want to become rich, even if there is not much chance of it happening. But the central paradox of Western attitudes towards money is this: people in the West tend to feel awkward about money and often have alarmingly conflicting views towards it, but they nevertheless continue to pursue the making of it with all their energy.

In the developing world, where the possession of money can literally mean the difference between life and death, and often does, people are refreshingly unequivocal in their attitude towards money. They want it and they know its importance, but there is much less guilt and confusion about it than in the West. India, for example, is perhaps the most spiritual country in the world, but the people have a healthy respect for money and its importance. In the West, where an effective welfare system provides a cushion against starvation, people want money just as badly as in developing countries, and they are usually more successful at getting it. But traditional Christian morality tends to conspire to make people feel a certain guilt in pursuing money with vehemence. In most cases, this feeling of guilt does not actually *stop* people from pursuing money, but it does create a serious ambivalence in their attitudes towards it.

The brief interchange from *Fiddler on the Roof* quoted at the start of the chapter sums up the situation. The highly articulate young Jew Perchik, who is also a communist revolutionary, states what is in effect the traditional Christian creed about money, which was, of course, wholeheartedly embraced by Communism. Tevye's reply is very much that of modern Western man. He is expressing a thought millions would echo: 'Yes, it may be the world's curse, but I'd like to have more of that curse.'

This interchange says just about everything one needs to say about Western attitudes towards money. What you, as a breakthrough consultant, need to realize is just how deeply ingrained these attitudes are in Western culture and how much they will probably affect all of the following:

- your attitude to making money;
- your clients' attitude to paying you what you think you should be earning;
- your clients' attitude to seeing you make money;
- the attitude of your family and friends to seeing you grow rich.

We look at these attitudes in more detail before we move on.

In Western mythology and culture, the rich person, or the person who vigorously pursues money, is almost always depicted as wicked. Even where this is not the case, the person is usually portrayed as unfulfilled and generally unaware of what life is really all about. In Shakespeare's *The Merchant of Venice*, for instance, Shylock is the classic example of a money-pursuing evil man. Dramatically masterly but morally confused, the play leaves us feeling dissatisfied because Shakespeare elevates Shylock to a tragic status that seems inconsistent with the trite moral game of which Shylock is the victim.

Shylock insists, with what Shakespeare depicts as pedantic cruelty, on getting his 'pound of flesh' because Antonio's ships have sunk. He has failed to pay on time, and the deal was that if he did not pay, he would have to forfeit that pound of meat. Shylock would have got the pound, too, if he had not been tricked out of it by what is nothing more than a piece of legal chicanery that Shylock would have been roundly condemned for practising if he had used it himself. Shylock is no saint but, as he himself observes, he is treated very badly by the Christians, and one might add that he is treated very badly by the plot, too.

If one views the play from the strict standpoint of business, the real villain is actually Antonio, who did not have the sense to take out marine insurance! More seriously, the play's fundamental hypocrisy is revealed at the end when the young people who have essentially defrauded Shylock out of his money and property are more than happy to make off with it and enjoy it. Suddenly, the love of money does not seem to be such a bad thing after all.

This fundamental moral confusion and hypocrisy recurs throughout literature and in the most popular modern global art form: the movies.

The movie business is a multi-billion dollar industry, where the rewards for success are fabulous. The principal question in Hollywood is whether audiences will pay to see a movie in cinemas and on video/laser disk/DVD afterwards.

So the movies have always faced something of a moral dilemma over money. On the one hand, no art form that is only going to make a profit if it can appeal to millions of people who are *not* rich can afford to depict poor people in a negative light. On the other hand, the financial and lifestyle aspirations of people who write and direct movies are so blatantly materialistic that the possibility of financial hypocrisy is almost genetically textured into the movie business. A subsidiary point here is that many of the most successful movies have derived from stories written under the influence of anti-materialistic Christian morality.

In any event, the facts speak for themselves. The vast majority of movies depict rich people as greedy, selfish and ruthless, with heroes and heroines usually being poor or comparatively indifferent to money. Examples abound. A moral template for thousands of movies, from *High Noon* to *Beverley Hills Cop* and *Die Hard*, is the struggle between a lone hero who believes in the good and appears indifferent to personal ambition, and the bad guys who on the face of it appear to have an overwhelming superiority in strength and who are in most cases simply out to make as much money as the plot will allow them to.

Similarly, in romantic stories where there is rivalry between men or women for the love of the hero or heroine, the less wealthy rival almost always wins. The 1997 movie *Titanic*, for example (which by the end of the 20th century was the most successful film of all time), was, for obvious reasons, never going to derive much dramatic tension from the fate of the ship, so a romantic story was put at the core of the movie. Essentially, the story of *Titanic* is a classical romantic rivalry between the wealthy (by inheritance), spoilt, emotionally congested son of a millionaire businessman, and a bohemian, confident and romantically adept young artist. Both are depicted as attractive in their own way, and it is to the film's credit that the wealthy rival is presented with some moral ambiguity – by the time he starts to lose the heroine, we believe that he truly loves her. Yet the outcome is never really in doubt.

Fortunately, the convenient self-sacrifice of the penniless young artist removes any obligation for the heroine to deal with the consequences of her decision to throw away the prospect of wealth in order to be with him. This particular dilemma is usually avoided in movies, either by the expedient of one of the lovers dying or by a sudden stroke of good fortune catapulting them to wealth in the final frames. Evidently, screenwriters and movie directors are happy to succumb to the need to make good characters poor for the duration of a movie, but they like their own perception of fulfilment to intervene at the end.

So there we have it, a brief summary of Western morality on the question of money. Ignore it at your peril: this moral universe is where you are, or will be, plying your trade, and the developed world's moral confusion about money is not going to get any better, if only because everybody at least has the sense to know that they cannot take their money with them when they depart this Earth.

To summarize, we invite you to consider developing your attitude towards money (at least the attitude you bring to your business dealings) around the following points.

1 Accept that the acquisition of money is, or will be, an essential measure of your success as a consultant.

2 Accept that earning big money will be a major motivating force in your work. By the way, don't forget that earning money should be a *pleasure*.

3 Accept that your clients will not mind paying you well – indeed, will be only too glad to do this – but will expect you to make them all the happier the more they *are* paying you.

4 Don't imagine that money will solve all the problems and challenges that life throws up. (You may, however, decide that you don't mind having the problems and challenges as long as you also have the money.)

5 Remember that there are many wonderful things in life that do not cost a penny, but also that many wonderful things in life *do*.

6 Don't spoil your family, particularly your children. Remember that the spoiled children of wealthy parents often have unhappy lives, resulting from the feeling that they have nothing to strive for. Children deserve security, but they also need the freedom to make their own way in life and feel that their struggles are real ones.

7 When you invest your money, find investments that offer you comparative peace of mind so that you can focus your attentions on your consulting work.

8 Once you have achieved financial success (how you define success in this capacity is up to you, of course) look for good causes and give them your support. Remember that you can't take your money with you when you're gone.

Now let's look at how you are going to make money in the first place or, if you are already making money, how you are going to make more.

Making money from consulting

For most people, the desire to make serious money – in some cases *very* serious money – is the principal motivation behind their desire to become consultants. It should indeed be a main reason for embarking on this fascinating career, but it should not be *the* most important one. *Your principal motivation for becoming a consultant should be that you are genuinely interested in your specialization and that you are also genuinely interested in deploying your skills to help others.*

Just as nobody ever becomes a best-selling novelist without having a genuine love of words and telling stories, you are never going to become a star consultant without genuinely finding your clients interesting and wanting to bring your skills to their service. Great storytellers find that money comes to them by a natural process resulting from millions of people wanting to read their books; great musicians and composers find the same thing. Great consultants need to love what they do first and money will flow to them ... by a natural process? Well no, not entirely. For they operate in the harsh business world, and they need to do things properly if they are to make the money from their hard work and talent that they deserve.

In this chapter, we assume the following:

○ you are genuinely interested in your specialization and have significant expertise in it. Precisely what constitutes 'significant' in this respect usually depends on how much experience your consultant rivals are likely to have, but – as we have suggested – you will probably need at least five years' practical experience in any field in which you are hoping to consult;

❍ you love helping people;

❍ you have a healthy attitude towards money, developed along the lines of the suggested guidelines above.

If any of these points do not apply to you, rethink them and try to develop a positive approach relating to each of them. If you don't, what you are about to read will be less useful to you than it should be.

The secret to making money as a consultant

The secret to making money as a consultant is simple, so simple that you are probably going to wonder why on earth we would bother wasting our time (and yours) telling you it. We would not need to if there were not so many books for consultants that make the fatuous point that you should approach the business of pricing yourself as if you were a consumer product composed of various parts, all of which need to be carefully costed. You are *not* a consumer product. You are a person. You are a person whose skills, energy, intelligence, advice and general talents are desirable in the marketplace, ideally because you have managed to establish a significant incremental competitive advantage along the lines we have already discussed.

As a person who is offering a service to a market that wants that service, your procedure on setting your fees is simplicity itself: *You should charge the greatest amount that the market can bear.*

We will leave aside the fact that most star consultants will on occasion reduce their fees for a special reason. Any true consultant will sometimes undertake *pro bono* work where he may provide his services free of charge or at a heavily discounted rate. We are not talking about that kind of work, we are talking about your typical workaday consulting assignment.

Let us repeat our guidance: you should charge the greatest amount that the market can bear.

There is nothing cynical in this advice, nothing immoral or greedy or money-grubbing about it. It is pure common sense. If you are good at what you do, why on earth should you not charge the most you can get for your services? After all, the whole idea of capitalism is that prices are set by market forces, and if the market permits you to charge a certain high rate, why should you not charge that?

This reminds us of an anecdote about the great Spanish artist Picasso. It sounds like an apocryphal anecdote, and perhaps it is, but the lesson is so important that it does not really matter whether or not it really happened. When Picasso was an old man and at the peak of his profession (by the way, most great consultants find that consulting keeps them young, just as art kept Picasso young), he was enjoying a glass of wine with friends in an outdoor café in the Montparnasse area of Paris one fine summer day. A lady, an art-lover who had been a fan of his for many years, was thrilled to see him sitting near her table. Mastering her nerves, she went up to the great man, handed him a paper napkin and explained that she was a New York millionairess and would be happy to pay anything he liked for a quick drawing on her napkin.

Picasso smiled, thought for a moment, and then drew a few well-chosen squiggles on the napkin. History does not record exactly what he drew, but that isn't the point. The lady looked at it, exclaimed it was wonderful and asked him his price. 'Fifty thousand dollars,' he said.

Suddenly the lady looked a great deal less pleased. 'But Señor Picasso, that took you only ten seconds to draw! Surely you can't expect me to pay that vast figure?' 'Madame,' said Picasso, 'the drawing did not take ten seconds to draw, it took me fifty years.'

Your expertise has taken you your entire career to date to master. Who is to say what that expertise is worth? Nobody but the market, and if the market will pay it, you should feel entirely comfortable about charging it.

Charge your time out at the highest rate the market will bear

This is our first guideline for making money as a consultant. We strongly recommend that the basis for your charging should be the consulting day. It is much better to base your charges around this concept than to quote for a particular project or quote on a monthly rate. Even if you are going to receive a monthly or quarterly fee, the basis for your charging still needs to be the consulting day. There are four reasons for this.

1   Approaching charging in this way is the best method of ensuring that you get paid properly for your time.

2   It is an important discipline for you to estimate in advance how many cumulative days of your time the project will take to complete.

3   Clients like to feel that they are paying for a certain number of consulting days in a given period. That way, they know they can expect the specified number of days to be devoted to their cause.

4   A consultant who charges according to the number of days he is devoting to the project sounds professional and gives the impression of knowing what he is doing.

Imagine for a moment that you are a client. You have a job that needs doing, and you have a shortlist of two consultants, both of whom seem perfectly qualified. One quotes you a monthly fee, but does not provide any breakdown of how much time he will be devoting to the project during that month. The other comes to you and says: 'Having considered the project carefully, I will need ten consulting days each month to carry out the job. My total monthly charge will therefore be based on ten days of my consulting time.'

Which of the two consultants are you most likely to hire? Even if the first consultant is charging less than the second one, isn't the second one going to have a level of credibility which the first doesn't have?

Do remember that if you are going to base your charges around the consulting day as a unit, your client is entitled to know at the end of the month or quarter what exactly you have done on those consulting days. That is only fair. The reports you provide of your activity are a particularly familiar feature of public relations and marketing consulting. Known as activity reports, or sometimes contact reports, they are increasingly frequently seen in other types of consulting. We believe all consultants should base their charges around the consultancy day unit and should also submit activity reports.

So far, so good. However, there is another essential point to make here.

Don't be afraid to ask for a day rate that may be many times what you earned per day as a salaried employee

This is the second guideline for making money as a consultant, and is a crucial point. If you don't ask, you won't get. But remember that you must justify that 'multiple' in the quality of your work, and in the value that your work has to your client.

Many consultants new to the industry undercharge and fail to get taken seriously as a result. If one of your incremental competitive advantages lies in your fees being lower than those of other consultants, you need to be careful that the differential does not become so great that prospective clients wonder what the catch is. In practice it is probably easier to lose business by *undercharging* rather than by charging too much.

When a Massachusetts-based PR consultant we know was launching his public relations consultancy in the late 1980s, he was able to attract significant business from the outset because his location, about 50 miles outside Boston, gave him low overheads that he could pass on to his clients in terms of low fees. He won many valuable mandates through demonstrating to clients that he could provide the same quality of service that they would expect from a Boston-based consultant but charging about half the price that a Boston firm would charge. However, while he was busy, he was not particularly profitable, and eventually came to see that the 50 per cent differential was too great. Not only was his profitability being compromised but some heavyweight clients were not taking him seriously at the rate he charged. He subsequently increased his daily rate to a differential of only about 30 per cent below what Boston-based consultancies charged.

Now on to the next crucial issue: how many consulting days you should be aiming to charge out in a month.

The world's largest consultancies generally expect their consultants to charge at least 75 per cent of their time to clients. Law firms, on the other hand, are normally much tougher: they expect their lawyers to charge out pretty well all their time to clients. Some, especially in the cut-throat world of American law, aim even higher than this. One of the most interesting episodes in John Grisham's book *The Firm* is where the young lawyer is being told by his superiors to think about client business even when he is driving to work, as this makes it legitimate (at least from their perspective) to charge that time to clients.

Our advice here is uncompromising, and it forms the third guideline.

You should cultivate the aim of charging all of your time to clients

There is no room for compromise here. As a consultant who wants to be a star, you have only 20 working days in a four-week month and 25 in a five-week month. There is no reason why you should not aim to charge all that time to clients. After all, what else should you be doing but working as a consultant? Running your consultancy? If by this you mean 'handling accounting and administrative matters', there is no reason why these tasks cannot be fitted in around client activity on particular days. Besides, you will probably want to recruit somebody to handle these matters.

You may say that you need time for internal meetings with your colleagues. Yes, you do need time for these meetings, but it should be easy to keep them short, sharp and to the point. You are consultants, not a debating society. Writers write, artists paint and draw, musicians make music, consultants consult, end of story. The rest, as Gordon Gekko might have said, is just conversation.

The only really legitimate use of your time apart from devotion to client activities is hunting for new business. However, you should be able to delegate much of the research aspect of the task (and as we will see, some research is always necessary in a new business initiative) to your administrative staff, if you have them. Some consultants who make a very good living from home get their spouse to do this kind of research for them, which can make sense because under most tax dispensations the spouse can claim a tax-free allowance every year, thus frequently making it sensible to give them a salary of some kind.

What about time required for new business meetings? You will need to fit those in, but you should be able to fit them in with other meetings in the city centre. If your prospect is located far away, you will probably have to swallow the time needed to get to the meeting. The subject of winning new business is explored later in this book; in the meantime, suffice it to say that it is possible to waste a hideous amount of time on pitching for new business, and this is something you need to guard against.

Other key practical guidelines to making money in consulting

There are other important practical points we need to make about money. Of these, the most important is the following.

Never forget that one great way of making money is avoiding spending it!

Like many of the principles in this chapter, this is also an obvious one, but it is all too frequently forgotten even by experienced consultants, particularly when they are caught up in the supposed excitement of starting a consultancy or consulting division. Trust us, there is nothing exciting about starting *any* business that lands you in financial hell. Financial hell is very, very bad news, and not in the least glamorous. It means being in debt and not being able to clear those debts. It also means – usually – losing control of your finances. Too many consultants wind up in this situation, and the reason is almost always the same: they have spent too much on setting up their consultancy without having done their initial research.

In the next chapter, we provide a blueprint for setting up a particular type of consultancy that starts small and aims to fund its growth from the revenue it generates. Using the consulting model means that entering financial hell should not be a possibility because you are not taking the risks that would lead you to this hell.

When you start any kind of consulting activity, keep your expenses to a minimum. Do you really need a secretary if there are only a few of you and you are all proficient typists, use voice dictation systems or compose your own word-processed documents on your lap-tops or similar. Too many small consultancies hire secretaries who are expensive and basically have nothing to do but answer the phone. Modern telecommunications techniques mean your clients can contact you wherever you happen to be and whenever you are available. Once you reach a critical mass, you may decide that a secretary-cum-receptionist is an essential requirement, but do not take this step too soon.

As far as your office resources are concerned, you should keep expenditure to a minimum. If you and your colleagues are spending most or all of your time working at client locations, for example, it is not even necessary for each of you to have your own desk. This is especially so given the remarkable power of the new generation of laptop computers, which today's top consultants carry around with them rather as if they were an extension of their brain.

In a book such as this, where we assume a reasonable amount of business knowledge on your part, there does not seem much point in going on at length about the need to minimize your expenditure. We hope you will have the sense not to spend much money on your premises until you have a guaranteed income stream. You will not (we hope) spend $3000 on a large filing cabinet system if you do not really need it, and even if you do, you should try to buy it second-hand first. We are not saying you should have premises that are shabby and look unprofessional: the more successful you become as a consultancy, the more often clients will visit your premises, and they need to be convinced that you are operating a professional and tidy ship. What we are saying is that you do not need to give the impression that you are a high-profile advertising agency and waste money on interior design and decorating. What are you selling? You are selling knowledge and expertise. Where is that located? In your consultants' brains. And so your consultants need a comfortable and business-like place in which to work and, above all, think. Making your premises so trendy, over-designed and over-decorated that they distract you and them from working is counterproductive. Even more to the point, it does not give your clients the right message.

You need premises that are businesslike, economical to run, fairly minimalistic and which, above all, allow you to get on with the job.

Part of your management information should be a knowledge of what the consultancy is costing you to run per month, with such items as rent, secretarial expenses, heating, light, telecommunications and computer peripherals all included in the reckoning. But if you are following our guidance of aiming to charge out to clients all the consulting days you work, and if you are charging the maximum amount that the market will bear, you can hardly fail to be profitable.

Our other advice for maximizing the money you make as a consultant is presented here in the form of additional guidelines.

Resist any temptation to over-service your clients

Be careful to avoid over-servicing your clients. While you must, of course, work hard from the outset to keep your clients happy and to maximize the likelihood that they will want you to work for them in the future, there is a danger that in your enthusiasm to make your consulting activity a success, you will give your clients *too much* value for money, i.e. you will devote more time and effort to their interests than is required by the agreement you have with them (we will look at the details of the agreement in the next chapter).

There are three big drawbacks with over-servicing. First, and most obviously, if you devote much more time to one client than you need to devote under your agreement with them, you will be less profitable because you will not be earning the additional revenue you might otherwise have earned from that time. Second, rather than necessarily being deeply impressed with you, the client will – not unreasonably – come to expect you to keep up the same level of over-servicing for the whole time you are working for him. Third, not only will that client's account not be very profitable for you, you may also wind up neglecting your other clients as well as opportunities that may arise for winning new business.

Ensure your agreement covers all activity you will be carrying out on your client's behalf

When you agree to work for a client on a retainer or *ad hoc* basis, you must have a provision in the agreement for what happens if:

○ the client makes additional demands on you not covered by the original agreement;

○ the complexity of the project was not fully clarified at the outset.

You can guard against this danger to some extent by being quite certain, before you quote for the project, what work needs to be undertaken, but the problem can still arise.

We suggest you include in your agreement a provision that additional days of activity will be charged on a pro rata basis, but that you will undertake any additional work only if you receive *written* permission from the client to do so. You need written permission because, as we have discovered, it is all too easy, in the heat of the moment and when the client is under pressure to get the job done, for one of the client's managerial staff to ask you to do the additional work and then, when you have solved the problem, for the client to turn round and say you have overcharged.

Charge expenses at cost

When you make an agreement with a client, charge out-of-pocket expenses (e.g. your telephone and fax charges, postage, rail fares etc.) to them at cost rather than, as many consultancies do, adding a fixed percentage to the expense (the 'mark-up') when invoicing. The small amount of additional revenue you will lose from not imposing a mark-up will be vastly outweighed by the goodwill that this aspect of your pricing policy will create for you with your clients.

Note that this advice does *not* apply with major expenses that you may incur on a client's behalf. For example, if you have arranged for the printing of a brochure for your client, it would be foolish for you not to mark up the printing cost, as this mark-up is a legitimate part of your income from the project. Your mark-up should be in the vicinity of 15 per cent. And don't lay out the money: get it from the client first.

For advertising agencies – which are in their own way a form of advertising consultancy – the mark-up on media spend is an important part of the revenue deriving from a client, even though advertising agencies are increasingly using fee-based structures in addition to mark-up.

Time spent travelling on a client's behalf can be a legitimate expense

This is true, but you need to be sensitive here. Clients can be expected to pay for travel time when you are making a substantial journey in order to undertake the mandate. For example, if you are based in New York and are asked to go to London to work on a project (or vice versa), it is reasonable for you to charge an extra day of your time at the start and end of the project in order to cover the time you spend travelling, although if you are going by Concorde, you may find that the client expects you to confine your claim to two half-days!

On the other hand, the client may balk at being asked to pay travel time from your home to their office. If your office is out of town and you charge out-of-town consulting rates, you might get away with pointing out to the client that they are benefiting from your lower consulting rates, but not every client will be impressed by this argument.

Our advice here is simple and unequivocal: *discuss travel time with your client and ideally enshrine it in the agreement*. Tell them what travel time you are expecting to incur and decide between you how to treat it.

Do not expect to be able to charge travel time at the same rate you charge your full-steam-ahead, maximum-focus consulting activity. Don't jeopardize the quality of your relationship with the client for the sake of a few hours of paid travel time here and there. But do have a provision in the agreement whereby travel time can be renegotiated if the nature of the mandate changes and more travelling suddenly becomes necessary. Do not forget that time spent travelling on a client's behalf *is* time for which you can legitimately charge, although you should use tact and discretion to avoid annoying your clients.

Many kinds of projects you undertake for a client could not be completed without time spent travelling. For example, if you were visiting a certain number of a client's offices around the country, you would naturally expect your client to pay for the time for you to travel from your base to the first of your client's offices, and then from the first to the second office and so on. Similarly, if your office is, say, an hour's journey time from your client's office and you have to go to the client's office for a meeting that lasts two hours, it would be perfectly legitimate for you to regard this as half a day of your time.

The only problem that arises here is when you are making a passing visit to your client's offices, such as to drop off a document or pick something up. You should show some sensitivity and tact here, particularly if you have other clients nearby and are also visiting *them*. In such cases, you should be fair and spread the travel time equally among all the clients you are visiting. Only charge travelling time when you have genuinely made the journey purely on the client's behalf. By following this rule you may occasionally lose out on some travel time, but your client will appreciate your honesty and will, with any luck, bear it in mind when next thinking about giving you more work or renewing your retainer contract.

You will, of course, charge the expenses of your travelling to the client, whether these are the train fare, air fare or an agreed petrol cost.

Seek to agree 30 days' credit terms

The reason for this should be self-explanatory. You (and your colleagues, if applicable) are people providing a personal service, and people need to eat. Thirty days is quite long enough for you to have to wait to get paid. If your prospective client pompously informs you that they pay invoices after 60/90/120 days, politely explain that those terms are not acceptable to you. You can certainly expect to be treated in a special way: after all, you are supplying consulting services, not pig iron or photocopying paper. If the client is a large and financially reliable organization, you may be prepared to wait a while longer than 30 days, but by this we mean maybe 40 or 45 days, not 60 or something beyond it.

We think you should reconsider whether you want to work for a client who expects you to wait months to get paid. Remember that all the time you are waiting you are having, in effect, to fund *their* business and are incurring financial risk. A client who agrees to pay you after 120 days and goes bust on day 119 will not give you any preferential treatment as a creditor because you have already waited so long – they will treat you like all their other creditors, and if they *have* gone bust, you probably won't get a cent.

Send out invoices promptly

Proper timing in sending out your invoices is essential to your cash flow and consequent general morale. We recommend that you adopt the following approach to the timing of your invoices.

For *ad hoc* projects, the precise timing will usually be part of the agreement you reach with clients. If it is a small project (requiring, say, less than ten days of your consulting time), aim to invoice the total agreed fee for the project when you have completed half the number of agreed days. That way, by the time you have finished the project, you should be well on your way to being paid.

Clients' creditworthiness is also a factor here. You can (and should) obtain details of a prospective client's creditworthiness from their bank or from a credit reference agency, although this kind of investigation is of limited use only because even organizations with a superb credit track record can go bust. Therefore, if you are considering embarking on an *ad hoc* project for a new client whom you regard as only a moderately good credit risk, you should invoice for 50 per cent of the fee *and* all the planned expenses (i.e. disbursements) before you begin the project and do not start work until you receive this money and the cheque has cleared.

If the client will not agree to this, do not work for them. After all, if the client is unwilling (or cannot afford) to pay you for your planned disbursements and half your fee *before* you start the project, is there any reason to assume that they would be willing to pay you (or be able to afford to pay you) your expenses and the full fee *after* you have completed the project. When they want nothing more from you?

For a larger *ad hoc* project with an entirely financially reliable client (and do not embark on a large *ad hoc* project unless you are certain your client *is* financially reliable), you might seek regular monthly payments, or else may be willing to make payments dependent on specific measured deliverables within the lifespan of the project (known as 'milestones'). The good thing about milestones is that the sooner you attain them, the sooner you get paid, so they represent a real incentive for you.

When invoicing for retainer projects, we recommend you invoice in full the fee for a particular month's work at the beginning of the month in which you will be doing the work. This sounds pushy, but in fact it is not because even if the client pays you within 30 days, you will only be getting paid by the end of the month in which you do the work, i.e. after you have done the work. If the client takes longer than 30 days to pay you, you will still receive your payment within a reasonable period after completing the work for that month. On the other hand, if you do not invoice until the *end* of the month in which you are doing the work, even if the client takes only 30 days to pay you, you will still not get paid until at least a month after you have completed the work. In the meantime, you will have done another month's work, so that you are always at least two lots of one month's work behind in terms of getting paid. It is not in your interests to do business in this way.

Clients are unlikely to object to being presented at the start of a month with an invoice for that month, as long as they know from the outset that this is the way you do business. Submitting an invoice to them in this way does not put any immediate pressure on them to pay you, it simply means that – as your clients will most likely decide when to pay you on the basis of when they receive your invoice rather than when you did the work – you will be a month ahead, in terms of receiving payment, on any system that involves invoicing them a month later.

You also need to get to know who to address your invoice to, whether or not it needs a purchase order and, if it does, what that number is, who will authorize the invoice for payment, and who will pay it. It is good to get to know who all these people are so that you know who to talk to in the event of a hold-up.

Ideally, aim to get into a situation whereby you submit your regular monthly invoice, with a proper purchase order number filled in if necessary, to the same person roughly at the same time of each month. If you can do this, the payment of your invoice will probably become a regular part of your client's operations, and you are likely to find that you get paid every month, by a certain day.

Avoid errors on your invoices

Take great care not to make any numerical or factual errors on your invoices, whether these relate to the amounts you are charging under different headings, your adding-up of the various amounts, or your calculations of any additions to the invoice deriving from the imposition of statutory taxes. If you make errors on your invoices, you run the risk either of charging your client less than you are due (and it is not always easy to rectify this by sending another invoice without annoying the client) or charging your client more than you are due, when the client will almost certainly query the invoice, thereby delaying payment and planting at least a seed of suspicion in the client's mind that you were trying to get more money out of them than you were due.

Never put any chargeable item on an invoice unless the charge has been agreed by the client. If you do, you will merely delay the payment. For more information about this, see below.

Keep a record of every piece of activity carried out on the client's behalf

Once you start working for several clients, you may find it easier to prepare invoices if you have kept a record of when you worked for a particular client, how much time you spent on them, and what you did. If you have several clients, it is likely that on days when you are working in your office you will be acting on behalf of more than one client during a day. It is useful for your records to keep what is known as a 'timesheet' for each client. This is a record of the hours you spend on a particular client's behalf on the various days in a specific month. You can then add up all the hours you spend and invoice the number of hours. You can also keep tabs on whether you are under- or over-servicing a client's account.

Timesheets are a great help when it comes to preparing activity reports. It is very easy, by the end of a busy day, let alone at the end of a busy month, to forget what you did for the client earlier in the day. They are also extremely useful when you reach the stage of employing (or working with) other consultants and want to find out exactly how they are spending their time.

Never send out an invoice unless you are confident your client is expecting it

This is the most important rule of invoicing. Like many of the most important rules in this book, it is a simple and straightforward rule, but it is all too often ignored. In fact, there really is no other way to run the invoicing side of your consultancy or consulting division than to have a policy of never sending out invoices which will upset your clients.

Far too many businesses – particularly those run by professional advisers such as lawyers, accountants and consultants – send out invoices that are either larger than the client is expecting or, worse still, that the client is not expecting at all. We think businesses that do this are either being run by fools or by people who are so arrogant that they actually think their clients should consider themselves privileged to receive that invoice.

No client ever considers himself privileged to receive an invoice, even if the invoice is accurate and is what he expected. Where the invoice is either too high or is unexpected, the client will feel only annoyance and contempt for you. Even if he does pay up, that is the last you will see of him. There is absolutely no reason to send a client an invoice that he is not expecting unless you are foolish enough not to agree precise terms with him before starting work, or you are inconsiderate of your clients. If the latter is true, the money you spent on this book has been wasted.

Do your utmost to avoid accruing bad debts

Unfortunately, perhaps, if you are running a business-to-business organization such as a consultancy you will need to offer credit to your clients. Sadly, the implications of this are a terrible headache for many new consultancies and frequently a cause of their premature collapse.

As we have suggested, you can insist, tactfully, on your clients agreeing to pay you after 30 days, but you will still face two dangers:

○ they may not *want* to pay you when payment is due;

○ they may *be unable* to pay you when payment is due.

In theory, and to some extent also in practice, the types of business that suffer most from extended credit are manufacturing businesses that must pay for raw materials before they can produce any goods. If their customers do not pay up, insolvency is never far away. As someone running a consultancy, you should be able to supply your services without having to incur large financial commitments. But you will still have fixed costs from setting up your consultancy, and there will also be your regular operational costs. Your financial risk in trading may not be as great as that accrued by the manufacturing company, but you still cannot afford to work without getting paid for what you do.

Although most people regard a 'bad debt' as a debt that is never recoverable, we regard bad debts as also consisting of those that are not *readily* recoverable, which includes debts that are paid only after you have initiated legal action against the debtor, or debts that are paid only many months (say, more than six) after you have completed the work.

You must, from the outset, resolve to take every possible step to avoid accruing bad debts if you possibly can. Bad debts are very, very bad news. Not only is it disastrous for your morale to accrue bad debts, it is literally better to go fishing, watch television or stay in bed rather than undertake work for which you will not be paid because you will have incurred expenses in carrying out that work that you would not have incurred if you had not done the work.

You should also bear in mind that the cost of a bad debt to you is not only the expenses that you have incurred by carrying out the work but also the revenue that you would have earned if you had devoted the time to working for a client who *would* pay you. Economists call this 'opportunity cost'. Furthermore, all the time and effort (and legal costs, not all of which will necessarily be recoverable from your debtor) you devote to trying to recover the funds you are owed will also be a cost to you.

Accruing bad debts is a particular danger when you are just starting out as a consultant because in your eagerness to win and work, there is a hazard that you may work for clients whose ability to pay you is questionable. In fact, you may even have strong reasons to suspect that their ability to pay you is in doubt, but you may be willing to work for them nonetheless. After all, they *might* pay you.

They probably won't. Generally speaking, clients who are bad payers look as if they are. Their offices are dirty and untidy, their staff are demoralized and do a lot of complaining, phone calls take a long time to be answered and the client himself is full of grandiose plans but does not seem to have achieved very much to date. Beware such clients, for almost every consultant encounters them at some point or another. They want your assistance so that they can use it to make money, but they do not see why you should complain if you do not get paid for six months, if at all.

Do not work for clients whose willingness or ability to pay you seems questionable without first having received the fee and expenses up front (and having waited until the cheque has cleared). If they refuse to go along with these terms, don't work for them.

Ignore this advice at your peril.

Try to cultivate an ability to spot bad payers. Trust your hunch here, it is likely to be right. You can investigate an organization's credit record, but this will tell you only what their credit record has been like *in the past*; it does not tell you what it is going to be like in the future. Besides, bad payers know all about credit reference agencies, and are forever creating new organizations that are too new to have managed to build up a bad credit record. Yet.

Only lay out a minimal amount on expenses on a client's behalf

It should be obvious that one excellent way for a new consultancy or consulting division (and, indeed, one that is long established) to descend into financial hell with great speed is to lay out a considerable amount of money on a client's behalf (or incur debts on behalf of the client) and not to get reimbursed for the money. There is absolutely no room for compromise. *Never* – and we *mean* never – incur anything but a modest expense (say, up to about $500) on a client's behalf without having cleared funds in your bank account from the client to cover the expense. Making this mistake just once can wipe you out. No ifs, no buts, no special cases.

Even if it is last thing on Friday and you need to get things moving and the client says he will pay you first thing on Monday, don't do it. Get that money up front. Don't be rushed into a financial commitment which you may regret for ever.

Incidentally, if a particular mandate would require you to buy some expensive equipment (say, a CAD/CAM system or a computer screen with a very high resolution) in order to carry out the mandate, why not suggest to the client that *they* buy the expensive equipment and let you use it?

Infuse your client relationships with goodwill

Other things being equal, a client who likes you and respects you will treat you fairly and pay you on time. Even if a client is doing badly financially, if he likes you and respects you he will almost always provide you with a fair warning of potential payment difficulties, thereby giving you the opportunity either to stop working for him or to reduce the amount of work that you do for him until all your payments have been received.

While it is generally true that you should steer clear of an organization that is doing badly financially, in practice consultants sometimes have the option to work for organizations that are going through a sticky patch financially (or that are already clearly insolvent). Indeed, the financial problems may be precisely why they have asked you to work with them. In this eventuality you will need to protect yourself thoroughly against not getting paid, and if an organization is on the verge of being insolvent (or actually is insolvent) you would be crazy to start working for it without receiving *all* your fees up front. Alternatively, if you can afford it, why not arrange to have all or part of your fees paid in equity (if it is a private corporation) or in equity options (if it is a corporation listed on a stock exchange)? Why not arrange to benefit personally from the brilliantly successful turn-around you perform on them?

Don't get into debt yourself

The object of being in business is to accumulate debtors, not creditors. Just as you need to be rigorously on your guard against accruing debts that will not be paid to you, you must also take steps to avoid incurring debts yourself which you are not able to pay within the time limits requested by your suppliers, or within statutory time limits in the case of official payments such as for income tax.

The way to avoid incurring debts that you cannot readily pay is to follow our advice about keeping in mind at all times that you make money by not spending it. You should also plan your finances with sufficient precision so that you will always have funds available as debts become due.

Good financial planning is, for obvious reasons, especially important when you are launching your consultancy, when the income you may make is far from certain.

You need a well thought-out and realistic financial plan that provides financial forecasts that are as reliable as reasonably feasible. Further, you must have a contingency plan so that if things do not go well, you have a fall-back position. If you are a start-up, you will need to decide at what point you reconsider your entire consulting venture and go back to the world of employment. Of course, we very much hope your consultancy will succeed, but heroic and painful struggle is no fun, and sometimes it is necessary to cut one's losses and accept – sadly, wisely – that something has not worked.

If ever you do find that you need more time to make payments, the golden rule is to tell your creditors at the earliest opportunity. They will appreciate this. Furthermore, do not make pledges to pay by instalments, for instance, unless you will be able to keep to them. What creditors cannot stand is where a debtor does not have the courtesy to contact them and ignores letters and demands that the creditor sends.

Never forget the importance of insurance

Before you start trading, you need to consult a reputable insurance broker to make sure you have all necessary statutory insurances in place. These vary from country to country, and in the US from state to state, so we do not provide any more specific information about these here. You certainly need to insure your premises and your office equipment against hazards such as fire and theft. A new consultancy or new consulting division could be killed off in its early days if all its office equipment was damaged or stolen and if no insurances were in place to fund the purchase of replacement equipment. Make sure that any insurance cover you do take out will enable you to buy new equipment to replace the old, not cheaper versions of this.

You and your consultant colleagues should each also consider taking out an insurance policy that will provide you with an income in the event that you suffer a serious illness or an accident and are unable to work. Also take out life insurance, to protect your dependants if you die, and remember to check the status of any life insurance you may have had while working for your last employer; it may be that this will have lapsed when you left your job.

You will probably already have effective medical insurance in place, but now is the time to review it. You need comprehensive cover that will give you preferential treatment. Should you fall ill, you will want to be treated as speedily and effectively as possible so that you can get back to work with minimum delay.

Find a good, cost–effective accountant

Unless your consulting speciality is financial management, in which case you will probably have accountancy training yourself, make sure you find an accountant who will prepare accounts for you and undertake other tasks such as preparing tax returns. Do not try to carry out this work yourself: it is a specialized skill, and besides, you should be able to charge out your consulting time for more than it would cost you to pay an accountant to undertake these relatively modest jobs.

Do not incur unnecessary accountancy charges, however. Some accountants make a fortune by writing up every single item of expenditure or revenue that their clients receive. You do not need this service. In any case, you should do your own book-keeping. This is essential because you need to know how things are going financially now, today, this morning, *not* when your accountant prepares the figures in a couple of months' time.

Particularly if you are a start-up, find an accountant who understands that you want a minimalist service that is value for money. Sometimes there is a strong case for avoiding large accountancy firms and choosing a freelance accountant who will give you really good value for money and understand that you see accountancy expenditure as a necessary evil.

Don't be ostentatious

When you start to become wealthy – and if you are a really good, dedicated and hard-working consultant who follows the advice in this book this *will* happen – remember that your clients will often be resentful of ostentatious wealth. This is particularly true of client organizations that are going through financial difficulty, but generally clients feel, quite reasonably, that you are their *servant* and that servants should not be obviously far more wealthy than their masters. People are susceptible to envy at the best of times; avoid fanning those flames!

Therefore, even if you love driving your new Porsche, Jaguar or Aston Martin, don't drive it to meet your clients, or if you really insist on doing so, park nearby (not in their car park) and complete your journey on foot. You do not need to wear your solid gold Rolex either. You are supposed to be a thinker and a doer, not a walking catalogue for luxury goods manufacturers.

You may think this point trivial, but many star consultants alienate clients by unnecessarily ostentatious displays of wealth: don't do it.

Final thoughts on money

Having set down the above practical guidelines about making money – the fruit of our collective experience as consultants over more than 30 years – there are a few final points we ought to make.

First, you must know your cost basis at all times. This means you need to know how much it costs you to deliver your consulting service. If you don't know this, how can you possibly be profitable? Elements that will comprise your cost basis should be according to what they cost you per month. Some costs will be fixed, such as the cost of capital equipment; others will be regular monthly costs. It makes sense to apportion your fixed costs over the life of the equipment, with a maximum of two years, since after this you may well look to buy new capital equipment, especially if the equipment under consideration is information technology. So, for example, if your computer resources have cost you $3000, cost this at $125 per month for two years. Other costs will include:

- rent/mortgage;
- heating/lighting;
- capital equipment;
- stationery;
- furniture/fittings;
- staff salaries (and your own if you are trading through a limited company);
- travel (including car) that you cannot claim back from clients.

Add up your monthly expenditure and produce a grand total. In principle you are profitable if you are earning more per month than that figure, after allowing for income/corporation tax on your earnings. However, you will want to do more than simply hover around the break-even point. You need to earn at least three times your monthly expenses in order to turn in a healthy profit, and five times the expenses in order to be very profitable. Beyond that, the sky is the limit.

Second, what do you do if you have quoted a carefully arrived-at fee for a job (whether it is a retainer or an *ad hoc* project) and your client informs you that their budget for the project is less than the amount you have quoted? What you mustn't do is immediately capitulate and say you will do the job for the lower rate. Not only does this make you look stupid and weak, it will also raise in the client's mind the possibility that you were trying it on with your original quote, not that your rate was based on an intelligent appraisal of the work needed.

You must stick to your guns. Once the client knows that you really do believe the project will require the input you have proposed, they may be prepared to increase their fund allocation in order to hire you at the rate you propose. After all, budgets are not edicts delivered by God; they are almost always flexible.

That said, there will be occasions when a client says, in effect: 'I really like your proposal and the number of days you have quoted for this job makes sense, but we simply can't afford to pay the total amount you are proposing.' In this case, you should feel free to walk away from the job. After all, if you see something in a shop that you want but can't afford, you don't expect the shopkeeper to bring the price down, not unless you are haggling in a Turkish bazaar, anyway.

On the other hand, you may be willing to find ways to reduce your charge for the job by cutting down the time you spend on it. Whether you should be prepared to do this is something you will have to decide. The only advice we can give here is that you must never reduce the number of days to such an extent that you cannot do the job properly. It is much better to walk away, or come back when the client *can* afford to hire you.

We mentioned earlier that sometimes offering to receive part of your payment according to the results you win for your client can be a good way of distinguishing yourself from other consultancies. If you do this, however, remember the following points:

○ as we have already emphasized, there is no sense in making your payment dependent on factors that are beyond your control. Remember the example of the public relations consultant: he cannot possibly be held responsible for the amount of business his client wins from editorial coverage because that is out of his control. On the other hand, he may be prepared to agree a charging system whereby he receives a bonus each time, say, his press campaign results in more than a certain number of mentions in key media;

○ *do not allow 100 per cent of your remuneration to be dependent on results.* Payment by results does *not* mean that you only get paid if you get results. You are not a commission-only salesman, you are a professional consultant. The payment by results agreement should essentially be a bonus agreement whereby a particularly high level of success brings you extra money;

○ the level of your additional payment should be realistic. If, for example, you have helped a client build a new front-office trading system that makes them $1 million in its first year of operation, there is little point in a payment by results agreement that gives you, say, $100 per $1 million your system makes for your client. You need a proper share of the action. Fortunately, clients are increasingly receptive to the notion of sharing risk and reward.

CHAPTER FIVE

The mechanics of setting up and running a consulting practice

Introduction

In this chapter we cut to the chase. We confront, head on, the mechanics of setting up your consultancy or consulting division. Our aim is to provide you with the practical information you need to have the best chance of making a great success of your enterprise, and to avoid the pitfalls lurking all over the place.

In order to help you, we propose a consulting business model that is essentially an almost fool-proof way of making your consultancy succeed or, if your consulting idea is not strong enough, will keep your financial risk to a minimum. We have both used this model successfully.

Introducing the 'self-fuelling consultancy' (SFC)

We have named the business model we recommend to you the 'self-fuelling consultancy' (SFC). We use the term to describe a consultancy that is, from its earliest origins, 'self-fuelling' in that its growth and development are linked closely to the demands of the marketplace. Furthermore, the expenses of setting up and managing the SFC should, with very few exceptions, be funded by revenue that the SFC is itself generating.

This is the whole idea. The SFC is a kind of breeder reactor. A breeder reactor is a nuclear reactor that can create more fissile material than it uses in the chain reaction. The SFC, like such a reactor, is fundamentally self-feeding and self-sustaining. Basically, the SFC cannot go wrong because it is designed by its very essence to be manageable, controllable, and to make rock-solid financial and business sense.

In particular, the SFC:

○ starts small;

○ pares everything down to essentials;

○ does not involve you in risking a large amount of money in setting it up;

○ funds its growth as far as possible from revenue;

○ grows organically, in response to marketplace demand;

○ is run by people who are intelligent, committed, unpretentious and hard-working, with extensive and in-depth expertise and experience and proven track records;

○ is fun to run and operate;

○ offers you real possibilities for earning a high income;

○ can be expanded to any size, given that the marketplace demand is there.

Can this be true? Is it really possible to set up a consultancy that requires minimal financial risk and is fun to run and operate? Yes, such a consultancy is possible. The SFC is not a pipe dream but a reality. Indeed, almost by definition, all successful consultancies once were, and many still are, SFCs.

Start small and grow organically

The guiding principle of the SFC is that you start it small and let its size be dictated by the amount of work your clients give you. On the face of it, this guideline is so obvious that there should hardly be any need to set it down. The trouble is that, however obvious the guideline is, most start-up consultancies fail to follow it.

Instead, what usually happens is something horrific like this. Someone, somewhere, decides to set up a consultancy, whether alone or with various friends or business colleagues, and before you can say 'let's get into debt' the new consultancy has acquired an expensive office, expensive equipment to fill it, a charming secretary, letterheads, compliment slips, company cars and the usual paraphernalia, and the consultant and his colleagues have given themselves important-sounding job titles and are raring to go.

Except that, because they have devoted their efforts to giving themselves the illusion of running a business rather than going out and getting clients, they don't have much to do. So they start bickering among themselves, typically over whose job title is the most important and who is responsible for what. Job titles are important only when a consultancy has got off the ground and a distinction needs to be made between the prime animator(s) who got the consultancy going in the first place and the 'lieutenants' who were recruited subsequently. Immediately post-formation is no time to be bickering about this.

They finally agree on job titles and responsibilities, but there is still no work coming in, so maybe, if they have any money left, they employ a public relations consultant and/or advertising agency. By going down this route they are forgetting that public relations and advertising are all very well, but that these are essentially *additional methods* of attracting clients. The prime method of obtaining clients is the exploitation of existing contacts and/or clients, coupled with the widening relationship that goes with doing good work.

Not surprisingly, the new 'consultancy' finds that its efforts to win business through public relations and advertising do not work but merely cost it more money. Perhaps, by this point, the consultancy has – through one consultant's contacts – been offered the opportunity to pitch for a potentially lucrative piece of business, but the consultancy's overheads are already so high, and the consultants themselves are getting increasingly desperate to start making some money, that the consultancy pitches its price for doing the piece of business at much the same level as the estimate provided by larger, longer established consultancies. As one might expect, the potential client cannot see any reason to use the services of the new consultancy if it is not offering a cost-saving, and so the client gives its business to the larger, longer-established consultancy. If a newcomer cannot demonstrate an unarguable edge, it is likely that the business it might otherwise have won will be awarded to the large, long-established consultancy, simply because this represents the safe, sensible decision. No one ever got fired for appointing Andersen Consulting/McKinsey/PricewaterhouseCoopers.

Result: morale at the new consultancy falls to an all-time low, and one of the consultants panics and takes a salaried job offered to him by someone with whom he used to work. Once he has gone, the others, realizing in their heart of hearts that he was probably right to leave, secretly start looking around for their own bolt-holes, then bicker even more intensely when these are not forthcoming. Finally, six months or so after starting out, the secretary leaves when her last salary cheque bounces; the telephone service is cut off due to non-payment; the office equipment (most of which has been obtained on expensive leasing arrangements) is repossessed; and the landlord, whose rent has not been paid for two months, changes the locks on the doors and exercises his right to recover the premises.

The ex-consultants do their best to forget the experience and to return to the world of the regular salary, except that now they have all got embarrassing six-month holes in their CVs, to say nothing of bank loans that must be repaid. This financial pressure makes it difficult for them to accept salaried jobs at a similar salary to what they were earning before they left to set up the consultancy, and so they hold out for more lucrative positions, only to find that these are not forthcoming. Finally, they accept jobs at salaries that only just cover their living expenses and debt repayments. Their lives have taken a distinct turn for the worse, but sadly it does not occur to them for one moment to blame themselves for going about forming their new consultancy in a foolish way. Instead, they blame the recession, or what they regard as the pitiful lack of courage their potential clients displayed in being unwilling to trust a new consultancy to do the job.

This nightmarish scenario is not far-fetched but is repeated again and again around the world, every week of every year. A significant proportion of new business failures are failed consultancies. Indeed, where a new consultancy is being run by people who have allowed themselves to forget, even for a moment, that a consultancy is only the sum of its relationships with its clients, and does not have any genuine existence apart from that, it is difficult to see how the new consultancy can do anything but follow this rocky road to ruin.

So the guideline that a new consultancy's size and growth should be dictated by the amount of work it wins is a pretty obvious one and in many ways can be reached by the simple application of common sense. This being the case, why is it so often implicitly disregarded by those who set up new consultancies? There are two reasons for this, and both represent faulty business philosophy.

Two big misconceptions

First, many people who start consultancies believe they will be able to win business only if they give their potential clients the impression that the consultancy is already well-established, with its own premises, staff, secretarial assistance and so on. This idea is both a complete misconception and a dangerous one because it provides the groundwork for financial hell. The danger of believing that, as a new consultant, you need to expend a great deal of effort and money in order to give your consultancy the pretence of being successful already (and of course it *will* be only a pretence) is so dangerous that it is essential for us to warn you very strongly against it. Do not follow that path: unless a miracle intervenes, you will surely live to regret it.

'But,' you perhaps think, 'if I don't give my potential clients the impression that my consultancy is already successful, how on earth can I expect to win any business from them?' Please, please do not think like this. Why should your clients want to see a falsehood? Why should they want to do business with an illusion?

Instead, what they want is sincerity, honesty, thoughtfulness, proven expertise, a first-class track record, and a real commitment on your part to listening to their needs and bringing all your skills to bear to meet them.

If you need to be persuaded further, go back to Chapter Three and reread what we said about the need for you to bring something to the market that existing consultants in your area are not already offering. Look again at the pages that follow, where we talked about the need for significant incremental advantage and showed you the type of incremental advantages or unique selling propositions you might be able to display. It is because of those incremental advantages that you can expect to win clients even though your consultancy is, in every sense, new and untested.

Trying to convince your clients that you must have something to offer them because your consultancy looks as though it has been around a long time is not only deceitful and insincere but is also horribly expensive. Also, it may be counter-productive because the effort of setting up a 'pretend' consultancy will probably blind you to the incremental advantages that you and your colleagues can actually offer.

The second type of faulty business philosophy one often sees at work in start-ups (and we include here new consulting divisions started by existing successful consultants; they often have misconceptions, too) is where people hold the dangerous belief that setting up a new business is some sort of exciting game. They imagine that renting premises, employing a secretarial assistant, buying word processors and telephone equipment, and getting your letterheads and compliment slips printed is somehow all part of that game. If you really believe this – and many people do – thank your lucky stars we are around to advise you otherwise.

We are not going to waste time stating the obvious reasons why any idea that business is some sort of game is clearly nonsense. Just take it from us: *business is not a game but a deadly serious battle in which there are no prisoners taken and in which everybody – your clients and your suppliers – will basically be out to get from you whatever they can.* Yet despite that unnecessarily pessimistic view of what business is all about, it *can* be fun, too. There is no reason why, in the medium to long term, you should not be able to establish relationships with your clients and suppliers that are amicable, sincere and mutually beneficial. But, and it is a big but, those relationships do not happen overnight, any more than the loving, mutually trusting relationship between a couple who have been together happily for several years can be compared with the relationship between a man and a woman who meet each other for the first time at a party and are not yet quite sure what they think of each other.

Like the woman at the party (or indeed the man) you would do well when setting up your consultancy to cultivate a healthy distance from the people you encounter while setting up your embryonic business, at least until you have good reason to trust them.

We cannot help thinking that the media must shoulder part of the blame for giving people the idea that business is a sort of game where mere determination to succeed and the courage to set up in business by oneself are the qualities that will, by a sort of magic, bring you success and financial prosperity. They won't.

It is too easy to conclude from the success stories one reads in business magazines and business sections of newspapers that success stems from energy, enterprise, courage and determination. It doesn't. Just as you will fail to conquer (or survive) Mount Everest if all you bring to the mountain is energy, enterprise, courage and determination, these qualities will not sustain you in the consultancy business either.

In fact, all successful businesspeople have only one thing in common: they have found a market niche and have been able to supply at a profit to that niche. The whole thing really is that simple.

How does this square with our earlier precept that in consulting it is personality that wins business? Simply because there is no conflict with it. The personality you need to bring to practising as a consultant should be an attractive and inspiring one, but the personality you bring to setting up and running your consulting business needs to be hard-headed, tough and good at facing reality. If this sounds as if you need to be two different people – a charismatic consultant and a hard-headed businessperson – you are right, you do.

But even this is not enough. You need to cultivate business sense, too.

Cultivate business sense before you begin

We described above the bad business philosophy that leads to the establishment of a consultancy that is not really a consultancy at all but a *pretend* consultancy which is as lacking in real substance as a scarecrow. Being aware of the dangers of pursuing a bad business philosophy is extremely important for anybody who wants to start a high-income consultancy, but it would hardly be fair of us to introduce you to *bad* business philosophy without showing you what *good* business philosophy is all about.

Good business philosophy – or 'business sense' as we prefer to describe it – is not something people are born with but something they have to learn, often through sad and costly personal experience. In essence, business sense is the possession of a realistic awareness of the operations of that part of human life that concerns itself with buying and selling, and a knowledge of how to get the best possible deal for yourself from the buying and selling world.

This awareness and knowledge is by no means necessarily linked to your intellectual capacity.

One of our favourite business stories concerns a fellow who was hopeless at arithmetic at school and who is still hopeless at arithmetic but who, by virtue of his business sense, is a millionaire at the age of 30. One day he is visiting his local bar, where he bumps into a man – also 30 years old – who at school had been consistently top of the class in arithmetic. This chap is now an accountant and makes a good living, but he is certainly not a millionaire. The accountant buys the beers (the millionaire doesn't mind letting him do that) and the two men chat about their respective careers. 'I'm really pleased to hear that you've done so well,' the accountant says after a while. 'Maybe there's something you can teach us. What's the secret of your success?'

'Well,' says the millionaire, 'it's like this: we just happen to have this product that we buy for $5 and sell for $10. It's amazing how much money you can make on a five per cent mark-up.'

In his book *Growing a Business* (Simon & Schuster, New York, 1988), Paul Hawken uses the term 'tradeskill' to denote what we call business sense. This is what Hawken has to say about tradeskill (the parentheses in the passage are his):

> *'Tradeskill is really the set of skills that spell the difference between success and failure in business. It is the knack of understanding what people want, how much they'll pay, and how they make their decision. It is knowing how to read the signals of the marketplace, how to learn from those signals, how to change your mind. Tradeskill gives you a canniness about how to approach a given product, market or niche. (The geniuses of tradeskill are the turnaround "artists" who don't even need to "know" the business they are in. They perform radical, successful surgery on the patient simply by knowing what the disease is.) Tradeskill becomes a sixth sense that gives those who have it the ability to make decisions quickly, cutting through months of meetings, brainstorming and bureaucratic shuffling. Tradeskill is knowing how to handle money, how to buy and how to sell.'*

In the movie *Big*, starring Tom Hanks, Hanks plays a 13-year-old boy who has grown into a man overnight as a result of making a wish at a mysterious magic puppet machine at a funfair. Hanks moves to New York City and finds himself a job as a lowly clerk at a corporation that designs and manufactures toys. He does not linger in his humble position for long, being promoted to the role of official toy-tester when his boss, played by Robert Loggia, notices that Hanks, who is at heart still a child, possesses a remarkable ability for assessing whether or not a toy is likely to be successful in the marketplace. An extremely revealing sequence from the point of view of defining tradeskill occurs in the Fifth Avenue toyshop FAO Schwartz. Loggia and Hanks bump into each other: Loggia having come to the shop to see what the competition is doing, Hanks because he likes toyshops. During their conversation Loggia casually refers to a particular marketing report that he has been perusing, at which Hanks – whose character genuinely has no idea what a marketing report is – asks: 'What's a marketing report?'

Loggia takes the question as indicating that Hanks does not have a high opinion of marketing reports. Giving Hanks a look that indicates a high respect for Hanks' perception, he murmurs, 'exactly'.

Possessing true business sense, as contrasted with the kind of dry, theoretical business lore taught by the vast majority of management books and most business courses, is the difference between how the characters played by Hanks and Loggia regard the toyshop. Hanks walks around the shop with an instinctive feel for which toys were likely to appeal to children, whereas Loggia were all too aware of his dependence on the purely cerebral, theoretical aspects of his business knowledge.

There is no reason why a highly intelligent and well-educated person should not also possess true business sense, but business sense is, in itself, anything but cerebral and theoretical. Rather, it is instinctive and born out of a living, dynamic awareness of what business is and how business works. There are no substitutes for it.

In particular, pure theorizing is no substitute for business sense because, ultimately, theorizing merely forces a preconceived theory of behaviour on the dynamic elements – in particular market demand and how your clients view you – that will make or break your business. Business sense, on the other hand, appraises these dynamic elements in a holistic and genuine way and draws realistic, instinctive conclusions about which course of action is likely to be in your best interests.

Having money is no substitute for business sense either, although far too many people think it is. In fact, possessing too much money when you are thinking of setting up your own consultancy can prove a real handicap, not only because it may tempt you to make the fatal mistake of creating a 'pretend' consultancy that is not allowed to grow in organic harmony with the level of business that you can win, but also because the possession of too much money may blind you to the mistakes you are making until it is too late to do much about them.

Consider carefully the implications of this last point. It is absolutely central to making a success of a new consultancy and minimizing your financial risk, but far too many people are unaware of this guideline or think it unimportant.

There is a perceptive passage in *Growing a Business* that neatly sums up what can happen when theory and money rather than true business sense are the bases for a new business. The passage relates to the retail industry, but the lessons it has to teach us are profoundly important for anybody who is planning on setting up a consultancy.

> *'Because California is immodestly affluent in some places, there are many businesses started up by professionals from other fields, including many couples who worked for large corporations and set out on their own. The results of these businesses, usually retail stores, are sometimes painful to watch. Because the owners are well educated, well connected and have "good taste", they believe they have the advantage over other merchants. They don't – unless they have tradeskill. We have all seen the food "shoppe" or toy boutique with the cute name, expensive custom-designed logo, well-chosen inventory, costly fixtures, beige carpet and articulate help. Nice touches, but why does the shop feel dead? We as customers sense a lack of hands-on knowledge, authenticity, and market sense. We want our businesses to be run by businesspeople, not by hobbyists. We're more comfortable in the hands of a pro than an amateur. Without tradeskill, a business seems a caricature of itself.'*

You cannot acquire business sense by following a set of rules. There are no rules. You cannot even know whether you possess business sense until you have gone out into the marketplace and made a success of running your own business – in this case your own consultancy. Unfortunately, it is possible to rise to a high corporate position – even, if the corporation is very well-established, the *top* position – without possessing much in the way of business sense. This can happen because a corporation is, in essence, somebody else's business idea; someone with true business sense has already been there and established the business before you joined it. When you work in a corporation that is already successful, the personal skills required boil down to conformity, restraint, getting on with the job, thinking up sensible ideas, and projecting oneself within a group of people. These qualities are all very well and good if you are content to remain an employee all your life, but they do not, of themselves, add up to the possession of business sense.

Sadly, many people think they do, which is why every year millions of people throughout the world assume that as they have attained a high position in a corporation they must be good at business. So they leave their nice, safe, salaried job behind and start their own business (frequently a consultancy), only to discover, in many cases, that they cannot make the business work. And the reason they cannot make the business work is that for all their achievements in their last corporate position, they do not possess business sense.

It would be absurd – and incorrect – for us to suggest that *nobody* who has done well in a corporate environment is ever going to make a success of running their own consultancy, but we want to drive home the point that your previous corporate experience will not *of itself* mean that you will be successful as an independent consultant. The skills that make a top-grade corporate executive are not necessarily those that will make you a good independent consultant.

We suggested earlier that you need five years' experience in the field in which you intend to consult as a minimum if you propose to consult independently. We realize that this experience can in most cases only realistically be gained within a corporate environment. Yet there is no contradiction here. We have nothing against corporations. What we do object to – because it can be so dangerous – is the assumption that success at a corporate level will easily lead to success when running your own consultancy. It might do, or it might not, but if it does that is because, in addition to your specialized knowledge of the areas in which you are consulting, you possess business sense.

As we have said, there is no way of telling whether you have business sense until you get to grips with the actual business of setting up and running your consultancy. All you can do, therefore, is follow our advice and keep your consultancy small at first, absolutely minimizing your financial risk, and growing only in response to the need to service the business that you are able to win.

There is no reason why you should not set yourself specific objectives in terms of how much new business you are aiming to win in, say, your first year of trading and in successive years but we still maintain that you should start small and grow in response to market demand. That way, if you do discover that you are ultimately much happier working in a corporate environment, you can bail out in the manner that we suggested earlier, with whatever work you have done for your first client being a useful addition to your CV and with no nasty debts inhibiting your enjoyment of your return to the corporate fold.

We do not believe anybody can teach you to have business sense, but we are convinced that there are certain fundamental principles which, if you follow them, will give you at least the beginnings of business wisdom. They may even prevent you from making many expensive mistakes. We have already touched on some of these principles, but since it is time to move on to the specifics of starting your own consultancy, you might find it useful for us to end this section by setting down the 12 most important principles that will enable your consultancy to be guided by business sense.

1   Start your consultancy small and grow only in response to your clients' needs, not in response to your own wishes and ambitions. When you *do* grow, expect the new consultants you recruit to look after a volume of business, annually, equivalent to at least three times whatever you are paying them during that year (including bonuses, of course). Do not recruit *anybody* unless you have cash on deposit in the bank amounting to at least *three months* worth of underlying costs for the consultancy, including the salaries of all staff (the new recruit included).

2   Never forget that while business should be fun, it is also going to be an ongoing battle.

3   Take every possible step to minimize your financial risk.

4   Make sure you have a significant incremental competitive edge that justifies the formation of your consultancy, but remember that only practical contact with your marketplace can tell you whether your business will succeed or not.

5   Always do a superb job for your clients and spare no effort to look after them.

6   Devote the maximum time to working for your clients and winning new business, and the minimum time to running your business. If you would like guidance on what proportion of time you ought to spend actively looking for new business (which includes attending new business meetings) rather than working on existing client business, we recommend that you try not to spend more than one-quarter of the time looking for new business that you spend on working for existing clients. Of course if, at an early stage of your SFC, clients are rather thin on the ground, you may want to spend proportionately more time on looking for new business, but when you start to get a good influx of work, we recommend that you go back to the 25 per cent rule.

7   Trust nobody – whether supplier, client or colleague – until they have shown themselves to be worthy of your trust.

8   Don't be afraid of admitting to yourself that you have made a mistake, but make sure you *learn* from those mistakes.

9   Do not use the hours during which you should be running your consultancy to indulge in hobbies or charity work.

10 Do not allow your consultancy to ruin your personal life. An unhappy consultant is rarely a good consultant.

11 Take every step to make yourself – and keep yourself – fit and healthy. If you do not already have a good doctor, get one.

12 Try to find a mentor, someone off whom you can bounce ideas and with whom you can share your triumphs and disappointments over a beer or a glass of wine. A mentor should ideally be someone who is experienced in the business world, senior to you, and for whom you have respect. There is no reason why it cannot be an uncle or aunt, or even your mother or father, if these people meet the qualifications. However, a mentor should not be someone who is actively involved with your consultancy because such people will not be able to view your problems and queries with the objectivity required. A mentor can be immensely beneficial for your morale, and can put your difficulties and tribulations into perspective, thereby making it much easier for you to deal with these problems and, if things ever get really tough, survive them.

There is a 'thirteenth rule' here, by the way – you should not regard advice that others give you (including the advice in this book) as gospel until you have found it to work for you!

The practicalities of starting a self-fuelling consultancy

We now turn to what you need to do in a practical sense to start your self-fuelling consultancy. We have broken down the process of starting your consultancy into six stages, which we have set down in sequence and will discuss individually.

Stage one: decide whether you will form your consultancy alone or with others

Our advice on this subject is quite categorical and entirely thematic with our most fundamental advice above: form your consultancy with others only if you are unable to undertake the work from your first client or clients without the help of others *and* if you have good reason to believe that you and your fellow consultants will be able to maintain this high level of business activity in the future.

Say, for example, your first client, a bank, awards you a mandate that involves the need to visit the client's 100 branches throughout the country and spend a day at each branch, gathering material for a lengthy, in-depth report that will make recommendations on how your client's business could be improved. Obviously you could not undertake such a large project yourself. On the other hand, it may be that this is the largest project you can reasonably expect to acquire in your first year of trading. That being so, you would be foolhardy to start your consultancy with two or three other people merely because you were lucky enough to win such a big piece of business when starting out.

You would do much better starting your consultancy by yourself and hiring some other specialists on a temporary basis to help you out with this project – a temporary basis that could turn into a permanent basis if you keep winning good and profitable business. Generally, aim to hire people with skills that complement your own. After all, a good team is composed of specialists in different, complementary fields: how many soccer teams have 11 goal-keepers or 11 centre-forwards?

Even if there is clearly going to be plenty of work for several people from the word go, there is no reason why you need to start a consultancy in which you share your ownership with others. That will dilute the equity in the consultancy, and if your business is going to be a winner from the outset, you may want to keep your hands on all the equity yourself, so that in, say, ten years' time, when you are employing 100 people and are turning over $10 million annually, you have the option of selling your business and retiring to the Bahamas. (Except of course that, as we have already observed, any consultant who builds up a business in this way will be so much in love with his work that the last thing he will want to do is retire.)

Given these factors, why do so many new consultancies start out with four or five directors (each with their own painstakingly worked-out job titles) and a secretarial assistant? The answer is that the people who found the consultancy have no idea what they are doing.

We cannot emphasize enough that trying to start some sort of 'ready-made consultancy' with several consultants and secretarial assistance is ridiculous if you do not have ample business to justify such a complex creation. And even if you do have enough business to justify this, you will probably do much better starting the consultancy on your own and employing the other consultants.

Maybe you feel inclined to protest, 'Listen, guys, I've worked with Rick, Dick and Mick for ten years and we've always had a dream of setting up a consultancy together'. Sorry, but that isn't good enough. If you are thinking of creating a consultancy because you want to indulge in a dream, take our advice: keep your daytime job and have a week's holiday in Las Vegas to get all your desires for earthbound dreams out of your system. The few hundred (or thousand) dollars you lose doing that will be a cheap price to pay for being able to resume a life of reality at the end. Starting a consultancy is not about indulging dreams, it is about facing up to hard commercial realities about what the market is likely to want and whether or not you can provide it.

Don't let us put you off starting your consultancy with a few friends or colleagues if you already have some very interesting business in the bag and you are utterly convinced – and we mean *utterly convinced* – that you and your prospective co-founders are truly talented people who are sure to make a big success of setting up your consultancy together. But if not, set up your consultancy by yourself. The road to the happy land of success in running a high-income consultancy passes through the valley of the shadow of anxiety, the sun-baked plains of hard work, the deep forests of confusion and self-doubt, and the muddy trenches of inertia and exhaustion. It is infinitely easier to give your consultancy the flexibility and adapt-ability it needs to negotiate these hazards if only one person (i.e. you) makes the big decisions, but you will also want that promise of financial success to give you courage for the journey.

Don't worry if you 'feel' that a business started by one person is not a 'real' business. Recognize this feeling as a leftover from the days when (probably) you worked in a corporate environment and were surrounded by people all day. Reflect that the average corporate person probably does only around three hours of real work a day if you factor in coffee breaks, excursions out of the office, chats with colleagues about personal matters and the attendance at largely pointless 'internal meetings' where half a dozen highly-paid people spend an hour deciding, for example, which brand of coffee machine ought to be purchased for the canteen on the second floor.

Resolve to work solidly and with complete concentration for *at least six hours* a day, and more if the mandates you are working on require it. That way, you will be doing the work of two corporate employees every day of your new-style, independent working life. With that your consultancy will already have doubled in size before it is even properly under way.

As regards how you organize the legal status of your new consultancy, we strongly advise you to start by forming your consultancy as a sole proprietorship, and only incorporate when (and if) you grow your business to employ at least four or five other staff, by which time the tax advantages of running a corporation, and the advantage which a corporation offers in most countries in terms of limiting your liability, will have started to become an important factor.

Otherwise, follow the basic rule of running an SFC, and keep the consultancy small, perhaps ideally a sole proprietorship. The precise benefits of starting your SFC as a sole proprietorship will depend on the laws of the country in which you are based, but in general the main benefits of a sole proprietorship are as follows:

○ there is no legal requirement to file detailed accounts, although of course you will need to keep copies of your invoices and receipts so that you (or your accountant) can produce a truthful statement of your income during the year for income tax assessment;

○ the costs of setting up a sole proprietorship are minimal, since in essence all you are doing is trading under a trading name;

○ all income that your SFC generates can go straight into your pocket (you must, of course, keep records of your income for income tax assessment). With a corporation, on the other hand, you will need to invoice the corporation for your salary.

Against this, the sole proprietorship has the following possible disadvantages:

○ your liability is unlimited. For most consultancies this will not be a problem until they start to employ several people, at which point you will run into the problem that one of your staff might do something silly such as libel someone in a report they are writing or make a recommendation to a client that leads to the client suffering financial loss. For some consultancies that specialize in areas where the possibility of being sued is a very real one (e.g. construction and engineering), the sole proprietorship might not be suitable even when your consultancy consists of just you and perhaps a secretarial assistant. You may want to take out professional liability insurance to prevent yourself suffering substantial financial loss if you are sued successfully, but such insurance is very expensive and not always available, and limiting your liability through incorporation will possibly be a better idea, given that you must obviously check the legal aspects of your incorporation to confirm that your liability is indeed limited. Professional indemnity insurance is almost always available more inexpensively through a professional institute than on the open market, so if you are a member of your respective professional institute it is worth your while investigating whether it offers this insurance facility;

○ as a sole proprietor, you will be taxed on the basis that the profit you derive from your SFC is simply another element of your personal income (which it is). In some cases you would pay less tax on your profits if you had incorporated than if you are a sole proprietor. However, whether this is true or not in your case is something that only your accountant can tell you, and any possible tax savings after incorporation must of course be set against the costs of setting up a corporation and the higher accountancy charges that go with it;

○ some business books try to persuade you that for a consultancy, the sole proprietorship is unprofessional and clients will prefer to work with consultancies that have incorporated. We do not believe this; it smacks of encouraging people to create 'pretend' consultancies, and you already know our views on those. If you are not offering consulting services in an area where you consider there is a high risk of being sued, we see no reason why the fact that you are not incorporated from the outset should prejudice your chances with prospective clients.

The advantages and disadvantages of forming your SFC as a corporation can be summarized as follows:

○ advantages of incorporation:
  – limited liability;
  – possible savings on tax and National Insurance. These can be complex and you need to talk to an accountant about them. For example, if your consultancy is really successful, there may be opportunities to receive part of your income in the form of company dividends, to which a lower tax rate and lower National Insurance may apply;

○ disadvantages of incorporation:
  – costs of incorporation;
  – the expense of preparing detailed accounts to meet legal requirements;
  – income accruing to the corporation is not automatically yours;
  – lack of flexibility. For example, if you are a sole proprietorship and you want to change your trading name, all you need to do is change it. To change the name of a corporation, however, will cost you;
  – you will in effect incur a form of double taxation. Your corporation's profits will be taxed, and your income will also be taxed.

The final option is the partnership. The precise legal attributes of the partnership will depend on which country you are operating in, but in general partnerships involve joint and several unlimited liability, which is a nice way of saying that if you go into partnership with someone and that person screws up, you (and your other partners if you have any) are as liable for the screw-up as is the person who caused it.

In some professions, where the professional is not allowed to limit his liability, partnerships are the usual method of forming a firm. But if there is nothing to stop you from forming your SFC as either a sole proprietorship or a corporation, we advise you to forget about starting a partnership. Not only are partnerships inherently unstable as partners are always falling out and blaming each other for what is going wrong, there are several complex legal niceties of forming a partnership, and the last thing you want to be bothered with when starting an SFC are legal niceties.

Choosing a name for your SFC

You need to think of a name for your SFC. One option is simply to put the word 'Associates' after your name and leave it at that. But put 'Associates' rather than '&

Associates' which is pretentious and outdated. If you are going into business with someone else and have decided to form the consultancy's name out of both your surnames plus the word 'Associates', (e.g. Dembitz Essinger Associates), the inevitable argument over whose name comes first will soon make you wish you had followed our advice and set up in business alone. 'Maybe "Essinger Dembitz" sounds better.' 'No, it has to be "Dembitz Essinger" or else ...'

The rationale for basing your SFC's name around your own name is that what you are selling is your expertise and personality. And as we hope we made clear in Chapter Two, ultimately it is personality that wins business for consultants. This being the case, it makes sense to be up front and straightforward about the fact that, at least in the early days, it is essentially yourself and your experience and expertise that you have to offer. Besides, what was good enough for Messrs Coopers and Lybrand, Messrs Touche and Ross, and Arthur Andersen should be good enough for you.

We have always basically distrusted consultancy start-ups that call themselves silly things like 'Capable Consultants' or 'Consultancy Expertise'. However, if your name is either rather boring or rather embarrassing, we do not necessarily advise you to set up your consultancy under that name. But if you need to pluck a name out of the air, choose one that is straightforward and unpretentious. One good strategy is to choose a name that summarizes what business you are in. For example, if you are an agricultural consultant and you do not want to include your name in that of your SFC, calling yourself 'Agricultural Consultants' is simple, unpretentious and effective, although you will have to check that nobody else is using the name.

Sometimes consultants prefer not to use their own name in the name of their consultancy so that, if it does not succeed, they can return to work as a salaried minion without any stigma attached to their name. This was a factor in Alex's decision to name his consultancy IDOM: an acronym of 'Innovation, Development, Organization and Management'.

Stage two: drawing up a business plan

It is by no means always the case that you need a detailed business plan to start a self-fuelling consultancy. You can, of course, draw up an imposing-looking document with lots of figures and financial projections, but even if you were to find such a document genuinely convincing (which we doubt), it is unlikely that professionals – and particularly your bank manager – would attach a similar level of credibility to it.

If you were planning to start a business that manufactured mousetraps, you would need to have some idea in advance of how many mousetraps you could expect to produce in your first year, how much wood and wire you would need to order, and what you would need to pay for your materials, machinery and labour. Similarly, you would need to know how much you could charge for your mouse-traps, and you would be well advised to plan for contingencies such as the Great Mouse Exodus to Hamelin, or a dramatic increase in the population of cats during your first years of trading.

But you are not starting a mousetrap factory; you are starting an SFC. And we cannot see a business plan serving any function for you other than wasting time that would be better spent on clarifying in your head exactly what incremental advantage you can offer as a consultant and on winning your first client.

If your answer to this is 'Yes, but we need a detailed business plan so that we can apply to our bank manager to take out a loan to start the consultancy', then reread the previous chapter where we explained how getting into debt to start your new consultancy is a very bad idea. In fact, as someone who is planning to start an SFC, the only business plan you really need is one that contains answers to the following five questions:

1   What consultancy services will my SFC offer?
2   What incremental advantages will I be offering my clients?
3   Who is my first client?
4   What will I be doing for them?
5   How will I set about getting our next clients?

You should already have answers to the first four questions. The answer to the fifth is covered in the next chapter, which is all about winning business.

By all means draw up a formal business plan if it makes you feel more comfortable, but keep it short and to the point. Above all, keep it realistic. If you do want to draw up a more formal business plan, it should contain answers to all the preceding five questions, as well as realistic financial targets (i.e. targets for profitability and income) for the first three years, plus details of contingency measures you will take if you fall below your targets, and if you exceed them.

Beyond those three years, you cannot know what will happen. You are a consultant, not a fortune-teller.

Stage three: choosing your premises

Knowing what you know by now about the SFC, it will not surprise you that we strongly recommend that you at least consider starting your SFC at home, or in modestly-sized and priced premises. There are very good reasons for doing this.

1   You need to pay your rent or mortgage anyway, so if you are working from home your premises will in effect not cost you anything extra.

2   You will probably be able to claim a proportion of your rent or mortgage as an allowable expense against income tax, although seek advice from an accountant here since if you own your home it may be that making this claim may oblige you, in some national jurisdictions, to pay capital gains tax on any profits you make when you eventually come to sell it. The reason is that your first home, which would otherwise be exempt from capital gains tax, may be treated as non-exempt business premises if you are claiming some of your rent or mortgage against income tax.

3   You will probably want to have an office in your home even if you are planning to set up office elsewhere. This being so, why bother to set up office elsewhere?

4   You will have no costs of travelling to work, and you will not waste time travelling to and from work.

5   Particularly in the early days, establishing a consultancy can be an anxious and lonely matter, and you will find it reassuring to have your home comforts around you.

Stage four: choosing your equipment

If you are initially going to be running your SFC as a one-man band, you will need the following office equipment as a minimum. You can scale up this list to take into account what your colleagues will require.

Personal computer

Get the best and most powerful PC you can afford. There are really only two types to consider: IBM-compatible or the Macintosh.

If you are going down the IBM road, should you buy IBM or non-IBM? The answer is that it depends on the deal you are offered. Clones are so good nowadays that it makes little difference whether you buy a clone or an IBM machine.

At the very minimum your PC needs to be loaded with:

○ a suite of office programs. The current version of Microsoft Office is the most obvious choice, and probably the best. At the most basic, the suite needs to contain a word-processing package, a spreadsheet facility and a slide presentation program;

○ a computerized voice dictation system. IBM VoiceType and ViaVoice are excellent, as are the various types of voice recognition software from Dragon. With all these systems, you have to persevere to get the accuracy you need, but once you have done so, you will be astonished at how much time voice dictation can save you. Many users find that with practice they can regularly achieve 95 per cent accuracy;

○ Internet access (ideally via a well-known Internet service provider) and e-mail facility. E-mail is rapidly becoming *the* dominant means of business communications; you must have an e-mail address if you are to be taken seriously. Many consultancies stay on-line to the Internet all day.

Increasingly, businesspeople are preferring lap-tops or notebook-type palm-tops (i.e. palm-tops with a keyboard rather than a stylus-type input device) or subnotebooks (i.e. palm-tops with a smaller than standard keyboard) as their personal computer, instead of a desktop PC. The huge advantage these non-desktop machines offer in terms of portability is only partly offset by problems such as restricted memory, reduced processing power, comparatively poor graphics, and short battery life (a particular problem at present with lap-tops). These problems are sure to disappear in the fairly near future.

Telephone and fax

We recommend you begin with a straightforward telephone and fax, keeping in mind the principle that you are going to be starting small and ought to minimize your outlay on equipment. Combined telephone and fax machines are not a bad idea, except that they tend, by definition, to be rather large and may not always leave much room on your desk. Obviously, if there is more than one of you, you will need two telephone lines – in fact generally you need as many telephone lines as there are people working in your office.

You will certainly need your own fax machine, ideally with its own dedicated telephone line. Dismiss instantly any thoughts of using a bureau service to send/receive faxes. As a consultant, you will use the fax a great deal, and the cost of doing so via a bureau is exorbitant. It must be said, though, that the dramatically increasing importance of e-mail is causing a big dent in the popularity of the fax. Fax machines may, in time, become close to obsolete as a result.

Answering machine

There is definitely something to be said for having someone available to answer the telephone at all times. This is why, if you do not want to work from home, taking space in a business suite is a good move. In most cases the telephonist in a business suite will answer the telephone by saying the name of the suite and will then put the call through to your office if you are in, or will tell the caller that you are not in and will suggest they leave a message. Sometimes it is possible to arrange things in business suites so that you have your exclusive telephone number on the switchboard and the telephonist can answer the telephone with the name of your firm. Obviously, when you start to grow, you will probably have someone in the office all the time.

The only problem with incoming calls arises if you have decided to start your SFC at home. As we say, we strongly recommend this option if you are starting your consultancy by yourself, but we do concede that when a prospective client calls it does not always create a good impression if they get the answering machine.

If you are working from home, there are three ways of resolving this problem. First, you can train your spouse (if you have one, and if they are at home during the day) to answer the telephone professionally on your behalf, although this does not, of course, solve the problem when your spouse is not at home. (As we have said previously, in some instances it can be efficient, from an income tax and National Insurance perspective, to pay your spouse a modest salary for doing this and other jobs for you. You will need to ask your accountant to clarify this.)

Second, you can get yourself a mobile telephone and include the number on the outgoing message on your answering machine. That way, people who want to talk to you when you are out have the option of calling you on your mobile. This should also have a message facility. In the US, the national mobile system is disappointing compared with Europe, where the widespread availability of the GSM standard enables Europe-wide communication.

Third, you can rely on your answering machine. If you choose this option, it is advisable to ensure that you are in the office on days when you are expecting more than the usual number of calls, such as the first or second day after you have sent out a mailing in search of new business.

Photocopier

Get your own photocopier only if you regularly make a large number of copies or your office is a long way from a bureau. Competition keeps the prices of copying relatively low (this should also apply to the prices fax bureaus charge but it doesn't seem to, presumably because there is less demand for fax services than for photo-copying). Besides, photocopying anything other than a very short document is a tedious task and if you can get someone else to do it for you, at a modest cost, so much the better. Also, many photocopying bureaus (e.g. Kinkos, which is already very big in the US and becoming big in Europe) are open round the clock, so if you are desperate for a photocopy at three in the morning, you won't need to wait until after breakfast.

Furniture

Office furniture – which we take mainly to include desks, chairs, filing cabinets, bookshelves, bookcases and waste paper baskets – is something you should try to obtain as inexpensively as possible when starting out. The only exception to this rule concerns office chairs. The comfort of the chairs in an office is a major factor in the morale of the people who work in that office, even if the only person is you. Bad backs and even more serious problems such as repetitive strain injury (RSI) are common among office workers, and much of the problem stems from sitting for long periods on an uncomfortable or unsuitable chair.

It never fails to astonish us that many people who work in offices are prepared to sit on those dreadful little metal chairs with short backs shaped like the end of a canoe paddle. Since you will be spending many hours sitting on your office chair, the least you can do is make yourself comfortable, which means that you need a chair with a high back for the best level of back support and ideally with side supports so that you have somewhere to rest your elbows while you are typing.

One final point about office equipment: if you can afford it, never buy any piece of office equipment on a leasing arrangement. The money you will save by following this piece of advice should itself outweigh the cost of this book several times over. Leasing agreements are almost always nothing more than legalized theft. If you really cannot afford to pay cash for a piece of equipment that you need, consider taking out a bank loan – the interest rate will probably be lower than that 'offered' by leasing companies and you will not be tied to some extortionate agreement.

Stage five: filing

An essential element of the effective and efficient administration of an SFC – indeed of any business – is the maintenance of a good filing system. The key to this is twofold: simplicity and an awareness that the best filing cabinet of all is your waste paper basket.

Above everything else, keep your filing system simple and up to date. Use jacket files to keep all relevant papers relating to the current work you are undertaking for each of your individual clients, and use a different coloured file for each client so that you can easily distinguish between them. Keep your clients' 'current files' close to hand, so that you can grab the file when a client calls without keeping them hanging on the telephone for five minutes while you search for it. For some clients you will also need back-up files to keep background information that is not needed for the current project but that ought to be accessible.

Keep another file containing copies of all invoices you have issued, and wait until your clients have paid before putting the invoices into yet another file, which should hold all the receipts, copies of paid invoices, and other items which your accountant will need. Put receipts into that file as and when you get them. Remember that you will usually need to show receipts for any legitimate business expenses in order to offset them against tax, so try to obtain receipts for all expenses. If, say, you are planning to claim for a regular small cash expenditure, such as a daily copy of *The Wall Street Journal* or the *Financial Times* that you buy from your local newsagent, he will probably be prepared to give you a receipt for these on a weekly basis.

You will also need a separate file for client agreements unless you prefer to put these into the respective client files. However, it is probably best to keep these very important documents separate from the files in which you are keeping records of day-to-day client activity.

Keep a 'day file' where you can put all letters you receive through the mail and that are significant for your business. You can include copies of important letters that you send. Day files need sifting through every month or so to remove items that are no longer current. These can either be binned or placed in an archive file if necessary.

You will also require an efficient method of keeping names, addresses and telephone numbers of contacts, as well as the business cards that you are given and want to keep. A rotating business card file that allows you to store the cards in alphabetical order can be very useful here, although it does not solve the problem of what to do about those contact details you want to jot down yourself and retain. Another option is to use an alphabetic notebook into which you can paste important business cards and also write down key contact details. Whichever method you use is a matter of individual taste.

When it comes to filing, there are three rules that you ought to keep in mind. First, when you have anything to file, file it immediately. This particularly applies to your incoming mail. When you have sifted through your mail and binned what you don't need, it is tempting to put the remaining mail in a little pile somewhere in your office and get on with whatever job you are working on. Don't do this. Instead, get into the habit of filing your incoming mail immediately.

Second, always be alert to the dangers of filing something in the wrong place. Analytical scientists would tell us that paper is a lifeless substance; a mere wood product which, by the time it reaches us, has been pulped, pulverized and bleached to the extent that what remains bears no resemblance whatsoever to a living tree. Don't you believe it. In fact, paper has a life of its own, and it is a strange aspect of running a consultancy that the more critical and crucial a particular letter or document is, the more likely it is to attach itself by a sort of magic to the underside of a sheet that is ready for the bin, or the more probable it is that the prized piece of paper in question will manage to get itself filed with a routine document that you bury in one of your other files. Then, when you are sifting through the file a month or so later, you find the document whose apparent loss caused you so much heartache and inconvenience.

The only way to prevent this problem is to take great care with documentation and to concentrate when you are handling it, rather than imagine that documentation is something so mundane that you can file it away with one hand while you are holding the telephone receiver in the other hand and making an important call.

Third, don't be afraid to use the wastepaper basket as an important part of your filing system. Generally speaking, most businesses, and consultancies in particular, retain far too much documentation on file. This is all very well if the business is a long-established organization where keeping a letter that Mr Milquetoast wrote to Mr Feeble back in 1856 is a way for the organization to remind itself of its origins. However, you are starting an SFC, and the more streamlined you are, the better.

Of course you have to hang on to documents for several years (typically five or six) where there is a legal requirement to do so (this applies to your financial records used for accounting purposes, for example). You need to know what the particular legal requirements are in the jurisdiction where you operate. But apart from that, it is usually better to bin papers that are no longer part of your current activity. We would say that in general you should not bother retaining any paper or documentation that is no longer being actively used for longer than six months unless there is a very good reason to do so. However, if you would feel safer keeping every single document that passes through your office, don't let us stop you.

Stage six: choosing your stationery

As you will know by now, we believe passionately in the need to start an SFC small, run it as cost-effectively as possible, and take every step to relate its growth strictly to the volume of business that you generate. However, while starting small and running your SFC cost-effectively will mean that you need to cut corners with some expenditure, you must make every effort to furnish yourself with professional-looking and attractive stationery.

The reason for this is simple: your stationery is the way in which you present yourself to the business world through the mail. If you are offering an intelligent, thoughtful and resourceful service, it will not matter that you are working from home and (for the moment) paying yourself only a minimal salary. Nor does it matter, really, that when you are not in the office your prospective clients will (for the time being) have no alternative but to leave a message for you on your answering machine. You are just starting out, and by keeping things simple and even slightly primitive you are minimizing your expenditure and ensuring that you focus all your efforts and energies on working for your first client or clients and on searching for new business.

But you cannot economize on stationery. If you do, your clients will (with reason) regard you as being amateurish. We are not suggesting that you need to spend thousands of dollars doing what large corporations do and getting some hyped corporate image firm to design an entirely new corporate look, with a custom-designed typeface. But if you seriously think it is in the best interests of your SFC to send letters to your prospective clients typed on plain paper, you are wrong.

What we recommend is that you go to a local commercial designer and ask him to provide you with samples of typefaces suitable for stationery, given that you will probably need one typeface for the relatively large letters that present the name of your SFC and another for the smaller letters and numbers that present other information. You can also ask the designer for suggestions on the colour. Keep to just one colour in order to minimize printing costs. Dark blue is a strong, attractive, business-like colour, but you may have other ideas.

Some franchized chains of printing shops offer special deals on stationery design and printing to new businesses. If you shop around you will probably find that you can get your stationery designed and the first batch of it printed at a very reasonable cost. You will, as a minimum, need to equip yourself with the following.

Letterheads

These are the flagship documents on which you present your SFC through the mail. The letterhead is the piece of stationery on which the first page of your letters appears. It must contain the following information:

- the name of your consultancy;
- the address of your consultancy;
- the telephone number, fax number and (if you have them) e-mail address, website address and mobile telephone number. If you have a serious expectation of being able to win business from abroad, a pleasant courtesy to your prospective foreign clients is to put your country's national dialling code on the letterhead.

You can include other information such as the names of your fellow consultants, if you have any, or your name and job title. It often looks better if the name or names of personnel are at the foot of the letterhead rather than at the top. If you are running your SFC alone and want to put your name on your letterhead but don't know how to describe yourself, call yourself 'managing consultant'. This is simple, unpretentious and – best of all – true.

Some consultants like to put relevant tax numbers and any incorporation numbers on their letterhead. This is a matter of taste.

Continuation sheets

These are the sheets of paper on which you type (ideally with a word processor) your letters and other documents after the first page, which will go on your letterhead. Many consultants do without continuation sheets, preferring to use a sheet of plain paper. However, we recommend continuation sheets for two reasons.

First, they make your letters and documents look professional. Second, it is very likely that the type of paper (which is determined by factors such as the weight of the paper and the watermark on it) that has been used for your letterheads will not be the same as your everyday plain paper. If you do not use a continuation sheet, you may find there is an unprofessional-looking contrast between the appearance of your letterhead and that of your successive sheets.

Your continuation sheets should be the same type of paper as that used for the letterheads and should simply carry, in the top right-hand corner, the name of your SFC as it appears on the letterhead, but the name should be reduced in size by at least half. This makes for a neater and more professional appearance than if your SFC's name is reproduced on the continuation sheet the same size as it appears on the letterhead.

Big labels for packages and large envelopes

Big labels (with peel-off sticky backs) that you put on large envelopes and packages are extremely useful. They need to have plenty of space in the middle for you to write or word-process the address of where they are going. They will, of course, have your consultancy's name and address on, either at the top, the bottom, or divided between the two. Quite apart from enhancing your corporate image (and providing the postman with a return address for any package that goes astray), they are cost-effective as they allow you to recycle used envelopes and padded postage bags.

Compliment slips

You should include a compliment slip whenever you send somebody something (e.g. an invoice or a cheque) that does not require an accompanying letter. It should give the name of your firm and all the contact details, plus the words 'With Compliments'.

Invoices

Now we come to the mighty invoice, the life-blood of any business, and the one thing you will never regret giving away. An invoice is usually a one-page document – the same size as your letterhead – with one or more copy sheets underneath. You send the top copy to the lucky recipient and you keep the bottom copy or copies for your files so that you know which invoices you have issued and can keep a track of those that are still outstanding. You can also keep a record of your SFC's revenue.

There are many ways of composing invoices and all we would say is that if you are imposing a statutory tax on the amount invoiced (e.g. value added tax in the UK) you should put your registration number for this tax on your invoice (in some countries you are legally obliged to do so).

As a minimum, your invoices should contain the following information:

o the name of your SFC and your contact details. These are normally placed at the top of the invoice, and there is no reason why they cannot simply be 'lifted' from your letterhead;

○ a space for you to write the number of the invoice (incidentally, when you get round to issuing your first invoices, don't make yourself look silly by starting with invoice numbers 1, 2, 3 etc.; instead start with 101, 102, 103 and so on. This is not insincere or dishonest, simply the application of business sense);

○ a space for you to write the date of the invoice;

○ a space for you to write your customer's name and address;

○ a space (which should be the largest space on the invoice) for you to write details of the activity you have performed (or are performing or are about to perform) and which is the reason for sending the invoice. Remember to distinguish clearly between consultancy time for which a fee is payable and agreed expenses;

○ a column in which you write the various sums of money involved. If you are charging a statutory tax in addition to your own charges, you will need to create an extra box for this and a box for a sub-total prior to setting down the total;

○ you might like to state your payment terms at the foot of the invoice. If you do this, do not make your words sound menacing. 'Payment Within Thirty Days Would Be Appreciated' will usually get things moving without annoying clients.

Business cards

These are obviously essential. As with your other stationery, they should conform to whatever typeface and colour scheme you have chosen. We recommend that you keep what appears on your business cards simple and functional. You will need to put the name of your SFC and your contact details, so we suggest that again you simply lift these from your letterhead.

Apart from those details, you need to put your name and job title on the card, not forgetting to include any letters after your name such as those accruing from a first and second degree or a doctorate, as well as any letters you have by virtue of belonging to a professional institution that allows you to use those letters. Do not use letters after your name that you are not entitled to use – somebody is bound to find you out sooner or later.

That, then, is an overview of your minimum stationery requirements. Other materials you may want to create for your consultancy will relate to your marketing activity. These are covered in the next chapter.

Your agreement with your clients

Tom Lambert is absolutely right to point out in his book *High-Income Consulting*

(Nicholas Brealey, London, 1997) that the contract with clients should be seen as part of your marketing activity. He says:

> '*The basic use of a contract is self-evident; it states what you are bound to do and what you are entitled to receive. It does a great deal more and what it does says much for your professional status. The fact that you always insist on a contract immediately identifies you as a serious professional, it adds to your status, and your ability to attract and retain business is based firmly on your status.*'

There are basically three reasons for a contract:

○ to promote a crystal-clear understanding between yourself and your client of what you will be doing for them;

○ to furnish a document that can be used as a working brief for carrying out the mandate;

○ to promote your status as a professional.

These three objectives should be the overriding considerations here. They are more important than anything. In particular, the contract should improve the quality of your relationship with your client, not worsen it. The problem with using ultra-formal legal contracts is that it will raise your client's hackles and he may suspect (not without reason in the case of some consultancies we have heard of) that your motive for producing such an intensely legal document is to trap him into signing something it is not really in his interests to sign. This being so, he will subject your draft contract to intense scrutiny by his own legal team, and once lawyers start squabbling over contracts, all that happens is that lawyers generate fees for themselves.

Obviously, in business there *are* occasions when you need an ultra-formal legal contract, but your relationship with your client should ideally not be like that. Your winning of the mandate, and subsequently carrying it out, should be a positive process, and if the whole thing is going to be tense and unpleasant from the beginning it rather raises the question of whether you are managing the client relationship properly.

Generally, therefore, we recommend that rather than drawing up a contract written in tough legal language, you write your client a letter that is formal in the sense that every contingency is taken care of, but that is not so tough that it frightens off your client. There is a certain comparison between wooing a client and wooing a prospective spouse. How would you feel if, the day before your wedding, your beloved presented you with a ten-page legal document covering various aspects of your life together? In America pre-marital agreements are common, but nobody is saying they make the marriage more likely to succeed: very possibly they indicate a level of distrust that is bad news from the beginning. One expects one's marriage to be based on co-operation and collaboration, and that is exactly how your relationships with your clients should work.

This does *not* mean that the letter should be so informal or casual that crucial points are left out. As we made clear in the Introduction, it is essential that you base consulting work on a clear agreement and that you do not start working until that agreement is signed. Just to recap, the agreement should cover all the following points:

○ precisely what you will be doing for the client;

○ precisely what benefits they can expect from your work;

○ when you will be starting to work for them;

○ when you will be stopping working for them;

○ how much time in aggregate you will be spending on their behalf and when you will be charging for this;

○ how much you will be charging as expenses and what the basis is for a cost qualifying as a rechargeable expense;

○ when you will be sending invoices and how much the invoices will be for;

○ when you expect your invoices to be paid;

○ when the client can expect a written report and how long this is likely to be;

○ any other key issues relating to your work for the client;

○ the resources the client needs to make available to you, including access to people, systems and premises.

This is not supposed to be an exhaustive list. There may be other points you need to include, especially if some aspect of your remuneration is going to be based on results.

Take great care to avoid making your agreement ambiguous – you and your client need to be absolutely certain what everything means. Remember that this is a collaborative exercise: invite your client to discuss any points of query or uncertainty before he signs it. It is in both your interests to know where you stand. In particular, *make your credit terms crystal clear rather than springing them on the client once you have started work*. If you have drafted your agreement properly, there should be no reason for you or your client to have any dispute about invoices unless your client decides that you have not done what he expected you to do in carrying out the mandate.

After a while you will find that your agreements with clients are basically similar and you will probably formulate a kind of pro forma agreement that can be adapted as and when you need it. Your early agreements, when you are still finding your feet, and your pro forma agreement definitely need to be scrutinized by your lawyers before they see the light of day. But ensure that you retain control of the situation, and do not allow your lawyers to put so much legal verbiage and sub-clauses into the agreement that it looks like a contract to cover a merger between IBM and Hewlett-Packard rather than what should at heart be an amicable deal between you and your clients.

Your letters of agreement or contracts should be prepared in a good spirit. They are almost always drawn up at a time when there is plenty of goodwill floating around. Make sure they are robust enough, and protect you sufficiently, to cover eventualities when unforeseen problems have caused the goodwill to dry up or fade.

We call the agreement a marketing tool because your clients will respect you if you draw up clear, friendly agreements. As long as you do the work covered by the agreement to the standard they expect, they will think of you as a straight-dealing, ethical consultant who does what he says he will, and keeps the atmosphere pleasant and friendly. They will very possibly recommend you to their friends and business contacts as a result of this, which brings us to the hugely important subject covered in the next chapter: how you win business.

CHAPTER SIX

Winning business

Introduction

The first observation to make on the equally essential matter of winning new business is this: *as a consultant, and especially as a new consultancy, the world does not owe you a living.* You need to go out and win your living from the world.

In this battle to sell your consulting services, your only weapons are the ones we have already identified: your expertise, experience, sincerity, energy and determination to give clients value for money.

The second point to make is: *don't imagine that merely undercutting your competitors on price will win you business.* It probably won't. Pricing is certainly one area of potential business-winning competitiveness, but it is rarely enough in itself. In fact, it will be enough in itself only in the unlikely case that there are very few consultancies offering the service you offer and you can readily prove that you can offer at least the same quality of service they offer at a lower price. But generally price competition is far from being enough to win you new business, especially because many clients link the quality of the consulting service with the cost of that service. This means that you need to have other competitive attributes if you are to be successful, which means if you are to win new business.

The third point is: *you must create a sales resource within your organization, whatever the size of your consultancy, and you must ensure that it is active all the time.* This guideline is easy enough for a very large consultancy to carry out; many large consultancies employ people full-time to sell the consultancy's services, and by definition these people will be selling all the time and will be rewarded by the consultancy according to how successful they are.

Unfortunately, if you are a start-up (not an 'upstart' although some prospective clients will consider you one) it is highly unlikely that you will be able to afford to employ someone who can devote all his or her time to selling. If you are a one-man band, at least to start with, you will need to generate income for your consultancy by working on mandates. But even if you are starting your consultancy with several staff, it is unlikely that the economics of your business will make it possible for you to employ one person solely to sell. Winning new business is always partly a speculative exercise – indeed, some consultancies regard it as a numbers game, with a certain percentage of positive responses to be expected in relation to a number of approaches. Funding speculative sales activity is always difficult, and funding a full-time sales person is a privilege for anything other than a huge consultancy.

Consequently, you need to work out a balance that allows you to spend time both earning income and selling. We thought hard about making specific recommendations here for how you should divide your time, but we decided that these could be misleading and malproductive. You need to work out a balance that suits you, and that is clearly going to depend substantially on your selling abilities, on the success of your sales activity, and on how much time you feel you need to devote to working on paid projects in order to meet your financial targets.

The fourth point is: *at a psychological level, winning new business is not something you should compartmentalize from your day-to-day activities as a consultant.*

We have already emphasized that it is personality that wins business for consultants, so it is common sense that your best business-winning asset needs to be switched on at all times. And so everything you do as a consultant – your entire way of being in business, the way you talk to clients, the level of service you extend to them, the way you project yourself to the outside world, the way you deal with any problems your clients may have, and of course the way you carry out your consulting activity – is part of your business-winning process.

That business-winning process is, in effect, the projection of your personality to the outside world in general, and to potential clients in particular. A good consultant never stops selling.

But do not imagine that this means we advise you to be doing a 'hard sell' on your consulting services all the time. There are occasions when a consultant who wants to be successful needs to sell himself or herself hard: when you are faced with a wavering business prospect who is trying to decide between you and a competitor, for example. In that scenario, there is not much point being modest about your expertise, anymore than a presidential candidate is likely to get anywhere by being modest and suggesting that his (or her) rival is an equally strong candidate.

But generally the hard sell does not succeed in consultancy. Again, it has a lot to do with the psychology of why clients appoint consultants. The reason the hard sell does not work can be largely explained by the following observation: clients want to feel that they have made the decision to give the business to a consultant themselves, as a result of their own intelligence and judgement.

Let clients find out about you, and get to know your good qualities (by 'your' here we are talking about either you or your consulting organization/division).

Above all, give prospective clients the space and freedom to make the selection decision themselves.

We have already compared the process of wooing clients to that of wooing a member of the opposite sex. Men who are in love with a woman and want to win her (or, in these days of refreshing equality between the sexes, vice versa) will naturally want to make sure the beloved person knows how they feel about them. But it is essential for the would-be lover to give the other person the chance to make up their own mind, which means giving them the space and freedom to do what they please. If they are not allowed to do so, it is not affection but coercion, which does not belong in the modern world. And so it is when wooing a new business prospect in consulting.

Another key aspect of human psychology needs to be mentioned here. It is fundamental to human nature that we are most likely to bestow our affection on someone who does not demand it, and in many cases, the less they demand it, the more likely we are to bestow our affections on them. Conversely, the more somebody begins to demand our affection, the less likely we are to bestow it.

Naturally there are exceptions to this rule. It does not apply in the affection we extend to our children, for instance, or when those we love are facing a crisis that means they desperately need our affection and support. As Shakespeare wrote, 'love is not love which alters when it alteration finds.' In other words, if we cannot love unequivocally in this situation, it is not love anyway.

But the rule is profoundly true of very many human interactions, especially with people who are new acquaintances, or whom we do not know at all.

As far as your activities as a consultant are concerned, the rule is of enormous importance. Bearing it in mind at all times will remind you to avoid the hard sale in the vast majority of cases, and instead to give your prospective clients the space and freedom to discover for themselves that they like you. There is a kind of affection involved here, just like affection in your personal life, and of course the same fundamental psychology is at work. Consultants are appointed because clients – both existing and prospective ones – like the consultants as people and find them inspiring. It is true that many of the best consultants work for organizations, but preferences for organizations are always much weaker than preferences for people. Even where a particular client has pretty much decided to opt for a particular consultancy organization, the client will need to be finally convinced by meeting inspiring and likeable people from that organization.

It follows from all this that, in essence, the way to win new business as a consultant is to be a great consulting personality in every sense, that is:

○ to be highly professional in everything you do and say;

○ to be sincere with existing and prospective clients;

○ to work hard and give value for money;

○ to listen to clients;

○ to cultivate an attractive and inspiring personality that makes people want to queue up to let you work for them.

We will now focus on the actual mechanics of how you win new business. In this context, the 'mechanics' are the methods by which you consciously project your 'great consulting personality' to your existing and potential clients. And do not forget that your existing clients are a major source of new business, both because they may give you more business themselves, and also because they may give you references and referrals.

Generally, the importance of existing clients as a source of new business tends to increase the larger your consultancy becomes. Many large consultancies find that about 80 per cent of new business comes from existing clients, either directly or indirectly. A smaller consultancy is unlikely to find that this extremely high percentage applies to them, but even so, existing clients must always be nurtured as a direct or indirect source of new business. Furthermore, winning new business from an existing client removes many obvious sources of risk: for one thing, you will probably know how creditworthy (or not) your client is and can reasonably expect that favourable payment terms that have been extended to you in the past can be continued for the new product.

Moving on to the methods of winning new business, it is useful to identify four of these. We will consider them in order of importance.

Method one – referral business

By far the most important way of winning new business in consulting is by referral from an existing client. What typically happens is that your name or the name of your consultancy or division has been given by an existing client to a third party. The reason for referral business being so important is that the whole essence of consulting is the confidence clients have in the consultant. It is in practice extremely difficult for clients to get to know consultants with the requisite degree of intimacy to generate such confidence without actually hiring them. Consequently, a referral from somebody whom the client already knows – and in whose judgement the client has confidence – is one of the best ways for the prospective client to gain reassurance about the consultancy.

This does not, however, mean that as a consultant you should be passive when it comes to winning referral business. Clearly, you can take an active role in maximizing the chance that you will win such business by working hard, effectively and sincerely on behalf of your existing clients.

In business, as in other areas of human activity, word soon gets around if someone is very good at what they do. Or if they aren't.

Method two – getting your name around

The next most important way for you to win business is by consciously taking steps to get known in the industry, and in the area, where you are operating. Your aim should be to position yourself as a thoughtful, results-orientated consultant who is devoted to delivering value for money.

You also need to be subtle. Remember what we said about avoiding the hard sell? Your aim should be to position yourself as an authority who is genuinely interested in industry issues and in the practice of consulting. In other words, you should make it an objective to be seen to be an industry guru: selling yourself should be a distant second and in many cases you are best advised to avoid overt selling of yourself.

Be a guru. *Make* yourself interesting. Think of things to say about your industry and say them. Make yourself a spokesman and an inspiring authority on issues that are key to you. Keep in mind our principle that clients employ consultants because they want to feel they have the right person for the job, and they also enjoy the surge in their status that comes from employing talented and inspirational consultants. In a nutshell, give your prospective clients the space and freedom to make the decision to employ you. Don't be afraid of attracting fame and recognition.

So how exactly do you get your name around? The most obvious thing to do is to offer your services as a speaker to the organizers of relevant conferences and seminars. This is an extremely good idea because if you can win a conference-speaking opportunity, the potential promotional mileage may be considerable. Not only will you have the opportunity to project yourself, your expertise and your skills to the audience (who, if it is a good event, may be extremely influential people), but there is usually additional promotional mileage deriving from your inclusion in the brochure or 'flyer' promoting the event. Many conference and seminar organizers also announce events with press releases and even major editorial features which again can be extremely useful coverage for you.

In addition, you will find that the discipline of preparing a pithy and interesting presentation, and standing on a podium to deliver it, will concentrate your mind wonderfully, encouraging you to think hard about your attitudes to your industry, the role of consultants in it, and other important issues.

On occasion you will be offered a fee for your speech, usually a fairly nominal sum, but often this is not the case. In any event, the promotional exposure you gain will be very valuable and worth the effort required in preparing your presentation. You can, however, expect to have your expenses reimbursed.

Sometimes conference organizers are so aware of the promotional benefits to speakers that they actually expect them to pay for the privilege of speaking. Our advice is not to do this. For one thing, you should be able to find other organizers who do not expect you to pay (after all, you are already going to be providing your time for nothing.) For another, the important conferences that attract influential decision makers as delegates (i.e. the very people you want to sell to) generally do not expect speakers to pay. It is usually only the second-rate organizers who do.

Since we are on the subject of avoiding wasting money (remember our precept that you make money by not spending it?), we recommend that you avoid paying to appear in the numerous manuals, yearbooks, etc. which will contact you once they hear about you. Money spent here rarely brings in new business. There are some key manuals or yearbooks you may need to appear in, but generally the best ones will include your details – as a reputable member of the industry – without asking you to pay for the privilege. Sometimes such key directories will offer you the chance to pay for an 'enhanced entry'. You can decide whether you really want to do this.

So what should you talk about in your presentation? Above all, you should focus on key industry issues that are likely to interest your audience. Whatever you do, don't use the opportunity for a hard sell. Your audience will find this extremely irritating, as will the organizers, and you will not be asked back. More to the point, as we have seen, hard sell rarely works in consulting and all you will have done is waste an opportunity to make important contacts. Instead, stimulate your audience and make them think. Stimulated people are likely to want to get in touch with you after the event.

It is extremely important that you tell conference organizers that you want to distribute a three-page hard-copy summary of your presentation to delegates before or after you have delivered it. You must, of course, ensure that your contact details, and ideally a short biography, are fairly prominent on the summary. Distributing the summary is essential because it means that your name and experience will be in delegates' minds long after you have given your presentation. If the conference organizer will not allow you to do this, ask if you can send the summary to delegates yourself. If neither of these options is permitted, consider whether you really want to take up the speaking opportunity.

Some advice about writing and giving your speech or presentation. The purpose of a speech or presentation is to convey information to an audience in such a way that they want to absorb it. Whereas a speech will usually be presented to a fairly large audience at a conference, seminar or similar event, a presentation will usually be made to a more limited audience, such as to the people in an organization who are responsible for choosing a new marketing or advertising agency.

Should a speech or presentation be written down at all? Some experienced speakers would say no, and would argue that speeches and presentations should be prepared in note form, thereby giving the speaker the chance to make the speech come alive during the event itself. Certainly nothing is duller than a speaker reading out a speech in a monotonous voice that makes no concession to the simple, brutal fact that you cannot convey information to people in a speech or presentation unless you first entertain them.

Let us elaborate on this point before returning to the question of whether or not a speech or presentation should be scripted. The delivery of a speech or presentation is inseparable from its content. You can no more effect a separation between the delivery and content of a speech than you can expect a cinema audience, if the projector breaks down, to be satisfied by each being lent a copy of the screenplay of the film they were planning to see. This is why the names of the stars get far more emphasis in a cinema poster than the name of the screenwriter: the audience attaches more importance to the actor's performance of the dialogue than to the dialogue itself (although good dialogue helps, naturally).

The vast majority of consultants have little or no understanding of this fundamental point. They continue to allow senior managers to deliver speeches at conferences and seminars, even though the managers in question have no talent for public speaking and will bore their audience rigid. Similarly, too many organizations allow a presentation team to consist of people who may be great at getting on with the work they will win if the presentation succeeds but who have no real idea how to deliver the presentation so that the likelihood of winning the business is maximized.

Think of the conferences and seminars you have attended as a delegate. What percentage of the speeches interested you beyond the first ten minutes, or even beyond the first five minutes? During what percentage of the speeches did your mind *not* wander to thinking of that video you saw last night, what's for lunch/dinner, or the work you should be doing instead of attending the conference? Zero per cent? Five per cent? Any more than five per cent and you will deserve an entry in the *Guinness Book of Records* under the category of Least Distracted Conference Delegate.

We suggest you should only speak at conferences and seminars if you believe (and have evidence for this belief) that you have a talent for public speaking. If not, find someone else in your organization (if you have an organization) to deliver your speech.

If you are using visual aids in a speech or presentation, keep them straightforward and to the point, otherwise it is too easy for your audience to be put off by them and wind up focusing more on the visual aids than on the content of the speech.

To get back to the point of whether the speech or presentation should be scripted, our advice is that you should script a speech but avoid scripting a presentation. If you don't script a speech there is a serious danger that you will dry up. Almost as bad is waffling or wandering off the point. Your audience will not be tolerant of either. Make no mistake: if you don't hold their interest, they will stop listening to you, and some may even walk out. They are paying good money to hear you, and they want value for their money. Even more to the point, if you do not engage them you will have lost an extremely important – and comparatively rare – opportunity to project the quality of your mind to numerous potential clients.

You could write your speech in note form, a good solution if you are an experienced speaker and you know what you are doing. Be warned, though, that notes that seemed so full and detailed when you wrote them can seem horribly sparse and unhelpful when you are staring at them in front of an audience of 200 people and desperately trying to think what to say next. One solution is to write out the script of the speech in full, but not to be afraid of enlarging on it as you present it.

As for a presentation, if it is a shortish one and you are spreading the burden among several people, there is no reason why everybody shouldn't learn what they have to say by heart, perhaps using a visual aid as a cue. Otherwise, use notes, but make sure you know exactly what you mean by a particular note. Don't script the whole thing: it will be far too unspontaneous and forced. And make sure you rehearse it, ideally several times. We cannot over-emphasize the importance of rehearsing the presentation. The better your presentation and your delivery of it, the more effective a tool for subtle selling it will be.

Another way to enhance your profile is to write articles for professional or industrial journals. You can hire a public relations consultancy to do this for you, but it is not really necessary and in any case, the PR consultancy is unlikely to be able to do the actual writing anyway. To place an article in a relevant professional or industrial journal you don't usually need to do much more than telephone the features editor or editor and either tell them what you want to write about or send them a synopsis. They will usually expect to receive the article on an exclusive basis, at least within their industrial or professional remit. You may be offered a small fee if they like your article and want to publish it, but often your recompense will consist simply of the coverage you gain. Ask them whether they will publish your telephone number at the end of the article as well as your name and the name of your consultancy at the start. Many journals are more than happy to publish telephone numbers. But in return, they will expect an article that looks at important key issues and is authoritative. This is not the place for a hard sell; indeed, many editors will simply refuse to run a piece that is not objective.

Another option is to write a book on a subject related to your professional or industrial sector. This can be a powerful promotional tool. A book will frequently have a long shelf life even of many years and so can give you visibility in the profession for some time. The big drawback to writing a book is that it is an extremely time-consuming process, as we have every reason to know. Because business publishers do not usually give substantial advances to writers who are not big names, there is not much point regarding the writing of a book as a profitable activity in itself: you are much better off devoting your time to working as a consultant.

You could hire a ghostwriter to write a book for you after you have briefed them thoroughly. There will still be some input required from you, but it won't be anything like as much as if you were doing the book yourself. If you are already very well known in your field, you may be able to find a literary agent who specializes in putting together book deals for well-known business people; these kinds of agents will often find a freelance ghostwriter for you as well.

Finally, you might start or edit a newsletter for your profession or industrial sector. Again, the promotional mileage here can be considerable, but you must balance the time required against your need to make a living from your consulting.

There are always other chances to promote yourself: it is a question of being astute enough to spot them. For example, a well-timed letter to the editor of a quality national newspaper on a key subject can bring good visibility, as can appearances on radio and television. You need to be on the look-out for these opportunities.

Method three – making unsolicited approaches

The most usual way of winning new business is to make unsolicited approaches to prospective clients with whom you have not yet worked. While it is undeniable that this method is always something of a 'hit and miss', it is nonetheless the bread and butter way of winning new business. As long as the consulting services you are offering are, viewed generically, in demand, and as long as you have something special to offer (and, for reasons we have already explained, you should not be working as a consultant if both these conditions do not apply), it is inevitable that there will be clients out there who will want to work with you.

This method does, however, need to be handled with care if you are to receive positive inquiries back, and especially if you want to maximize the chances of your approaches having a reasonably high hit rate. What do we mean by 'reasonably high' in this context? We mean that you receive a favourable response from about 3 per cent of your mailings. A favourable response would be a willingness on the part of the prospective client to meet you, either at your offices or theirs. Obviously, you are not going to get any business without such a meeting.

Sometimes you may do very much better than 3 per cent – a 10 per cent response is not unheard of when a consultancy has an exciting new proposition to sell and has really done its homework with regards to which organizations it is targeting – but even a 3 per cent response can be very good if you follow them up with care and attention and convert a high proportion into mandates.

Remember, too, that when you look for new business through unsolicited mailings, your financial numbers are not the same as they would be for an organization selling by mail order, where the relatively small profit to be gained from each sale makes the response percentage crucial to the success of the whole endeavour. For you, it really is no exaggeration that a handful of responses to your mailing (or even a couple of responses) could transform your business both now and for many years to come.

In almost every case, your first approach to prospective new clients on an unsolicited basis should be by letter. The only exception is when an existing client or other contact has given you the name of a prospective client who has indicated that they may be interested in your services and who has asked you to call them. In this case you may be able to set up a meeting with them on the basis of a telephone call alone. Such a prospect is not exactly a referral but neither is it a completely cold approach either.

Otherwise, you should write a letter to new business prospects. The purpose of this letter is to create a dialogue with the prospect, hopefully leading to a meeting with them which will give you a chance to listen to their needs (always the prime requirement) and to tell them, in a professional, non-hard-sell way, what you could offer them and how you could help them.

If you do your preparatory work properly, the response rate to such letters can be surprisingly high, but that is the proviso: you have to do your background work thoroughly.

Should you send the letter by post or by e-mail? Obviously, in these days when the Internet has made such a prodigious impact in business generally and commerce in particular (an impact that is only going to grow in time), you may be tempted to feel that sending a letter of this nature by e-mail is a good idea. However, our advice is unequivocal: use the traditional postal service.

The problem is that e-mails, while an extremely useful method for communicating, are not really optimal for making an unsolicited approach. For one thing, it can be difficult to get somebody's e-mail address unless you know them already, which in this case by definition you won't, and if you don't know them (or their organization) you can never really be sure that you are e-mailing the right person. Another problem is that by the very nature of the e-mail it is not easy to say very much about yourself and/or your consultancy. And e-mails can go astray: you will not always get a message back that a particular e-mail was not delivered, so you won't have the comfort of knowing that the e-mail reached its destination.

When you make unsolicited approaches to prospective clients by mail, you need to do things in the following way.

Step one

Start by accepting that you ought to send a batch of new business letters to prospective clients every month as a regular and important part of your consultancy's marketing activity. You should do this even if you are up to your eyes in business already (it does happen) and cannot imagine how you are ever going to find a spare minute to work on any new business.

Sending out new business letters regularly is not only important for the general health of your consultancy, it is also good for your morale to come into regular contact with new business prospects, even if they do not need your services at present. Many prospective clients like to hear about what a consultant can offer them and like to keep the consultant's details on file. The new business activity that you undertake this week may not bear fruit in terms of fee-paying work for six months or longer, but having the prospect of that work in the future is very important if you are planning – as we hope by now you are – for your consulting to be the mainstay of your income for a significant part of your working life.

Step two

Next, do your basic research. This is essential to the success of any new business mailing. You need to identify organizations that are likely to use your services. The sources of this information will depend on your specialization, and may include one or more of the following:

○ business pages of your telephone directory (*Yellow Pages* in the US and the UK);

○ lists of members of professional associations;

○ listings in industry yearbooks/handbooks;

○ guides issued at major trade exhibitions;

○ lists of conference delegates. These are often available to people who attend a conference, although this is rarely a cost-effective way of obtaining these lists as the cost of attending a conference can be very high. However, sometimes you can do a deal with a conference organizer whereby, for example, you supply them with names and addresses of potential conference delegates in exchange for receiving details of all those who attended the event;

○ lists of exhibitors at exhibitions;

○ lists of visitors to exhibitions;

○ names of organizations that advertise in your respective trade publication (many consultants overlook this source of possible new business contacts, but it is an important one, if only because such advertisers have already demonstrated, by buying the advertisement, that they believe in laying out some money for the chance of making their business more successful and profitable);

○ names of organizations that you read about in the editorial pages of the trade press or in general business publications such as *The Wall Street Journal* or the *Financial Times*. Bear in mind, though, that you may not be the only consultant who is writing to organizations whose problems and/or objectives have been revealed in the media;

○ personal contacts. These will typically include friends, 'business friends', colleagues (if you are still working for a salary), former colleagues (if you aren't) and former competitors (remember that when you switch to being a consultant, the former competitors can become current clients!).

In practice, lists of members of professional associations, and guides to major exhibitions, tend to be the best lists for new business mailings. These lists are usually available at a very reasonable cost from the professional association, whereas lists of conference delegates or of exhibitors or visitors to exhibitions are likely to be expensive or difficult to obtain.

What you should aim to be doing from your basic research is to gather the names and addresses of at least 100 organizations that might be interested in using your services. When you have done that, you are ready for the next step.

Step three

Create a special list that includes all these organizations, and make the decision to write to no more than about 15 of them a week.

The key to successful business mailings is to write to a relatively small number of prospective clients a week, but to keep up these mailings on a regular basis. The reason for this is twofold.

1 You must personalize each mailing, which means that unless you happen to know the name of the person at the organization to whom you should be writing, you will need to telephone that organization and find out from the receptionist who that person is.

2 Other things being equal, your new business mailings should be thoughtful and discreet rather than wide-ranging.

The job title or role of the person to whom you should write at the prospective client organization will depend both on the size of the organization and the type of consultancy business in which you work. If you are writing to a small organization (this is something you might be able to ascertain when you make your phone call) you should write to the managing director. If, on the other hand, you are writing to a larger organization, you will have to write to the person you imagine would be most likely to be responsible for appointing you. This is something you will probably have to guess as you cannot really expect the receptionist to tell you who appoints consultants in a particular field.

It should not be difficult for you to guess what the person's job title would be, and you can then call the organization and ask for the name of the person who has that job title (remember not to assume, when you ask, that the person will be a man). If, for example, you are offering information technology services, you will probably need to write to the information technology director. If you are offering human resources consulting, you will need to write to the personnel manager or the human resources director (if there is one). If you are offering public relations services, you should write to the marketing manager.

If, when you make your telephone call to find out the name of the person to whom you should be writing, you are asked why you want this information, tell the truth – that you are a consultant working in such and such a field and you want to introduce yourself to the person in the organization who is responsible for such and such a function. The vast majority of people will gladly give you the name of the relevant person, but on occasion you may be told that they have no need of your services. Thank them politely and replace the receiver – it's their loss, not yours.

There is nothing to be ashamed of in wanting to sell your services. All successful people are in a sense sales people. Even the President of the United States is a salesman: selling his policies to the American people both before and after he has been elected.

It sometimes happens that your telephone call to find out someone's name leads to you being able to introduce yourself over the telephone to a potential client – you may, for instance, telephone a small organization and inadvertently wind up talking to the boss and telling him about your services. If this happens, great, but remember that the purpose of your call is not to sell yourself over the telephone (unless there is a very strong interest at the other end, we cannot recommend this course of action to any consultant) but to find out the name of the person to whom you should be writing.

Step four

Now write that letter. Use your letterhead and, as with other business letters, include the name, organization and address of the person to whom you are writing on the top left of the letter, starting below the bottom of the printed text at the top of your letterhead. Below this put the date, and then the salutation, which should be to 'Mr' somebody or 'Ms' somebody unless you already happen to know them.

It should hardly be necessary to emphasize the ultra-importance of avoiding spelling mistakes in letters that you send out to prospective clients, otherwise they are likely to be nothing more than a waste of a stamp, a letterhead and an envelope. This sort of letter makes you look either unprofessional or incompetent, and rightly so. If you haven't got a good dictionary in your office, get one: nobody can spell every word accurately from memory. A computer spellcheck will help here, but don't rely on it entirely. Computer spellchecks can get things wrong. It is also much too easy to press the wrong key while running a spellcheck and put a completely nonsensical word into the text. And computer spellchecks obviously will not spot correctly spelt words that are the wrong word in the context.

You need to decide what enclosures to send with your letter. Our advice here is, again, unequivocal: do not send anything at this stage apart from the letter itself and a one-page printed or photocopied sheet giving basic information about you and your consultancy.

An unsolicited mailing of this nature is not the occasion to send your brochure if you have one (we discuss this knotty problem later in this chapter). First, it is a waste of money to include an expensive brochure in such a mailing when a high proportion of the mailings are likely to be binned without even being read. Second, sending your brochure to someone who doesn't even know you will seem like overkill and makes you look a bit silly. It is rather demeaning to yourself, too, like sending a long fan letter to a movie star or pop star.

The one-page sheet can say whatever you want it to say. If you are a small consultancy, just starting out, you will need to focus on your experience, expertise and fitness for the task, as well as that of your colleagues. If you run a larger consultancy, you will probably want to say something about your consultancy's vision, completed projects, and clients, but make sure you have your clients' permission to publicize any sensitive details or you may find they don't stay your clients for very long.

For the actual letter, this is so important an element of your success in winning new business – and therefore to the overall success of your consultancy – that we ought to make some suggestions for how you compose your letters, even though basically your text is something you will have to work on yourself. What we would say is, keep this sort of letter to one page in length. Your prospect will not be interested in reading anything longer at this stage. In the next chapter we provide detailed advice about how to write well – an essential discipline for almost all consultants. In the meantime, the letter shown in Fig. 6.1 provides a useful template for you. This letter was designed to sell public relations services to the investment management sector and helped to win several valuable pieces of new business. Notice how it displays a clear, unostentatious knowledge of the sector. It focuses on the expertise of the individual making the approach, but this kind of letter can easily be modified to focus on the expertise of the entire consultancy. By tailoring the letter according to your target audience, type of consulting service and your experience, it can be used to sell almost any kind of consulting service.

A. Prospect Esq.
Executive Vice President
General Investment Management Inc.
[address]

[date]

Dear Mr Prospect

Have you ever considered the great promotional advantages, and
significant potential increase in revenue, that your organization could
enjoy from adopting a pro-active approach to obtaining editorial
coverage in the business press – and especially within investment
industry media – read by your existing and potential clients? **(A)**

I am a writer and public relations consultant with a substantial
involvement in the securities and fund management industry. I can
reasonably claim to be an expert on the fund management business,
having written the Euromoney *Investment Management Training
Manual*, as well as the FT publication *The Investment Manager's
Handbook.* **(B)**

In addition to writing under my own name, I am able to offer some fund
management organizations a comprehensive public relations service
directed around such elements as drafting, clearing and distributing
press releases and ghost-writing full-length 'thoughtpiece' articles that
appear in key financial and investment media under my client's byline.
Publicity generated by this coverage is an immensely powerful
marketing tool; much more useful, for example, than advertising could
ever be. The cost of this service is modest; my daily rate is $750. **(C)**

I would very much appreciate the opportunity to meet you (on an
entirely no-obligation basis, of course) in order to find out about your
promotional needs. If you are interested in meeting me, perhaps you
could let me know. I am enclosing some biographical details for your
information. **(D)**

Thank you for your time over this matter. **(E)**

Kind regards

Figure 6.1 Example of an unsolicited new business letter

We are not suggesting that your new business letter should read precisely like this, but you will probably find the various parts of this letter helpful when composing your own letters. Here are our brief comments about the letter, with the paragraphs being referred to according to the letters at the end of them.

(A) It is always a good idea to start a new business letter with a question. The question should be such that if the answer is 'no', the inference should be that your consultancy will be able to undertake this service area for the prospective client. Of course, the wording of the question that you ask at the start of your letter will depend on the nature of the consulting service you provide. Not only is a question inherently interesting because it involves the reader in having to formulate an answer, but a question like this has the huge advantage over a more pedestrian type of beginning (such as 'I am a consultant specializing in …') in that it focuses on the needs of the recipient, not on your needs.

(B) Here, you briefly introduce yourself and your consultancy and mention any specific experience you have in terms of the market in which your recipient operates. This letter was directed at investment management organizations, so the experience mentioned is obviously appropriate for that sector.

(C) Next you detail the nature of the service you are offering and how much it costs. If you believe that cost is one of your incremental advantages, don't be afraid to point this out, but do it in a fairly discreet manner, as here. Some might prefer to defer any mention of cost until the actual meeting, and that approach is also sound.

(D) Here, you request a meeting. It is important to emphasize that this would be a no-obligation meeting. You can also include in this paragraph a brief explanation of any enclosures you are sending.

(E) This is a pleasant and courteous way to end the letter, but don't put this in if it means that your letter will run to two pages. As we have said, you must confine your new business letter to one page.

Step five

Put the letter in an envelope and post it. One final piece of advice, though: *handwrite* the address on the envelope. There is a strong case for saying that recipients regard handwritten envelopes with more attention and interest than typewritten ones. Reflect on your experience of receiving a mailing: don't you always pay more attention to handwritten envelopes?

The envelope may of course be opened by the recipient's secretary, in which case it won't matter much either way, but some executives prefer to open their own mail, and if your envelope is handwritten and not obviously a circular it is particularly likely that it will be opened by its recipient. That said, do not write 'Private' or 'Private and Confidential' on the envelope. Nothing is more likely to annoy your recipient than for him or her to open what seems to be a personal letter only to discover that it is a letter from someone trying to sell consulting services.

Step six

Now we come to the crunch. What do you do next? Wait and see what happens! Some consultancies like to follow up a new business mailing with a telephone call a week or so later. Ask to talk to the client's secretary or assistant in the first instance. When you do, ask the secretary or assistant whether you can 'book' a telephone call with her/his boss. As long as your approach is thoughtful and intelligent, you are likely to get your booking.

Should you always follow up a mailing with a phone call? Sometimes you should, such as when the letter is not an entirely unsolicited communication but you have been asked to contact the organization. If you do make a follow-up call, be subtle about it. Don't, for example, ask 'what did you think of my letter?' Instead, say something like, 'I'm phoning to make sure you got my letter, and to ask whether you need any more information at this stage.' Remember the weaver bird? This, too, is the no-pressure, no-sweat option.

Of course, if you do say in your letter that you will be following up the letter with a telephone call, ensure that you make the call and ensure that the recipient of the letter knows you have made the call. Otherwise, you might be perceived as breaking the very first undertaking that you have made to your potential client, and they may be less than willing to become a real client.

But what if the mailing is an entirely cold mailing? Should you follow it up with a phone call in that case? It is important for authors of business books to avoid being so dogmatic that they give readers no room to exercise their tastes and preferences. If you are a highly extrovert person and you don't mind making, say, 50 telephone calls and getting only two or three positive responses (that is, agreements to meet you), don't let us stop you following up on your mailings with phone calls. But there is a school of thought that says that consultancy should not be sold in an intensive, hard-sell way, that if recipients of your letters are interested in meeting you, they will contact you.

That said, it is unquestionable that certain upmarket types of consulting service – especially strategic consulting – do need to be sold by a senior consultant making contact by telephone with a senior director of a potential client organization. In this case, follow-up by telephone is essential, but you would typically be calling only a relatively small number of people and approaching them with a view to meeting them so that you can discuss their needs and what you have to offer.

However, it may be that being too forward on the telephone will put prospective clients off when you are offering a commoditized service such as a public relations consultancy. The whole thing is very much a matter of taste and personal preference.

Method four – using traditional promotional techniques

You might ask: what about traditional promotional techniques such as public relations and advertising? The answer is that these can be effective, but you need to bear in mind two very important provisos.

First, public relations is an effective method of winning new business only for consultancies that are well established and have some good stories to tell. When you use the public relations technique you either hire a PR consultancy or delegate someone to do the job in-house and get your PR resource to maximize your editorial exposure in the print and broadcast media. This can be a highly effective way of promoting organizations in general and consultancies in particular, but it is expensive, and because PR activity is essentially news activity, there is not much point using a PR consultancy unless you do have some good war stories, plus clients who are willing to be written about. Not even the best PR consultancy in the world can gain useful courage for a client who has no stories to tell.

Second, advertising is likely to be of any use as a general positioning tool only for a large and successful consultancy that is already well known, has brand recognition, and wants to keep its name in the public eye. Many consultancies, including larger ones, adopt the view that advertising is a waste of time and money, and in general you are not likely to lose out if you adopt that perspective.

Advertising is great (indeed, essential) as a means of promoting consumer products such as chocolate bars, washing powder and hi-fi units, but the big drawback for consultants is that you do not have enough room (in press advertising) or time (in broadcast media advertising) to say the things you need to say to impress potential clients. Furthermore, advertising is extremely expensive. For example, a colour page in a trade journal will typically cost more than it would cost to hire a PR consultancy for a couple of months at three or four days per month. As for the comparison with the cost of winning business through unsolicited mailings, the price differential is astronomical because mailings are comparatively so inexpensive.

Henry Ford is rumoured to have said: 'I know that half of my advertising budget is wasted; I just don't know which half.' Even with sophisticated modern response-tracking techniques, it can be difficult to know which advertising gets the results. For consultants this is particularly difficult.

Generally, if you are a new or relatively new consultancy, we recommend you dismiss the idea of hiring a PR consultancy or an advertising agency and concentrate instead on building up your business by doing great work and getting referrals, and by undertaking some well-targeted and well-researched mailings.

Your stationery and literature

Consultancies of any size need to think hard about how they will present themselves to existing and prospective clients. We covered stationery in some detail in the previous chapter, but it is worth summarizing again what you will need as part of your business-winning presentation.

You will need:

- a letterhead (and probably continuation sheets, which always look much better than plain paper);
- business cards;
- big labels (with peel-off sticky backs) to put on large envelopes and packages;
- compliment slips;
- invoices (of course).

Remember that all your expenditure on the above is, like all your legitimate business expenses, tax-deductible.

Do you need a consultancy brochure? We agree with Tom Lambert, who emphasizes in *High-Income Consulting* that it is too easy to waste a tremendous amount of money on a brochure. On the face of it, producing a brochure is something every consultancy needs to do: how else can you communicate your message to prospective clients? The answer is that you should communicate by talking to prospective clients. Especially when you are starting out, brochures can actually be malproductive because, apart from costing you money you probably cannot easily afford, they may seem pretentious and off-putting. What do you really have to sell besides your expertise and experience? Giving the impression that your consultancy is a corporation with a hierarchy of job titles and a nice brochure seems to veer dangerously close to what a 'pretend' consultant would be expected to do, and by now you know what we think about 'pretend' consultancies.

Brochures also date with horrible ease, especially if your brochure mentions names of staff who may not be working with you a few months down the line. New consultancies often go through major structural changes while they are finding their feet, so a dated brochure may be a particular problem when you are starting out.

Your entire business direction, being client-driven, can easily change radically, too. It is perfectly possible, for example, that you might start a management consultancy with the intention of focusing on the financial industry, but then win a large mandate from a major travel company that keeps you and five colleagues busy for a year. Result: your brochure has become a waste of money. Furthermore, because it is crazy to send out an expensive brochure with unsolicited mailings, you only really need your brochure when you meet prospective clients, and by that point you are generally going to be more successful by communicating with them through listening and talking to them.

Nevertheless, the act of writing a brochure can help you define your overall objectives and culture, and frequently there *is* a case for giving prospective clients something to read after the meeting. Just don't expect your brochure to do the job of communicating your true strengths and true personality: you and your colleagues should be the ones who do that.

If you are set on producing a brochure, we strongly recommend that you don't do so until you have been trading for at least 12 months, by which time you will be in a better position to assess what exactly you ought to say in your brochure. If the basic business idea (i.e. the incremental advantage or advantages) behind your consultancy is any good, you should have no problem in trading successfully for those 12 months, after which time you may find yourself so busy that you will not want to bother with a brochure.

If you do produce a brochure, don't spend too much money on it. Forget about producing a 32-page, full-colour, glossy showpiece; you are promoting a consultancy, not launching a cruise line. A good ruse is to base your brochure on a 'folder' design that lets you slot in additional sheets of paper. This way you can update your brochure when necessary without a major overhaul.

Avoid using pompous and boastful language about what your consultancy can do for its clients and what your skills and expertise are. Keep what you say factual and to the point. We cannot write your brochure for you, but you may find the following headings useful when deciding on its structure. We suggest you divide the brochure into various sections, as follows, with the order in which we present them here being one possibility.

1   The name of your firm and its contact details.

2   A one-paragraph summary of what your consultancy has to offer.

3   An explanation of what your consultancy is and who is, or are, working for it.

4   A detailed but concise account of what your consultancy offers its clients. You should make sure that your significant incremental advantage is fully explained here.

5   Details of why you regard your service to be cost-effective, and, optionally, concise information about your charges. You may, however, prefer to keep these under your hat at this stage, especially if you are going to be offering different clients different rates.

6   Examples of your clients. If you do not have at least six clients to put in here, don't have this section. Instead, say something vague like 'references are available'.

7   Flattering comments, such as extracts from letters, that your clients have sent you. But as with the mention of the client in the client list, make sure the client does not object to your using these comments in your brochure. You should also say somewhere in the brochure that references are available from existing clients if required, and then if someone pursues this, you can put them in touch with the client whom you know most likes you and admires you.

8   The name of the person at your consultancy whom clients should contact, and that person's telephone number. There is no harm in repeating this.

Brochures have to look good as well as read well, so unless design is one of your specialized skills, get a designer to help you.

Competitive pitches

The final piece of advice we offer here in connection with winning business relates to competitive pitches, a difficult and troublesome subject. A competitive pitch occurs where a prospective client compiles a shortlist of consultants or consultancies, one of which is you or yours. This enables the client to 'compare and contrast' different consultancies according to a variety of criteria, and choose the one that seems the best fit.

If this actually happened during the majority of competitive pitches, and if it was always done fairly, they would make more sense as a means of gaining business. After all, as a consultant who is busy establishing a significant incremental advantage, you should be perfectly placed to win many competitive pitches.

Unfortunately, competitive pitches are very often not done fairly. What frequently happens is that the client is already pretty sure who he wants to go with, but does not feel comfortable about choosing the consultancy as straightforwardly as that, especially if he has to report his selection decision to more senior people. So he pretends to himself, or to the other consultancies, or to both, that there really is an opportunity here for a competitive pitch. By adopting this course of action when the selection decision has already been made, the client wastes the time of every other consultancy apart from the one that has been pre-selected.

Even where pretence is not at the heart of the matter, competitive pitches are often not fair because some preferred consultancies get told more about the prospective project than others. Another consideration is that people with time on their hands at work will organize a competitive pitch to hire a consultant, even if no budget has been allocated and no real decision to appoint a consultant is imminent.

The purpose of the competitive pitch here is to give the underemployed person something interesting to do, that also makes them feel important.

Of course, there are some competitive pitches that are sincerely organized and held in a fair manner, with the purpose being to select the best consultant for the job. But even where this is the case, it is by no means certain that you should be taking part in competitive pitches. If you have recently started your consultancy or consulting division, you should be able to find clients who will want to give you mandates because of your expertise and because of the competitive edge you have: clients who will not want to involve you in the nonsense of competitive pitches.

Most of the time, there should be so much going on in your business that there is too much to do to go down the competitive pitch avenue. When your consultancy starts to acquire a critical mass and move from being a successful start-up to being a successful established business, there will be some mandates (especially in the public sector, where competitive tender is part and parcel of public bodies' procurement procedures) that are inaccessible unless you are prepared to take part in a competitive pitch. But that is mainly going to happen when you have already built up your consultancy to a respectable size. By this point you and your colleagues may be able to spare time from your schedules to prepare and compete in those competitive pitches that you feel you have a good chance of winning.

The point is that taking part in competitive pitches is extremely time-consuming and also consumes energy and cash which in many cases would be better deployed on making the level of service you offer existing clients even better, and on finding new clients who will come to you because of who you are.

Don't let us stop you taking part in those competitive pitches that you consider to be genuine and that you think you can win, but do not let competitive pitches be the mainstay of your new business-winning activity.

Do not actively seek out such opportunities unless you really want to develop your business in the public sector. Instead, seek out clients who want to hire you and your consultancy because, for the job they have, you are the only consultant who could reasonably be considered. You achieve this enviable position by providing specialized expertise that your competition can't provide, by being proud of being the new kid on the block, and by setting new standards for know-how, attention to detail, sincerity, thoughtfulness, sensitivity to client needs and client culture, and ideally by becoming known as an authoritative expert in your chosen field, whose advice potential clients are desperate to get.

CHAPTER SEVEN

Writing proposals and reports

Introduction

This chapter concentrates on how to write proposals and reports: the two types of documents that are the lifeblood of any consultancy.

The consulting process is as much about *communicating* as it is about *doing*. Even in those sectors of the consulting industry where writing proposals and reports might not appear to be particularly important – such as information technology and other intensively hands-on sectors where implementation is virtually everything – the mandate almost always needs to be won in the first place by the writing of a specific proposal. And after it has been won, it is highly likely that the consultancy will need to write periodic reports about the activity being carried out – the payment of the consultancy's invoice may well be contingent upon such reports being submitted and any client queries answered.

This scenario describes the typical requirement for communication that falls on any consultant's shoulders. Basically you need to communicate in two ways as a consultant. First, you need to write proposals that tell your existing or prospective clients what you intend to do, and in particular details of the work you would like to carry out for the client before you actually carry it out. Second, you need to write reports that communicate to your client what you are doing, and what you have actually done.

Both these types of communication require writing skills. Even if you are presenting the proposal or report to your client verbally, you will almost certainly want to ensure that the client has a copy of the document.

In this chapter we aim to provide you with the intellectual armoury that will allow you to do a great job of writing proposals and reports. We do not do what many business books that aim to provide advice in this area do and suggest only the *structure* of these essential documents. Of course, structure is extremely important, and we will cover it, but we go one better here and start by giving you specific guidance about actual writing.

The secrets of good writing

Speaking well is easier than writing well. We speak at our best – that is, at our most direct, forceful and interesting – when we have urgent messages to convey: requests, commands, wishes, plans, pleas. When we don't, we flounder: we bore people by talking too much about ourselves or about a hobbyhorse that fascinates us, we give after-dinner or best-man speeches that send our audience to sleep, we present a dull discourse at a business conference and forget that speaking at a business conference is a performance art best left to the professionals or the experts.

Mostly, though, we have relatively few problems communicating through speech. Easiest of all is talking to one person rather than several; we can generally assume that the person we are talking to wants to be there with us (or, if this is not the case, we are likely to detect this and quickly get out of the situation).

Speaking well is also easier than writing well because we have more experience of it. As a species, we were talking for about 250 000 years before we began to write. As individuals, we learn to speak at least three or four years before we start to write, and at least ten years before we start to write with any degree of fluency.

Writing well is something we must learn even if we are fortunate to be born with some talent for writing. There are no short cuts to learning how to write well; it takes experience and practice. The ability to choose which word you want, the capacity for discriminating between the infinitely subtle differences in meaning, the ability to twist a simple idea into something verbally expressive and exciting: these are all a part of writing and to a large extent can be learned only the hard way – by working at writing.

Just as a musician needs to be able to play scales, arpeggios and all the simple tunes before being able to produce brilliant improvizations, a writer needs to learn the fundamentals of writing before producing brilliant proposals and reports.

Here we provide some of this fundamental information, which is discussed under two categories: structural and stylistic.

Structural guidance

The importance of structure in writing stems from two factors:

○ the need for your writing to communicate efficiently to your reader;
○ the strictly limited nature of the written word as a message.

When you speak to someone, what you say is only a part of the communication process. The tone of your voice, the facial and hand gestures you use, even your bodily posture, will also convey meaning. It is quite possible that what you are really saying will not be represented by your words at all. This is particularly the case when two people know each other very well: what they say to each other is often intensely at odds with what they mean.

When you write, you have no other communication tool except the words. Get the words wrong, and the communication will miscarry. It follows that to get the words right you need to structure them in such a way that the reader will understand what you are saying. The originality of expression and meaning that characterizes the best writing is what you should ultimately be aiming for, but you cannot strive for originality of expression and meaning at the expense of good structure. The best writing is both original *and* well structured.

Grammar

Grammar is the system of rules which spoken and written language must obey if it is to sound correct to a native speaker. Grammar is the skeleton of a language, without which nothing works. Like language itself, it is purely a convention based on what is regarded by the community of speakers as acceptable usage. It is important to point out that grammar is merely good, accepted usage. Too many people associate it with the formal rules of Latin and see it as something dead, dismal and threatening. It isn't. Sometimes, it can even be fun.

Sentences and phrases

The third edition of the *Shorter Oxford English Dictionary* defines a sentence as a series of words in connected speech or writing, forming the grammatically complete expression of a single thought. We often use sentences when we speak, but frequently we don't because the urgency of our message is more important to us than creating an elaborate sentence. If, for example, you fell into a river and found yourself swept along to a dangerous weir, you would be unlikely to call out to someone on the bank, 'I need a lifebelt, please'. You would be more likely to say, 'A lifebelt, for God's sake!' In fact, analysis of conversational speech, even in non life-threatening situations, reveals that not only do we speak with many hesitations and repetitions, we also do not always form what could be described as a good sentence.

There is no avoiding the fact that writing is a more formal way of communicating than ordinary speech. You *can* get away with short phrases and one-word chunks of meaning when you write, but often the effect is somewhat pretentious and impertinent. Generally, it is best to err on the side of caution and use proper sentences unless you are sure that the ambitious effect you are trying to create is going to strike home.

And yes, your teachers were right. Your sentences need a subject and a verb.

Getting your sentences the right length

Your sentences should not be too long. We realize this is something of a generalization, and no doubt you can think of many examples of writing in which lengthy sentences abound. However, our advice is to keep your sentences relatively short unless there are good reasons for doing otherwise.

The main reasons for writing longer sentences are:

○ when you are seeking to gain the effect of a series of features or advantages being heaped up against one another;

○ when you want your sentence to take the reader through a sequence of meaning that mimics the progression of a series of thoughts;

○ when the rhythm of the sentence is attractive it helps your meaning along. Good writers are essentially musicians, with the music being the creation of prose rhythms. If a lengthy sentence is well crafted, the beauty of its rhythm can give a lovely strength and vigour to the meaning.

How do you know for certain whether your sentence reads better as a long sentence than as a succession of shorter ones? There is one simple answer: read it aloud. After all, if you are producing writing that is supposed to have the urgency and vigour of the spoken language, your writing ought to sound good when you do read it aloud. However much experience you gain, and however skilled you become, one rule remains infallible: if in doubt, read it aloud.

Paying attention to meaning

What you write must have meaning, and – unless you are deliberately aiming for an ambiguous effect – only *one* meaning. Meaning is not something that will take care of itself if the sentence is well constructed and grammatical. It is something you have to work for all the time, a living dynamic that arises from the energy and expressiveness with which you use words. Of course, if your sentence is not grammatical, your meaning will not be properly conveyed, but don't imagine that grammatical correctness is somehow a substitute for putting every ounce of your passion, energy and determination into the meaning of what you write. In fact, it is possible for a sentence to be completely grammatical and yet meaningless. A classical example of such a sentence was concocted by the linguist Noam Chomsky. His sentence was:

Colourless green ideas sleep furiously.

We cannot teach you to make your writing meaningful. This is one of the areas of writing which is an art, and for which you must rely on your intelligence, experience of writing and ability to criticize your own work.

Meaningfulness is ultimately what good writing is all about, and if you can cram great swathes of meaning into a few words, your writing may have a chance of being great. The main reason why Shakespeare's work seems complex is that he compresses meaning so powerfully, economically and succinctly that a single speech (or indeed a single line) will have a world of meaning in it. The people who read your reports and proposals will not be prepared to make the same effort that we have to make to understand Shakespeare. Even so, your writing should as far as possible compress meaning with all the power, economy and succinctness of which you are capable.

One of the most obvious signs of an inexperienced writer is that his sentences – particularly the longer ones – do not have a clear meaning. It is usually safest to avoid being too ambitious and to keep your meaning straightforward and simple. Remember that the world's greatest writers (the classic example being Hemingway) have done the same.

Many business people, and far too many consultants, imagine that longer sentences are inherently more subtle and profound than shorter ones. They can be, but only if they are constructed with attention to meaning. In addition to the hazard of partial or complete lack of meaning, the other major hazard is that of ambiguity: where what you write can mean more than one thing. Sometimes the effect can be comical:

I know a man with a wooden leg called Harry.
You do? And what's his other leg called?

And there may be rare occasions when you deliberately want to create an ambiguous effect. This is often seen in advertising slogans. *Players Please* is an obvious example. The most common reason for a sentence being ambiguous is that the writer loses track of who or what is the subject of the sentence, or what is the subject of a qualifying phrase. There is no reason why the subject of a fairly lengthy sentence should not change as the sentence progresses, but you must keep track of who or what it is, and not permit any ambiguity.

Another common error is where the person or object to which a possessive pronoun refers is ambiguous. 'His' or 'her' can sometimes inadvertently refer to more than one person. Be careful about this.

Do not, under any circumstances, imagine that ambiguous sentences are acceptable because you get two meanings for the price of one. In fact, you get no meanings for the price of two.

Just as the only way to make sure your sentences have a clear meaning is to take care over composing them and reading them through once you have written them, the only way to guard against ambiguity is to check your sentences have just one meaning. The meaningfulness and clarity of what you write depends on how much trouble you are prepared to take over your work. If you feel yourself flagging or getting tired, or if you simply feel lazy, remember this comment from Oscar Wilde: *talent is the capacity for taking infinite pains.*

Remember, too, that what you write and get printed is going to be around for a long time, maybe for the rest of your life.

Spelling

The only way to master the eccentricities of English spelling is to learn spellings of individual words. As we all discovered at school, there is no way to avoid this.

Dictionaries and word processor spell-check programs help to relieve the burden of having to remember how everything is spelt, but they are not a complete solution to the problem. As in other areas of this complex structure we call language, there are inevitably grey areas where to some extent what is 'correct' is a matter of taste.

Some of the most important of these grey areas are:

Use of initial capital letters

This is often poorly understood even by otherwise highly educated and intelligent people, some of whom allocate capital letters rather as if they were writing German (which capitalizes *all* nouns). The following is typical of the kind of thing one sees in far too many documents.

Ever since the Information Technology revolution of the late 1980s, occasioned by the use of Personal Computers and the Microchip, the Company, from the Managing Director down to the man in the mailroom, has been striving for a constant policy of Excellence.

There is no excuse for this kind of erratic and haphazard capitalization, yet it is alarmingly common.

In fact, English has relatively straightforward rules about capitalization. You should use a capital letter only if:

❍ it is the first letter of the first word of a new sentence;

❍ it is the first letter of the name of a person, an animal or a thing;

❍ it is the first letter of a proper noun.

This last area is the one that causes the most difficulty because the definition of a proper noun is less rigid than many people imagine.

The best way of looking at it is to see a proper noun as one used to denote something that is both clearly identifiable as a specific, individual entity and that has some formality attached to it. If this sounds a fairly woolly definition, this only reflects the principle that the concept of a proper noun is a fairly woolly concept. However, the idea of the thing being specific, individual *and* formal is often extremely helpful when deciding whether or not a noun is a proper noun. For example, when the word 'government' is being used in a general sense, it should not be capitalized, but when it is used in a specific sense (e.g. the British Government) its formality means capitalizing it would be reasonable, although 'the British government' is a viable alternative. (Note that the *Financial Times* never capitalizes the word 'government' unless it is used at the start of a sentence.)

Our recommendation is that you should avoid initial capitalization unless you are absolutely certain it is correct. Under no circumstances capitalize the initial letters of job titles, which always looks dreadful. We realize many organizations do this, but there is no justification for following suit unless, of course, the job title is appearing somewhere on its own, such as on a card or on a door. The *Financial Times* does not capitalize the initial letters of job titles unless, as before, the first word of the title is appearing at the start of a sentence.

Some words cause particular difficulty here. The following is a guide to what is most likely to be regarded as correct.

○ initial capitalization required:

Christmas;

Easter;

January (and all the other months);

Monday (and the other days of the week);

names of people, animals and things (e.g. Henry, Fido, *The Titanic*);

all words that denote something identifiable as a specific individual entity and have some formality attached to them, e.g. the Big Bang, the New York Stock Exchange, the Second World War, the President, the Holocaust etc.

○ initial capitalization not required:

autumn, winter, spring, summer;

job titles;

all nouns that are not obviously proper nouns. This includes terms that have a certain generic weightiness but where the term does not refer to a specific one (e.g. there is only one Christmas) but rather to a general concept, e.g. information technology, microchip, personal computer.

Brand names

The only reason the writing of brand names causes problems is that too many people who write business writing are overawed by them. The correct form is really very simple: start the brand name with a capital letter and put the rest of it in lower-case letters.

What is true of brand names is also true of names of organizations that usually appear in capitals: you should restrict the capitalization in the body copy to the initial letter of the word. The only exception is where the name is obviously an acronym: in this case use full capitalization *without* full stops. So, for example, you should write:

Many ATM terminals operating on the Cirrus system now accept Visa cards.

even though LINK and VISA are normally written with capitals in these organizations' advertisements. But you should write:

SWIFT is nowadays the major interbank payment system

as SWIFT is an acronym (Society for Worldwide Interbank Funds Telecommunication). If you are unsure whether a word is an acronym or not, it is safest to assume it is.

Putting -ing on the end of certain verbs

We have already seen that the English language, like other languages, has areas where what is 'correct' is to some degree a matter of taste. One such area for some words is the decision relating to whether or not to double the consonant at the end of certain verbs before putting -ing at the end. This problem does not arise with short, familiar words because the way in which they form the -ing ending is well known. However, some less well-known words do present a problem. Everyone knows that the -ing form of transmit is transmitting, but do you write, for example, benefiting or benefitting, focusing or focussing?

In the case of many words like these, both forms are acceptable. However, our advice is to use the form that *avoids* the consonantal doubling, unless this obviously looks wrong.

Whether or not to use a hyphen

The hyphen (-) is often, but not always, used where two or more words are linked together in a regularly used combination. For practical purposes, there are three spelling options where words are used in such a combination. These are:

○ join the words together without a space;
○ join the words together with a hyphen;
○ don't join the words together (i.e. write them with a space in between).

Historically, many words now written together as one word used to be written separately or with a hyphen. For example, Jane Austen wrote 'today' as 'to-day' and 'tomorrow' as 'to-morrow'. Nowadays, the tendency is to use a hyphen unless writing the words together has become widely accepted.

The use of a hyphen is particularly necessary in adjectival combinations which use 'well' or a number, such as:

well-read
well-known
six-month
five-year
ten-year
nineteenth-century genius.

However, there are many words (particularly coined, technological ones) where the decision whether to use a hyphen or join them together is still a matter of taste, e.g.:

nonetheless/none-the-less
laptop computer/lap-top computer
palmtop computer/palm-top computer
online/on-line
jetliner/jet-liner
microchip/micro-chip.

In these cases, where both options are acceptable, you should use the joined-up form unless you feel the reader will find it precious or even pretentious.

There is often the choice between writing the words separately and using a hyphen, e.g.:

first class/first-class
second class/second-class
third class/third-class
front office/front-office
back office/back-office
state of the art/state-of-the-art.

One way to handle this is to write the words without a hyphen if they are being used in a noun (i.e. naming word) sense and with a hyphen if they are being used in an adjectival (i.e. describing word) sense.

The apostrophe

The apostrophe (') is used to show that a letter has been elided. For example:

He isn't coming today, and she's not, either.

where *isn't* is the shorter form of *is not*, and *she's* is the shorter form of *she is* (some people mistakenly write *is'nt* for *isn't*: don't do it).

An even more common mistake here is to confuse *it's* (the elided form of *it is*) with *its* (the possessive case of *it*). This is probably one of the most common spelling mistakes in English: it is too often seen in printed business writing and even in national newspapers. An example of the correct usage of each is:

The Novon's power and reliability, and its superb design, mean it's the best vacuum cleaner you can buy.

The simple rule is that if *its* is not obviously short for *it is*, don't use an apostrophe. We present the rule this way round because people often write *it's* when they should write *its*: they think that the 's' denotes a possessive, which it doesn't.

The apostrophe is, of course, used for the possessive form of nouns, where it replaces an 'e' that was used until around the year 1500. When the noun is singular, the spelling is well-known and rarely causes confusion, e.g.:
the car's engine
the marketing director's report.

Incidentally, the second example is a floating possessive: the possessive that can be applied to the end of what can be an entire noun-phrase, e.g.:
the Queen of England's corgi
the young man from Japan's poetry.

Normally, where the noun is plural, the apostrophe must be put *after* the 's' rather than before it, e.g.:
the cars' engines
the marketing directors' conference
the Factories' Act.

But note that the few English words that retain the Anglo-Saxon plural form require the apostrophe to be put *before* the 's', e.g.:
the children's toys
the oxen's carts
the brethren's habits.

Punctuation

Too many would-be business writers regard punctuation as boring and take insufficient trouble about getting it right. The proper use of punctuation, like the proper use of words, is both an art and a science: there are some areas where what is right or wrong can be assessed with mathematical precision, and others where you must make your own decisions.

We have tried to reflect the art and science aspects of punctuation in the following comments on different punctuation marks.

The full stop

The principal use of the full stop (.) is to show that a sentence has ended. Assuming the sentence is not the last one of a particular piece of writing, the full stop should always be followed by a capital letter.

The only points of difficulty relating to the full stop are where to place it if the sentence ends with a parenthesis (… .) or [… .], or with an inverted comma ('or'). The rule is that the full stop should always come *after* the parenthesis or *after* the inverted comma when the quotation forms part of a longer sentence, but *before* the parenthesis or *after* the inverted comma when the quotation is a complete sentence.

For example:

(Like all our vacuum cleaners, the Novon comes with a five-year guarantee.)

but

Some people call the Novon the 'miracle cleaner'.

The full stop is also used to show that a word or term has been abbreviated. However, unless the abbreviation is an extremely well-known one, it is usually better stylistically – and also better from the point of view of clarity – to avoid it and write the word or term out in full. What this boils down to is that you can use the following abbreviations, but ought to be wary of using any others.

Abbreviation	Meaning
e.g.	for example
etc.	etcetera (and others)
i.e.	that is (Latin *id est*)
viz.	namely

Be careful to avoid confusing e.g. and i.e.

Any familiar abbreviation used as a brand name of the name of a well-known thing (e.g. IBM for International Business Machines, NYSE for New York Stock Exchange) is, like an acronym (e.g. Anzac), not the same as an abbreviation and does not require a full stop after it. Full stops after each letter are not necessary either.

The comma

Proper use of the comma (,) is essential for readability. The difficulty that the comma appears to cause to so many inexperienced and experienced writers is all the more surprising as there is a foolproof rule for using it properly. This rule is: use the comma to mark places where you would want to pause and/or take a breath if you were reading the text aloud.

There is no mystery about why this rule works. Generally, writing is most effective when it has the feel and sound of the spoken language. The comma's role is not so much to break up sentences as to make them read well and sound good. So if you are uncertain where to put a comma, simply read out your sentence aloud and make a note of where you want to pause and/or take a breath.

Should you use a comma before 'and'? We raise this issue because many people are taught at school that you should avoid the use of a comma before the word 'and'. When you are listing items, this advice makes sense. For example:

The corporation heads the US domestic appliance industry, with a leading share of the market in the manufacture and sale of microwave ovens, refrigerators, freezers, toasters, electric kettles and bread-making machines.

Here, a comma before 'and bread-making machines' would certainly be redundant because when you read the sentence aloud you do not need a pause or a breath there.

The trouble with the rule about not using a comma before 'and' is that many people imagine it means you should *never* use a comma before 'and', and this is nonsense. Feel free to use a comma before 'and' where, as in the last sentence, the 'and' starts a new clause. What you must avoid is the habit, seen in many pieces of published reports and proposals, of using a comma simply because there have been a fair number of words since the last one and it seems about time to put one in. Stick to the principle of using a comma where you would pause and/or take a breath while reading the piece aloud, and you will be all right.

This principle is particularly useful for relatively long, complex sentences that would otherwise be difficult to punctuate properly. Here is the first sentence of a discussion about the future of payment technology. First we give it in its unpunctuated form. Where should the commas go?

Predicting the future is never easy but by extrapolating certain present-day trends in retail payment technology it is possible to gain a good idea of how goods will be paid for in the year 2010 and what consumer attitudes towards payment methods are likely to be.

By following our principle, the correct allocation of commas in this sentence is really quite easy:

Predicting the future is never easy, but by extrapolating certain present-day trends in retail payment technology, it is possible to gain a good idea of how goods will be paid for in the year 2010, and what consumer attitudes towards payment methods are likely to be.

Your aim should be to get into the habit of knowing instinctively where a comma is required and inserting it as you are writing the material. However, even when you have developed this facility, you will still find the principle useful, when you check over your work, as a way of making sure the commas are in the correct places.

The colon

There is little rigidity in the rules governing use of the colon (:) and semi-colon. To a large extent you are free to use them as you wish, given that you understand their primary function, which is to create a sense of an ending in a sentence which is not as final as that which would be created by the full stop.

In the past, this was the principal use of the colon; nowadays there is an increasing tendency for the semi-colon to be used in this way, too. It is probably best to use the colon only in the following four cases:

1 To provide a clear, but not final, break in a sentence.

2 Where you want to introduce a spoken quotation with some impact, and the comma seems too weak for the purpose.

3 Where you want to introduce a list of bullet points.

4 Where you want to introduce something that is italicized or otherwise separated in some sense from the preceding material.

The semi-colon

The semi-colon (;) is a tricky little fellow. He can perform many functions, and using him is to some extent a matter of taste. In particular, you can:

○ use the semi-colon as a kind of 'strong comma' when listing attributes, although bullet points are usually better;

○ break up clauses with it in a long sentence;

○ use it to 'tense' a sentence and make it more exciting. For example, you can use the semi-colon to build the sentence up to a kind of peak before you descend to the full stop, e.g.:

When our company started trading our sales figures were initially disappointing; then we began selling via the Internet, and they quadrupled overnight.

This sentence has a tension and suspense that would be absent if you made a new sentence after 'disappointing'.

Note that the colon could also be used here: whether you use the colon or the semi-colon in this example is a matter of taste.

The dash

The dash (–) is extremely useful, and unjustly neglected by many writers. The beauty of it is that it can give a parenthetical clause a sense of tension and dynamism without resorting to brackets. Like bracketed parentheses, the dash needs to be opened and closed, so you usually need two of them. You should use the dash when you need to make a subsidiary point but where using round or square brackets would seem pedantic and cumbersome.

Bracket parentheses

Unquestionably, one of the signs of an inexperienced writer is over-use of bracket parentheses (...) [...]. These are used far too often when what is really required is a semi-colon or a dash.

The trouble with bracket parentheses is that they stop the flow of a sentence to such a great extent that it is questionable whether they really belong in good business writing, except where they are being used to introduce an acronym. Where you are using them for this purpose, the correct form to follow is to write out the name – or whatever the acronym refers to – in full first time round, set the acronym after it in curved brackets, and thereafter use the acronym on its own. For example:

The New York Stock Exchange (NYSE) has today moved from being an open outcry market to a quote-driven electronic system. A spokesman for the NYSE said that this was a revolutionary development.

Brackets are often unnecessary, as in this example:

Novon vacuum cleaners come complete with full accessories and a five-year guarantee. (Note, however, that an additional charge of £29.99 is made for the full ten-year guarantee.)

The brackets give the erroneous impression that the material they enclose is unrelated to the preceding sentence. In fact, the brackets can be left out.

On rare occasions you may need to use a hierarchy of brackets. Where this is unavoidable, use the curved brackets to enclose the square brackets, as in:

All models produced in the Chicago factory (that is, models 18–28 [except 23 and 24]) are cold-forged.

But avoid doing this too often. As you can see, it looks fairly gruesome.

Inverted commas

Inverted commas (" and "") are used for two main purposes:

1   To indicate that somebody is speaking or that somebody is being quoted.
2   To emphasize that a word or term is being mentioned in such a way as to draw special attention to it.

There are two kinds of inverted comma: the single inverted comma (') and the double inverted comma ("). Which one you choose is up to you, but remember that where you are quoting additional material *within* the particular type of inverted commas you choose, that material must be put inside whichever type of inverted comma is not your main choice. This is necessary to avoid confusing the reader. For example:

Addressing the meeting at the corporation's headquarters in Detroit, vice-president Dick Jones said: 'I have reviewed Bob Morton's "Robocop" proposal and am firmly of the opinion that my own "Enforcement Droid" recommendation is far more likely to prove practically workable and cost-effective.'

There is a preference nowadays for the single inverted comma to be used as the main one of the hierarchy, but organizations and publishers differ in their approach to this. If you are not pioneering a standard of use of inverted commas, you will probably have to follow an accepted format.

The use of italics

Italics are not punctuation marks, but as they relate to the way in which your writing is presented on the page they can usefully be considered here. Italics offer four main potential effects in a piece of writing.

1 Emphasis of a word, phrase or sentence.

2 A useful alternative to inverted commas when you want to quote the name of a work of art such as a film, a book or so on.

3 The opportunity clearly to distinguish between different kinds of writing.

4 To distinguish foreign words that are not definitely part of English.

Using italics for emphasis can be useful and effective but – to make an emphasis ourselves – you must be careful to ensure it is the *words* that do the work and that the italics are, so to speak, the icing on the cake. Do not expect, or hope, that the use of italics here and there will somehow turn weak, lifeless writing into strong, vigorous writing.

The sort of thing you must avoid is:

The corporation's results over the past year show that they are doing *very* well and are set for a *successful and prosperous* future.

This is basically a dull sentence, and the italics do not make it any better. Try again, dump the italics, and aim to show the company's success by referring to a specific example where it has done well rather than by a baldly statement.

Stylistic guidance

Stylistic guidance to help you write well is more difficult to give than structural guidance. However, the following points are useful to keep in mind.

Become fairly obsessive about choosing the best word

Expert writers are never satisfied until they have chosen exactly the right word to express what they want to say. The French novelist Gustave Flaubert used to call this word *le mot juste* ('the precise word') and spent hours trying to think of the right one.

Granted, this discipline is not for everybody. But it is better to become moderately obsessive about your work and make your work astounding than to be calm and indifferent to it and produce words that leave the reader equally calm and indifferent.

Fortunately, you are not alone in your quest to find the precise word. A thesaurus, which lists synonyms and near-synonyms, can be immensely helpful when you know more or less which word you want but need to know which other words are available (or wish to find a different word in order to avoid repetition). Thesauruses are not a panacea; you may still not find the precise word you want, but they are useful, and no serious writer should be without one. We strongly recommend you buy a thesaurus that lists words alphabetically rather than according to word-classes (as the original *Roget's Thesaurus* does) because it will speed up the rate at which you find the word you want.

Try to avoid repetition

Apart from the short, common words (such as *and, or, if, but, the, a* and so on), repetition of a word too close to where it has already been used looks clumsy and reads badly. A good rule of thumb is to try to avoid repetition of a word within about one page of word-processed text, which in practice means every 250-300 words, depending on whether you are typing or printing out in double-space or one-and-a-half-space.

The best way to avoid repetition is to use synonyms, which you will find in a thesaurus or from your own vocabulary. Be careful, though, to make sure that the words *are* synonyms and not near-synonyms; otherwise your meaning will be compromised. Bad as repetition is, you must never sacrifice meaning in order to avoid it. And in fact repetition can be better than strangled attempts to avoid it. Your aim should be to write so that your reader is unaware you have made an effort to avoid repetition.

Deliberate repetition can be highly effective as a way of hammering home a point. Winston Churchill's famous 'We shall fight on the beaches' speech owes much of its effect to the repetition of 'we shall fight'. This is effective repetition because it adds to, rather than detracts from, the energy of the writing.

So how do you decide whether repetition looks clumsy or dramatic? This is one of those areas where you must rely on your skill for assessing your work objectively and self-critically. The only help we can give you is to say that where the sense of what you are writing deliberately *draws attention* to your repetition, there is a good chance it will be effective, but where this is not so, it is likely it will seem clumsy.

The problem of repetition does not arise with short, everyday words to anything like the extent it does with longer words, probably because the reader's brain is so used to these short, familiar words that it does not absorb them with the same intensity it applies to longer words. We do not mean you can repeat the shorter words with complete impunity; we just mean that as long as you are not using the same short word about half a dozen times in one shortish paragraph, you will probably be all right.

Avoid clichés

You must avoid clichés in your work. Those hackneyed expressions, most of which are metaphors or similes, may have meant something once, but they have become so well-worn that any life they once had in them has long been extinguished.

The best way to avoid a cliché is to compose your own metaphor or simile. That way, you can be sure it will not have been used before, and even if what you write isn't so brilliant that it is taken up by the rest of humanity – and 50 years or so later becomes a cliché in its own right – at least you will show your reader you have taken the trouble to do your own thinking.

Stick to the subject

Even if you write with energy, conciseness, originality of expression and a careful attention to the precise meaning of what you say, your writing will still be weak and amateurish if you do not stick to your subject. We have already seen that the stranger for whom you are writing will have no interest in you personally. If you don't astound and fascinate him, he is going to switch you off.

Textual guidance

We now move on to stylistic points that relate more to specific textual points than general advice. We cannot pretend to be able to give you a comprehensive list of every textual stylistic point that is likely to present a challenge. Style is expression, and expression is a personal matter, as well as being as infinite as the universe. We have merely compiled a list of the textual stylistic points we regard as representing particular challenges to us, and we hope you will find our remarks useful for your own writing.

Adjectives

The secret of good use of adjectives is to use them sparingly. The problem with adjectives is that they so easily become words that *tell* rather than *show*. To that extent they are a kind of crutch. On the face of it they do your work for you and save you the job of bringing your writing alive. But only on the face of it. They can amount to special pleading: rather than using lots of adjectives to describe why your consultancy is so good, why not *say* why your consultancy is so good?

You have probably been to one of those modern diners – usually part of a nationwide chain – where most of the fittings are made of plastic and resin rather than wood, where the waiters' and waitresses' smiles are so bright you need sunglasses, and where the menus have obviously been written and designed by some trendy Madison Avenue ad agency. Orange juice isn't orange juice, it's 'thirst-quenching' orange juice. Steaks aren't steaks, they are 'tender, mouth-watering' steaks. Eggs aren't eggs, they are 'farmfresh' eggs.

The menu is littered with so many adjectives that, when the meal finally arrives, good as it may be, it seems to bear about as much relation to what was described in the menu as hamburgers on the posters in fast-food restaurants bear to the squashed object you get passed over the counter. The menu's adjectives have strangled the credibility and honesty of the place, like fast-growing weeds.

Yet this is only to be expected. Using words carries with it responsibility, and if you are irresponsible in the way you use words, you should not be surprised if the result is that the time you have spent doing your writing has been wasted. In many cases – indeed, I would go so far as to say in the great majority of cases – adjectives simply are not necessary.

Shakespeare *did not* write: 'Shall I compare thee to a beautiful summer's day?' What he wrote was: 'Shall I compare thee to a summer's day?' He did not have Macbeth ask himself, 'Is this a sharp, deadly dagger which I see before me?' but 'Is this a dagger which I see before me?' Shakespeare would have known instinctively that sharp, clear nouns or noun-phrases – such as a summer's day and a dagger – not only do not need a qualifying adjective before them but would actually have their meaning diluted if one were used.

Don't imagine we are recommending that you do not use adjectives *at all* in your work: like all the principles in this book, this guidance on adjectives is only that, guidance, and you must have sufficient responsibility as a writer to have the courage to break any rule that doesn't seem right to you.

It would sometimes be artificial to avoid an adjective. Also, you often need to use another noun to portray the meaning you want, with the secondary noun playing a kind of adjectival role (such as *summer's* does in 'a summer's day'). All we are suggesting is that before you decide to use an adjective, test the sound of what you are writing to make sure that it doesn't sound better without it.

Incidentally, never write 'the best possible 'anything' (e.g. 'the best possible service'). This is a dreadful cliché, and in fact it is meaningless. Think of something to say that actually means something.

Adverbs

If adjectives are the crutches of writing, adverbs are the wheelchairs. The only good thing to say about adverbs is that there is less temptation to use them when writing reports and proposals than there is to use adjectives. When writing reports and proposals you are more likely to want to describe an object or a person than how something is done. On those occasions when you do feel an adverb coming on, try to suppress it. In almost every case where you are tempted to use an adverb, you could, if you tried, do the job much better by expressing what you want to say in a different way.

Why should adverbs be such weak, lacklustre words? We think that, like indiscriminately used adjectives, they do not give the reader any images, or any sense data, but just words that *assert* without offering the reader any reason to believe – or be convinced by – the assertion.

Conjunctions

Conjunctions – 'joining' words such as *and, because, although, while* and so on – cause problems even to experienced writers. Like adjectives and adverbs, they tend to be over-used. With the exception of *and* – which is often, but by no means always, unavoidable – they are ugly words that have an inherent, poisonous tendency to tempt you to make your sentences too long and sprawling.

Our advice is to avoid conjunctions if you can. The best way to do so is to make two sentences when you were planning to make one. Alternatively, use a semi-colon.

An especially ugly conjunction is *although*. Consider:

Sales of fishing tackle have increased by more than 30 per cent compared with the equivalent period last year, although two major new tackle suppliers entered the market in 1999.

A long, dull sentence. Using 'even though' is better than 'although' in this example (as it often is) but it is even better if you start the sentence with the preposition 'despite' and write:

Despite two new tackle suppliers having entered the market in 1999, sales of our fishing tackle have increased by more than 30 per cent compared with the equivalent period last year.

What about *and*? Surely we are not saying this should be avoided, too? The answer is *yes*, if it joins two clauses that would be perfectly workable sentences in their own right, but *no* if it connects two nouns or adjectives. So feel free to write, for example:

Jack and Jill
bucket and spade
law and order
crime and punishment
love and marriage

but instead of writing:

The new Novon has more than eight different attachments and is fully guaranteed for five years.

there is more force in breaking up this one sentence into two:

The new Novon has more than eight different attachments. It is fully guaranteed for five years.

The reason why two simple sentences tend to have more impact than a complex one connected by 'and' is that the reader's brain likes to absorb the first point and then move on to the second. This is particularly true where the 'and' connects two clauses with action in them.

Should you start a sentence with a conjunction? This should be avoided except where, on occasion, you want to create an effect of a sentence being dynamically linked to the preceding sentence. In this instance starting a sentence with 'and' can work, but many of your readers will merely regard it as bad English.

If/whether

The written language tends to be more conservative than the spoken one. A consequence of this is that what is acceptable in speech is not always acceptable in writing.

An important example is the difference between 'if' and 'whether'. Many people will say, for example:

I don't know if she's coming.

The chairman asked if sales had increased since the decision to incorporate a built-in fragrance dispenser into the Novon.

Both these examples are fine if you are speaking, but in writing them you should replace 'if' with 'whether'.

Former/latter

These words are clumsy, ugly and a huge turn-off. Avoid them if you can.

Paragraphs

Good paragraphing is an essential part of good style. It is not an easy thing to get right.

The overriding rule for paragraphing is that you should start a new paragraph wherever there is a distinct – even if only slight – change in the sense and/or the flow of what you want to say. It means you need to detect where the change in the sense or flow has come, and where to introduce a new paragraph. It is important to do your best to put the paragraph break in the most appropriate place; good paragraphing will help the reader onwards with the crucial process of obtaining meaning from what you write.

We now move on to looking at the structure of proposals and reports.

The structure of reports and proposals

Many people in business, and especially consultants, get hidebound by notions of structure in relation to proposals and reports. The guiding principle here is: do not become too preoccupied with rules about structure. What really matters is that your proposal or report communicates what you want to say.

Closely related to this is the preoccupation that business writers frequently have with numbering individual paragraphs of a proposal or report, and especially numbering them in a hierarchical way. You know the sort of thing we mean: where you number a section as '1' and then the paragraphs in that section as '1.1', '1.2' and so on. The problem with this kind of numbering is threefold:

- ○ it can be irritating to read;
- ○ it is too tempting to create numerous sub-headings, all of which have their own numbers, so that you are likely to end up with some paragraphs being numbered in a very complex way – e.g. '2.1.2.5.1.2' – which is gibberish;
- ○ if you have to make redrafts of a proposal or report (such as when you are adapting it for another client), the whole numbering system will probably have to be redone.

Avoid this numbering process unless your proposal or report is relatively short and you really don't feel comfortable allowing your paragraphs to be unnumbered.

Ultimately, the structure of your proposal or report should arise naturally out of what you want to say. Think hard about the issues you want to bring up, and draw up a number of headings that will cover all of these. We give here examples of headings you might want to use.

○ Headings for proposals

Contents

Introduction

Preliminary remarks

The strengths of the organization or entity under consideration

The weaknesses of the organization or entity under consideration

The objectives of your activity

The methodology

Details of the team who will be carrying out the task

Specific plan of action, broken down on a week-by-week or month-by-month basis

The budget

Conclusion (make this upbeat and positive).

○ Headings for reports

Contents

Introduction (this needs to say what you are hired to do)

Methodology (here you say how you did it)

Findings

Recommendations for further action.

These are only ideas; you need to think of your own headings, and it is likely that every proposal and report you produce will have slightly different ones.

The only area where we do want to be categorical here is in the presentation of your proposals or reports. We strongly recommend you adhere to the following guidelines.

○ Always give the document an upbeat title. Don't be afraid to be provocative here, but if you are, be so in a tactful way. For example, if you are making a recommendation for integrating a client's IT systems, don't just use the title like 'Proposal For Systems Integration'; give it an upbeat title such as 'Making Your Systems A Dynamic Competitive Tool'. Even better, refer to commercial objectives that you know the client has, for example: 'How Jones Computers Inc can Beat IBM at its Own Game.' You get the idea.

○ Use a new page for each new heading.

○ Have a contents page that lists all the headings and the pages on which they appear.

○ Wordprocess the whole thing so that you can readily make changes to it and adapt it to other clients. (This may or may not be possible, but you do at least want to have the option.)

○ Use one-and-a-half or double-line spacing. Single spacing is difficult to read for a long document.

○ Make liberal use of bullet points, especially where you are listing things. Bullet points are much easier to read than long lists.

○ Use the third person rather than the first person. Describing your consultancy in the third person always makes the document look more professional than saying 'we'.

○ Prefer the active voice to the passive voice when describing your consultancy's views (e.g. 'IDOM believes' not 'it is believed by IDOM' etc.).

○ Be rigorously consistent in all editorial matters. For example, if you decide to spell out in full numbers between one and ten, and use digits for 11 and above.

○ Don't try to be funny, or too clever. You cannot be certain that your readers will share your sense of humour or your mindset.

○ Overall, do not feel the style of the document needs to be unbearably formal. This tone may be necessary for some clients – such as government offices – but remember that the document is not only a way of communicating facts, it is also a means of communicating the *personality* of your consultancy.

CHAPTER EIGHT

How to make your clients think you're wonderful

Introduction

Movies embody much of the morality of the modern world, especially American morality. Occasionally one gets a movie that not only addresses the question of how to conduct our personal lives but also how to behave in business.

Movies about business have always been an important part of Hollywood's output. This makes sense – in an average day most people spend a good deal more time doing business than they spend pursuing their personal and social lives.

One of the key themes of the movie we discuss here – Cameron Crowe's *Jerry Maguire* – is that one should approach one's business life with the same sincerity and passion that one applies to personal relationships. *Jerry Maguire* is above all a film about business. It's worth briefly recapping the story: at the start of the movie, Jerry Maguire (played with customary energy and conviction by Tom Cruise) is a highly successful sports agent working in a giant agency and making, as he explains, an average of 246 phone calls every day on behalf of his 70+ clients. Various disheartening events in his professional life cause him to have a crisis of conscience, and he starts to realize that he is nothing more than 'a shark in a suit' who is more interested in the dollar than in the well-being of his clients.

So he writes an inspirational memo, entitled *The Things We Think But Do Not Say*, and distributes it to all his colleagues at the mega-agency. In essence, Jerry uses the memo to urge his colleagues to follow his lead and 'learn to do without the bullshit'. His advice is that the agency should be run on both a more human and humane level, that it should have fewer clients and relate more to them as people.

Within a week he is fired. His attempt to take his key clients with him is frustrated, in a piece of brilliant cinema, by one of his second-tier clients – the only one who *is* willing to stay with him – insisting on keeping him on the phone at a crucial time when his other clients are trying to return his calls. This frustrates his last chance to harvest key clients before being thrown out of the office.

Result: Mr Big is suddenly Mr Nobody, trying to set up a new agency that promises to be nothing more than an unsuccessful two-person band. (Two-person, rather than one, because a vulnerable, deep-hearted female account clerk – played with charm and intelligence by Renée Zellweger – is inspired by Jerry's memo to leave the giant agency and join him.)

The unfolding drama is an almost perfect morality tale on the theme that heads this chapter: how to make your clients think you're wonderful. Discarded by everybody but his new assistant and the second-tier client, Jerry is ironically forced to confront the very essence of the situation he urged in his memo: to have fewer clients.

The personal and professional relationship he forges with his remaining client challenges him to face up to the consequences of his crisis of conscience. The client is a black American footballer (an Oscar-winning performance by Cuba Gooding Jnr) whose truculence, self-pity and tendency to badmouth the team's management are conspiring to prevent him from fulfilling his potential in the sport. In effect, both men help each other – Jerry helps the footballer to put his heart back into the game; the footballer encourages Jerry to realize that he can be a success on the new terms he has defined for himself only if he sorts out his personal life and develops a heart away from the office.

Reactions to *Jerry Maguire* differ. Even those who praise the quality of the acting find parts of the film schmaltzy, but this may be because many of those who see it bring to the viewing precisely the type of 'mega-agency mentality' the film is attacking. What really matters is that the central moral lesson – that business should be about sincere attention to the client/customer as a person rather than merely seeing him as a source of revenue, and that one should expose one's heart in business as much as in one's personal life.

In fact, the challenges faced by sports agents and consultants are remarkably similar: how do you reconcile the need to offer outstanding and sincere personal service with the essential requirement to be profitable if you are going to stay in business? We have little hesitation in saying that the solutions suggested in *Jerry Maguire* – while easier to dream about than to carry out – are more likely to bring success in the long run than the behaviour of the giant agency whose emptiness and *in*sincerity becomes increasingly clear as the film progresses.

The overriding importance of client relationships

As a consultant, your working relationships with your clients are the most valuable assets you possess. Even if you have followed our advice and have resolved to start your SFC small, grow organically in response to demand and minimize your expenditure at every stage of your development, merely following these key precepts will only create the conditions that make success possible; they will not of themselves lead to success. In the final analysis, it is only the quality of your working relationships with your clients that will bring you the professional and financial success to which you aspire.

The way to nurture quality relationships with your clients is to work hard, effectively and sincerely on your clients' behalf. Working hard is insufficient if you are not also effective, and you can only be truly effective if you have a sincere empathy for your clients' aims. The reason you are working hard, effectively and sincerely on your clients' behalf is so that you can help them to become more successful. This fundamental aim is (or should be) the prime objective of a consultant's activities on behalf of his clients, and there is no short cut to this objective.

If you work hard, effectively and sincerely on your clients' behalf, and make their success your fundamental objective, you will reap the financial rewards for doing this, and you will keep on reaping them. It is perfectly acceptable for you to make your financial success an important private aim of your own, but you will achieve that financial success on a sustained basis only if you make your primary aim the provision of expert assistance to your clients to make them more successful.

Unfortunately for the consulting profession, there are consultants who do not make their clients' success their primary aim, but seek to gain short-term financial benefits from a client by devious means such as getting the client to sign a contract that has the effect of bringing the consultant considerable revenue for a minimal amount of work. Because clients are sometimes rather intimidated by consultants – particularly ones with expensive-looking suits and pompous voices – clients will, on occasion, sign these contracts and enrich the consultant in return for little tangible benefit.

Taking clients for a ride is no way to run a consultancy. Instead, you must make every effort to ensure that, from the very first moment they come into contact with you to the time (perhaps many years later) when you part company, your clients are continually convinced of your remarkable talents, your professionalism, your hard work and your total dedication to their interests.

In this chapter we take you, step by step, through the process of making initial contact with clients, starting to get professionally involved, and working for clients on an ongoing basis, so that at every stage you see how you can work to gain their maximum respect and admiration. Although some of the business practices we recommend consist of what are essentially tactical measures, underlying everything is the fundamental requirement to work hard, effectively and sincerely. We suggest some useful business practices to maximize the esteem in which your clients hold you, but we cannot teach you how to work hard, effectively and sincerely. That is something that you must have in you. However, we believe there are two secrets to working in this way: to love the area of specialization in which you are working, and to gain pleasure from looking after a client's interests and from seeing the benefits that your work has on a client's business.

The most important guiding principles of all

Before moving on to our step-by-step analysis of how to gain maximum respect and admiration from your clients, we introduce two fundamental principles that should underlie every single aspect of your dealings with your clients, whether these clients are business prospects or clients with whom you have been working for many years.

The principles are these:

1 Seek at every stage of your interaction with your client to imagine yourself in your client's shoes, particularly as regards an empathy with your client's commercial and cultural goals.

2 Strive at all times to bring your disinterested – but not *un*interested – objectivity to bear in solving your client's problems and facing up to his challenges.

Your client is entitled to take for granted that you will put these principles into action at all times. If you don't, you cannot, in our view, really describe yourself as a consultant in the best sense of the word.

What we most emphatically are *not* suggesting here is that you should agree with your client at every point. Putting yourself in your client's shoes and understanding that your priorities and time-frames are not your client's priorities and time-frames is something very different from agreeing with whatever your client says. Putting yourself in your client's shoes is a mental discipline that allows you to see (as far as you can know this) what is motivating your client to think and act as he does. Not only will this mental discipline greatly assist you to conduct an amicable and mutually beneficial relationship, but on those occasions when you have to disagree with your client – whether over an aspect of your relationship or when you advise them against a particular course of action you know they want to pursue – the client will listen hard to the reasons why you disagree with them, and will probably respect them. You may even be able to change the client's mind.

Let us proceed to our step-by-step guide to making your clients think that you are wonderful.

Step 1: the initial contact with clients

You must ensure that ultra-professionalism and a very high degree of ability infuse your relationships with your clients from the very first contact with them. In practice, this means that you must pay particular attention to your initial telephone calls to your clients, and also to the first letters you write to them. The advice we have offered regarding telephone calls and letters holds good for those calls and letters that you send your clients once you have established a good working relationship. However, this advice is particularly important for the initial stages of your involvement with your clients. Ideally, you should give them a level of expertise, sincerity and value for money that they have never experienced before.

Telephone calls

If your first contact with a client is by telephone and you are initiating the call (for example, an existing client might have spoken to your prospective client who has requested that you call them), make sure, before you phone, that you are absolutely certain how to spell and pronounce the name of the prospective client organization and the name of the person you will be telephoning.

Before you pick up that receiver or press the hand-free button, make sure you have worked out what the objective of the telephone conversation is. If it is to introduce yourself to the client and to seek to arrange a meeting, keep the conversation confined to those two objectives. The prospective client does not want to know about irrelevant matters, such as how hard you are working, how little you see of your family, the problems you have encountered since you started your SFC. At a later stage, as and when you have established a mutually beneficial working relationship with your client, there may be room for more personal types of conversation, but not now.

The above guidelines are just two of our guidelines for being professional on the telephone. Our recommendations are as follows:

○ know how to spell the name of the client organization and the client contact before you telephone;

○ work out what the objective of the telephone conversation is before you telephone, and stick to that objective;

○ leave out any personal talk in the conversation unless your client invites it;

○ avoid asking prospective clients very direct questions. Clients find these embarrassing and even slightly impertinent. Where you do want an answer to a specific and (for you) important question, find a way to express it in a more subtle way. For example, rather than saying, 'Do you want to employ my firm as a consultant along the lines of the proposal that we sent to you last week?', say, 'Were any of the ideas in the proposal that we sent to you last week of interest to you?';

○ avoid the hard sell at all costs. You are a consultant, not an insurance salesman. Nothing is more likely to put a client off than a barrage of 'hard sell' verbiage emphasizing how clever you are, how much expertise you have, and how inexpensive you are compared with your competitors. There is no need to be pompous about it, but you must give your clients the impression that you are as privileged to be working with them as they are privileged to be working with you. You can never work productively with a client unless you both feel you are working on equal terms, and the hard sell – for all its bluster – is really a form of grovelling;

O don't be afraid to ask questions;

O never, never, refer to anything negative about your consultancy, even as a joke. Prospective clients (and, indeed, existing ones) will always think you mean it;

O never criticize a rival consultancy. This always sounds terribly unprofessional.

If you are receiving the telephone call and are not expecting it, you will have to plan the conversation as you talk rather than beforehand. All the same, the above rules still apply.

Dale Carnegie's book *How to Win Friends and Influence People* (Simon & Schuster, New York, 1989) is a great instructional book, and, in our opinion, the best 'how to' book of all time. One of the few 'how to' books that actually delivers what it promises, this book amounts to a fascinating set of observations on how paying heed to certain aspects of practical human psychology can help you get ahead in life and in business. In many ways the book is a kind of bible for post-war capitalism. Its assumption that getting ahead in business is mainly a matter of putting these observations into practice seems a little naive nowadays, but you will get a great deal from Carnegie's book. If you have already read it, read it again, for you would do well to keep much of its advice at the forefront of your mind when you set out on your great task of starting your high-income consultancy.

There is one Carnegie principle that we regard as particularly important to a consultant who wants his client to think that he is wonderful: *the most important sound in the world to any person is the sound of their name.*

Letters

If professionalism on the telephone is a prerequisite for the initial stages of a relationship with a client, it is equally essential that the letters you write are marked by a high degree of professionalism from the outset.

You have already read about our recommendations for having your own stationery. Good, professional stationery is a starting point, but it is only a starting point, for what matters now is what you actually type on to the stationery. And you will, of course, need to type it. There is certainly room for handwritten letters in the consulting business; a brief, informal letter to a long-term client contact can sometimes be effective if it is handwritten, but the letters you write to prospective clients are going to need to be typewritten, which today means word-processed.

In Fig. 6.1, we gave an example of the type of new business letter you could write to a client. Here what matters is to point out the various standards to which your letters must adhere.

○ There must be no spelling mistakes. Anyone who sends out a letter with a spelling mistake because they cannot be bothered to check the spelling of a difficult word has no right to call himself professional. Many computer word-processing packages contain spellcheck functions, but you cannot always rely on these as they do not normally contain proper names or much in the way of technical vocabulary. In particular, it is fatal to misspell the name of the person to whom you are writing, or the name and address of his organization.

○ There must be no 'typos'. These are not spelling mistakes but errors in the typing. If you use a computer it should be possible to avoid typos completely by paying careful attention to the letter on the screen before you print it out. Be particularly careful with the words 'of' and 'or', and 'if' and 'it'. On a QWERTY keyboard the 'r' is immediately above the 'f' so it is easy to confuse the two. The letters 't' and 'f' present similar problems. The fact that they are very common words and your eyes usually only skim-read them makes errors here very difficult to spot.

Generally, until you get the hang of sending out letters with no typos in them, you would do well to ask somebody else to read through a letter on the screen and then print the letter out and check it again. It is always more difficult to spot typos in a document that you have written yourself rather than in one that someone else has written. Incidentally, remember that modern word-processing programs usually allow you to enter your most common typos and spelling mistakes into a special file that will correct them automatically. In Microsoft Word, this is the 'AutoCorrect' function, found on the Tools menu.

○ The letter should be written on your letterhead and should have the name and address of the person to whom you are writing on the left and starting about an inch under the text at the top of the letterhead. Below the name and address write the date out in full, e.g. 29 August 2002 rather than 29/8/2002 (or 02) which looks official and unfriendly. A couple of inches below the date write the salutation, e.g. 'Dear Mr Smith'.

○ Even in a completely cold new business mailing, always write to a named contact, never to a job title.

○ Do not use the forename of the person to whom you are writing in the salutation unless you have either spoken to them on the telephone at some length or else met them at least once. In North America and Britain, the business world is becoming increasingly informal, and forenames are used soon after a business acquaintance begins, but using someone's forename when you are writing to them for the first time and when you have never met them or spoken to them on the telephone in an other than cursory manner is stretching informality dangerously close to impertinence. When writing to women, use the increasingly acceptable 'Ms' in the first instance. If you have met the woman in question and talked in some detail, you can feel free to address her in the letter by her forename.

○ Keep initial letters business-like and to the point. There is no room for silliness, frivolity or anything in the least self-deprecating.

○ Keep initial letters to one page in length *at all costs*. You cannot expect someone to whom you are writing for the first time to read more than one page. Bear in mind that if the letter does not grab that person right from the start, he may not even bother to read that first page in its entirety.

Finally, remember when making an initial contact with a client, remember that from the first moment that your prospective client hears about (or is told about) your existence you are in effect on trial, with the client assessing you as a reliable business contact and (possibly) consultant worth hiring.

Step 2: starting to get professionally involved with clients

The two most fundamental aspects of good client relations when you start to get professionally involved with clients are:

1 knowing how to arrange meetings and how to conduct yourself at meetings;

2 writing proposals and reports for clients.

These two aspects of your activity are also important for when you are working with clients on an ongoing basis, but they are particularly crucial to your success at getting those ongoing client relationships established. As such, our discussion of this second step focuses on this.

Here is our ten-point guide to success when arranging and attending meetings.

1 Always write down the precise date, time and location of meetings in your diary as soon as they are arranged. Do not delay doing this; it is horribly easy to forget about a meeting, particularly if you are arranging several in conjunction with a new business campaign in the early days of your SFC. Obviously, failing to turn up for a meeting because you have forgotten about it is disastrous, but it is hardly much better to have to telephone the organization to check on the precise time and location.

2 When you write down the date, time and location of a meeting in your diary, always write down the client's telephone number next to the details of the

meeting. You will need this number if you are on your way to the client and get lost, or if you have been inadvertently delayed and want to warn them that you will be a little late.

3   Unless absolutely unavoidable, do not change the timing of a meeting your end. Doing this always looks unprofessional and silly. Of course, your prospective client may change the timing, and you will just have to put up with that.

4   Your personal appearance is extremely important when attending a meeting with a client, and particularly an initial meeting with a prospective client. Dress smartly. If you are a man, the crucial things to watch for are that your suit is well-pressed, that your tie matches and your shirt is buttoned up at the top, and that your shoes are polished. If you are a woman, aim to be stylish. We have already mentioned that when people hire consultants, they usually do so in the first instance to boost their own ego rather than because the problem they are hoping you, the consultant, will solve is oppressing them. Even if it is oppressing them, they will still hire you basically for reasons of ego-boost.

   This explains why your personal appearance is so important at the initial meeting and at successive meetings. People want to do business with other people whom they perceive to be successful. As Mark McCormack states very succinctly in *What They Don't Teach You at Harvard Business School* (Harper Collins, London, 1986): 'People want to do business with winners.' So you have to look like a winner from the outset. Of course, ultimately what is going to matter to your clients is the quality of your thoughts and the way you express those thoughts in words and in writing, but if you don't look the part from the outset, you are not going to have a chance to show your clients what a good brain you have because they won't hire you.

5   Do not be late for a meeting unless an unavoidable emergency has occurred. When you attend a meeting with a prospective client, you are in effect trying to sell something (i.e. your services) and good salespeople are never, *ever* late. If you have never visited the client's premises before, give yourself plenty of time to find where you are going. Indeed, it is always a good idea to aim to arrive 15 minutes or so early for a meeting. You may want to freshen up before the meeting, but even if you don't, the receptionist will not object to your sitting in the reception area until it is time for the meeting.

6   When you meet the prospective client for the first time, give them a warm smile and shake hands. The first visual image that they have of you is important, so make sure that it will be a positive one.

7   When inside the meeting room, do not put your briefcase on a chair or table, but on the floor.

8　You must know exactly what you are seeking to get from the meeting before you go into it. Essentially, all meetings between a consultant and a prospective or existing client take place to discuss an aspect of the client's activities with which the consultant hopes to assist the client. This being the case, what you should be aiming to achieve at the meeting is either to obtain sufficient information about that aspect of the client's activities for you to be able to go away and prepare a proposal, or to obtain definite agreement from the client, there and then, for you to go away and undertake that action. In this case, you will, of course, need to get from the client a signed agreement relating to the activity prior to starting it.

You cannot always know in advance which of these two possible outcomes is likely to occur, but do your utmost to steer the meeting in one of these two directions, given that you must, as with your initial telephone conversations, avoid the hard sell …

9　Make sure that you take any relevant documentation to the meeting. This would include business cards (these are essential), any of your corporate literature, any visual aids such as flip-charts and overhead projector foils, and – something that we have always found very useful – a file containing numerous clear plastic jackets in which you can place examples of work already completed, flattering letters that clients have written to you about the excellence of your services, and other items. If, as a completely new start-up, you have no such documentation to show off from your time as a consultant, there is no reason why you should not include material from your time as a salaried employee if it has some relevance to the activity you are proposing to undertake on the client's behalf.

10　The key to attending meetings as a consultant is to *listen*. After all, the reason you are there in the first place is, presumably, because your client has a problem (whether temporary or ongoing) and needs your help. On the other hand, you cannot necessarily leave it to the client to say the first thing at the meeting. Even if the client has requested to see you as the result of having heard about you from one of his business contacts, he may still prefer you to kick off the meeting. And don't forget that clients are sometimes rather in awe of consultants, even a little frightened of them, so it may be up to you to break the ice.

The way to do this is not to fire a couple of party poppers at the ceiling but to introduce yourself briefly and summarize your experience. Then, if you know what problem the client has, ask him to tell you about it. Otherwise, tell him you would be very interested to know what he is doing in terms of whatever specialization you are offering as a consultant. Let the conversation develop from there, but above all, *listen*.

Step 3: working with clients on an ongoing basis

Managing the ongoing relationship with a client in the most effective way is beyond doubt the real essence of how to make your clients think you're wonderful. The initial stages of the relationship should result in the client being impressed by your professionalism, quality of service, knowledge of the field and attention to detail. The quality of the questions you ask your client is also of immense importance, because this will reveal how much – or how little – you understand of their business, and even more important, how much you care about them and their challenges.

As with other areas discussed in this book, it is not possible, in the final analysis, for us or anyone else to teach you how to work devotedly and professionally on behalf of your clients. The level of service that you provide as a consultant is a function both of your inherent skill and expertise and also of your willingness to spare no effort on behalf of your clients. However, by keeping the following guidelines in mind, you should maximize your potential for making your clients think that you are wonderful when working for them on an ongoing basis.

1   Cultivate a sincere interest in and empathy for those business problems which your clients have that relate to the specialization you are offering as a consultant. This is the most important guideline to making your clients think that you are wonderful on an ongoing basis because inevitably you will only be able to achieve this if you are sincere. You may be able to fake such an interest and empathy for a while, but it will not last long.

Cultivate a genuine interest in and empathy for your clients' business problems by reminding yourself that if you can solve them, those problems will help make you rich.

2   Resolve to spare no effort to help your clients. This precept is simple, powerful and essential. You must spare no effort on your clients' behalf, even if this means sitting up until 3a.m. to finish a report that your client wants to have on his desk the following morning. But if you do sit up until 3a.m., there is no harm in discreetly mentioning this to your client.

3   Ensure that your hard work is visible to your clients. Only religious martyrs or persons of an excessively self-deprecating temperament like hiding their light under a bushel, and as you are a consultant or are thinking of becoming one, we hope we can assume that you are not too keen on either religious martyrdom or excessive self-deprecation. The point is that if you want your clients to think that you are wonderful, you must take every step to ensure that they see your commitment. There is no room in the consulting business for modesty, false or otherwise.

This does not mean that you have to draw attention to your hard work in a flagrant and crudely boastful or conceited way. What you should do instead is recognize that there are three principal means by which your hard work will be visible to your clients, and never miss an opportunity to project yourself to the client by these means.

First, make sure you talk to your clients regularly on the telephone so that they can get a status report on what you are doing for them and what new problems/challenges/difficulties they are facing. While such telephone conversations may produce important new business leads for you, remember that the reason for the phone call is *not* to win new business but to communicate to the client what you are doing for them and that you care about them and their business.

If you are not talking to your client on the telephone at least twice a week during the period that you are working for them on either an *ad hoc* or retainer basis, you are speaking to them too infrequently. Of course, you must have something to tell the client or ask them about; it is not enough to phone them 'for a chat', unless you know them and know they will appreciate this.

You should, we need hardly add, have ensured that your client is paying for all your telephone calls by arranging a deal that includes a charge for telephone expenses that will pay for your regular telephone contact and for other calls that you need to make in the course of your work for the client.

Second, you can write letters and reports about your activity and send them to your clients. These are particularly important as they form a permanent record of your activity as a consultant. Unlike telephone calls, letters and documents can be filed by your client.

We recommend that for all your clients you get into the habit of producing a monthly project status report that lists in numbered summary form what you have done for your client during the month that is just coming to an end. Activity reports are equally important for *ad hoc* or retainer accounts, except that with *ad hoc* accounts you may need to consider preparing your activity reports on a more regular basis than once a month if the project is particularly time-intensive. (Incidentally, *ad hoc* clients need to be kept as happy as retainer clients – the *ad hoc* client of today may become the retainer client of tomorrow.)

Third, you can convey the information at a meeting. For retainer clients, you should be meeting them once a month, and more often if you are working on a particularly important mandate. For *ad hoc* clients, how often you meet them will again depend on how work-intensive the project is, but unless it is a very short project (requiring, say, less than six days of your time) we recommend that you meet the client to discuss progress (and to find out whether there is anything that they feel you are not doing) in the middle of the project as well as at the beginning and at the end.

4   Cultivate a habit of giving your client sincere flattery as and when it seems

appropriate. Apart from the basic human needs of shelter, food and sexual fulfilment, people want, above all, *to feel good about themselves*. Often, of course, they don't, but since you are being hired by your client to act as a consultant, you should not miss a chance of proffering sincere flattery to your client. Such flattery will, if it is properly done, endear you to your client and help him think that you are wonderful.

The key word here is *sincere*. You have to mean what you say or it will seem absurd and even outrageous. And really, how can you flatter a client sincerely unless you genuinely like them? So cultivate a liking for your clients above everything else.

5   When you judge an aspect of your client's activity, make sure your assessment is constructive. Anybody can offer adverse criticism, but only people who are thoughtful can criticize constructively, which basically means that you make positive suggestions to improve whatever is the subject of criticism. The word 'criticism' has become used to denote negative criticism, whereas the word's original meaning denoted a much more neutral, even constructive, process. Try, in your thinking and behaviour, to return the word to its original meaning. It is useful to recall that as a consultant you are not there to offer criticism but rather a critique – the word 'critique' does not have the same negative connotations as 'criticize' or 'criticism' and it is a better word for you to have in mind when you think about what you are seeking to do as a consultant, since the word implies constructive criticism.

6   Get into the habit of thinking before you speak. When you are running a consultancy, what you and your fellow consultants (if any) are basically being paid for is the quality of your thought. Therefore you must do your utmost to be regarded by your client as a thoughtful, perceptive person, which means that you must never give snap judgements, whether over the telephone or in a meeting. Always give yourself time – even if it is only a few minutes – to deliberate the matter. And don't say anything until you know that what you will say is going to be your best, most considered thoughts on the matter and that you would be ready to defend these thoughts energetically if necessary.

You should adopt the same policy in a meeting. Try to give yourself time to have a good think about the matter. Even if you are in a meeting where you have little choice but to give a rapid response to a question, sit in silence for half a minute or so and think about it. You have no idea how effective it can be in a corporate meeting for a consultant to sit there, thinking. And if that half minute is not long enough for you to reach a considered decision on the matter, say you need further time and will get back to them. But specify a time by which you will have got back to them, and make sure you stick to it.

7   As a consultant you should above all be playing a pro-active role in your clients' professional lives, and in particular you should get into the habit of initiating ideas that will assist your clients. Try to generate a genuine 'team spirit' in which you are part of the team. This guideline should be self-explanatory, although this does not make it any less important. As a consultant, you should always try to generate ideas and suggestions for activity rather than simply sitting back and being a sounding-board for your clients' ideas.

8   We have already referred to one of the psychological reasons why people hire consultants – to boost their ego – so bear this in mind and don't be afraid of being a little demanding, whether in terms of the fee that you are charging your client, or in terms of how you expect to be treated by your client (or his secretary). If you are a little demanding, what your client will think, in effect, is this fellow is a demanding person because he is talented and has abundant expertise. How clever we are to have hired him!

Of course, you cannot be *too* demanding because that would be impertinent, and you will, in the end, have to deliver the goods in terms of what you do for the client if he is to retain this high opinion of you. However, you are a consultant, and if you have been kept waiting for 20 minutes for a meeting that your client requested, you are entitled to an apology. If your client's secretary is rude to you or stroppy over the telephone without any cause, you are entitled to raise the matter discreetly with your client. Give yourself a high status, and your client will tend to believe that you deserve a high status.

9   Try to surround yourself with an aura of expertise and authority. You have to make your clients feel that your opinion is worth soliciting and that you are a person who is brimful with expertise. You can only do this by doing things for your clients, and by making suggestions that impress them, but even before achieving this you yourself need to believe that you are a person who is surrounded by an aura of expertise. If you believe this (given that you have good reasons for believing this), there is a much better chance that your clients will believe it, too.

10 Once you know that your client thinks you are wonderful, don't stop doing all the things that have made him think this. This is self-explanatory, too. You don't just want your client to think you are wonderful once; you want him to think this all the time.

Afterword

We wrote *Breakthrough Consulting* out of a conviction that there was a need in the marketplace for a book that not only inspired readers to regard the consulting industry as one that offered enormous potential for self-fulfilment, self-realization and very substantial income, but also provided the practical tools and general advice necessary to maximize the likelihood that the reader could make a success of consulting.

Ultimately, *no* business book wins your success for you – that is something you have to do for yourself. However, there is no doubt whatsoever in our minds that a business book *can* teach good business practice and good, money-making attitudes, and can help people avoid the numerous pitfalls which lie in wait for anybody with ambitions, and that are especially abundant in the consulting industry.

The fundamental point about consulting is that it is too easy to become a consultant without knowing what one is doing. In *Breakthrough Consulting*, we have aimed to give you the tools so that you *do* know what you are doing.

Unfortunately, most management training available to executives is directed at, and designed for, people who are already working for large organizations. Much of this training is comparatively irrelevant for anybody who wants to make a success of consulting. *Breakthrough Consulting* arose out of a determination to fill the gap.

We have set up a web site whose purpose is to promote this book and enable readers and consultants to ask questions on-line about issues that concern them. The web site address is: www.breakthroughconsulting.co.uk

We also welcome your comments on this book, and particularly comments on any areas which you would like us to address in subsequent editions. Please write to us, care of the publisher. We will ensure that all letters received are properly replied to, and if we take up your suggestion, we will give you an acknowledgement in the next edition.

May we take this chance to wish you every success with your consulting activity. You have chosen an industry in which it is probably easier to be delighted by your career than in any other industry in the world. May you make the most of the opportunities consulting brings you!

What the experts say

Introduction

Unlike most business books, *Breakthrough Consulting* does not contain any 'war stories': tales from the front line of business, replete with the cut and thrust of energetic, tough business activity. War stories tend to be written in an upbeat and – on the face of it – knowledgeable way, and the people involved are usually talked about as if they were characters in a movie rather than real people.

There are two reasons why we do not have any war stories in *Breakthrough Consulting*.

First, war stories are hardly ever genuinely instructive, and are in fact likely to be misleading. The point is that they tell the story of how somebody *else* did something, under conditions which, by definition, are going to be radically different from those in which *you* will do business. Indeed, many war stories are often dangerous to read because it is too easy for a reader to imagine that if they bring to the battle the same attitudes and mindset that the protagonists in the war story did, they will enjoy similar success.

In fact, it is very unlikely that they will. To focus on just one factor: all business activity is time-sensitive. If it worked, it worked at a particular time, but very likely – in many cases almost certainly – it would not work if it was done at another time. Microsoft, for example, has become a global sensation because it was launched at what, in retrospect, can be seen as the absolutely ideal time, when personal computers were just starting to make an appearance but when nobody could have dreamed of the impact they would have worldwide over the next 20 years. Bill Gates was able to base much of Microsoft's success on IBM's inability to see that it ought to own the rights to personal computer software running on its machines rather than be happy to buy it in from Microsoft. Of course, Microsoft has won many other battles since then, and the skills, talents and hard work of many thousands of brilliant people have combined to make the company what it is today, but all Microsoft's success has in a very real sense depended on the winning of that first battle.

To take another example, the enormous success of the British entrepreneur Richard Branson, founder of the Virgin Group, was by his own admission founded on the success and talents, in the 1960s and 1970s, of the musician Mike Oldfield, whose album *Tubular Bells* was one of the musical sensations of the 20th century. Reading the hundreds of column inches devoted to the personality of the affable and charismatic Branson, you would never think that such a simple commercial fact was what was really responsible for giving Virgin the financial muscle to conquer the world.

Fashions are also immensely important as to whether a particular initiative will be successful. By definition, fashions are time-critical, and what worked five years ago may not work now; indeed, what worked three months ago may not necessarily work now.

Furthermore, the particular mix of dynamics and personalities that helped a business initiative to succeed is something that cannot be recreated, ever. Even if you do manage to achieve success by imitating some success from the past, that will happen by a lucky accident, not by design. There is always a big luck factor in success, but war stories hardly ever acknowledge this: they tend to adopt the attitude that everything was brilliantly planned by the protagonists from the outset. That, too, is deeply misleading.

The point is, you need to *find your own success:* you won't duplicate it by imitating the success achieved by others.

Second, war stories are frequently misleading because they are often *not* true. They are written by writers and journalists who want to present a particular view of the issue under consideration, and so the war story is almost invariably slanted to support a pre-conceived argument. It is perfectly possible that the war story will contain factual errors, and even if it doesn't, the way in which it relates the psychology of the individuals concerned is likely to be inaccurate.

Success is never an illusion – it is very much worth having – but it always looks different viewed from the inside than from the outside. The great industrialist Lord Weinstock was once asked for the secret of his success. He replied – and it is rare that an industrialist or businessman will reply with this level of honesty – that all he had done was to pursue a course of action, and success had come to him as a natural result of that.

Most success happens in this way, but because such an undramatic point rarely makes good copy, writers usually prefer to over-dramatize the personality and ambitions of the successful person. This is all very well in the business pages of a newspaper, but you cannot base a personal business philosophy on it, still less use it as a base for your bid for success.

Reading the business pages of most newspapers, one would hardly imagine that the real key to success is the identification of a definite market niche and the steady, sensible, intelligent meeting of customer needs within that niche at a profitable price that the customer is willing to pay. Instead, business pages tend to give the impression that success stems from the brilliant cut and thrust of a giant business 'personality' in the boardroom.

The quest for the truth is not helped by the fact that when some people achieve success by the means we have just mentioned, they often start to believe their own PR and start to imagine that what created their success was their personality and energy. That might have given them the determination to persist on their path, but what created their success was, almost by definition, their ability to deliver value for money in a particular business niche.

War stories are all very well as entertainment, but they do not usually teach you very much, and can easily teach you the wrong things. So in *Breakthrough Consulting* we set out to provide you not with an endless succession of war stories but with the actual precepts and principles you ought to put into action if you are to become a star consultant.

This chapter broadens the material of the book, not by relating war stories but by looking at attitudes to consulting held by several successful consultancies in Britain and the US. We approached a number of consultancies – chosen on the basis of our knowledge of them as innovative, enterprising, and committed to the quality of the client relationship – and asked them the following questions.

1 Please state the full address of your head office, with contact details.

2 How do you describe your activities as a consulting organization?

3 How many consultants did you employ throughout your organization as of September 30 1999?

4 What is your total annual fee income (if you disclose this)?

5 What is your mission statement?

6 Please provide five examples of the kind of consulting work you undertake (e.g. strategic consulting, systems integration etc.).

7 What personal qualities do you believe a good consultant needs to have?

8 In your view, what is the secret to making your clients think you are wonderful?

9 What type of reports do your clients receive of the activity you have completed on their behalf? Please be as specific as you can here.

10 What are your most important methods of winning new business (e.g. client referral, advertising etc.)?

11 Most consultancies say they believe in team spirit. What do you do to encourage successful teamwork?

12 What procedures do you have for dealing with problems that your clients may experience with your service?

13 Do you believe in promoting your chief executive as a business guru? If so, how to you do this?

14 What training do you provide for new recruits in the first year of their appointment?

15 Consulting work is notorious for the long hours it requires. Faced with this pressure, how do your consultants retain a sense of perspective?

16 What advice would you give to any young person (e.g. a graduate) thinking of working in consulting?

17 How do you think the consulting industry will change as a result of the Internet?

18 How can consultants avoid getting a reputation for charging clients to tell them what they already know?

19 Why do you think there is pressure on consultancies to merge with others?

20 How do you think the consulting business ten years in the future will differ from the consulting business today?

The questions were designed to be detailed and searching, and some respondents decided not to reply to certain questions on the basis that the responses might have intruded on commercially sensitive matters. Naturally, we fully respected the right of the respondents – who were being very revealing generally about their answers – not to reply to some questions. Generally, these responses provide, in our view, a rich and varied picture of consulting in action.

Andersen Consulting

1 **Please state the full address of your head office, with telephone, fax and e-mail contact details.**

33 West Monroe Street
Chicago
Illinois 60603
US
Tel: 1-312 372 7100
Fax: 1-312 693 0507

2 **How do you describe your activities as a consulting organization?**

Andersen Consulting is the world's largest management consultancy. It possesses wide knowledge and in-depth experience across the full spectrum of business needs, spanning strategy, technology, operations and people.

3 **How many consultants did you employ throughout your organization as of September 30 1999?**

65 000.

4 **What is your total annual fee income?**

$8.3 billion revenue for the calendar year 1998.

5 **What is your mission statement?**

To help our clients create their future.

6 **Please provide five examples of the kind of consulting work you undertake.**

Change management, outsourcing, process design, strategic consulting, technology services.

7 **What personal qualities do you believe a good consultant needs to have?**

We recruit people who demonstrate confidence, good communication skills (especially orally), initiative and decisiveness. They also tend to have good analytical skills to solve problems and have interpersonal flexibility so they can build good relationships with individuals and in a team.

8 **In your view, what is the secret to making your clients think you are wonderful?**

Delivering value.

9 **What type of reports do your clients receive of the activity you have completed on their behalf?**

Respondent preferred not to reply.

10 **What are your most important methods of winning new business?**

Respondent preferred not to reply.

11 **Most consultancies say they believe in team spirit. What do you do to encourage successful teamwork?**

At Andersen Consulting we promote team spirit through a community structure and through project work. In these situations groups of people work together to achieve common goals. This brings out a very positive team spirit.

12 **What procedures do you have for dealing with problems that your clients may experience with your service?**

Effective client relationships are relationships of dialogue, discussion and debate. As we are working with a client over a period of time, their thinking will shift substantially or, often, our own thinking shifts substantially as we understand more about the context and the business problem. If you've got a situation with a client who is not open to debate or discussion, that is not a firm foundation for a consulting relationship. We regularly turn down work if we believe that a client is either not properly appreciating what they are getting into, not prepared to enter into sensible debate about the objective and the ways of achieving that objective, or if the client organization is not capable of achieving the change they say they want to achieve.

13 Do you believe in promoting your chief executive as a business guru?

Respondent preferred not to reply.

14 What training do you provide for new recruits in the first year of their appointment?

About three-quarters of Andersen Consulting's recruits join as graduates in their first year after university. The remainder join as experienced recruits, bringing at least two to three years' – and often considerably more – previous experience from a variety of fields, such as industry, banking, government and consulting. All recruits to our consulting business (and many more joining our outsourcing business) join one of our four competency groups: Change, Process, Strategy or Technology. Each competency group is responsible for all professional development activities – including training – of its members and for teaching the skills that its members will take to client engagements.

Andersen Consulting invests 6–8 per cent of its revenue each year in training. A similar proportion, on average, of consultants' time is spent participating in training, although this amount is weighted in favour of our new recruits.

15 Consulting work is notorious for the long hours it requires. Faced with this pressure, how do your consultants retain a sense of perspective?

Our consultants are recruited partly because they have achieved a great deal in their academic work, employment and external lives. They seem to thrive on being self-starters and getting involved in things. Because they have this ability to ensure they have outside interests, it means that they can ensure a good balance between their working and non-working lives. It is this that allows them to maintain a sense of perspective.

16 What advice would you give to any young person (e.g. a graduate) thinking of working in consulting?

Think about what motivates you. If you like hard work coupled with working with like-minded people to help resolve problems in the business world, it may be a good career to move into. If you also have confidence, good communication skills, initiative and decisiveness, you probably will enjoy it.

17 How do you think the consulting industry will change as a result of the Internet?

The developing use of the Internet as a business tool is providing, and will continue to provide, a significant shift in the things that businesses are going to have to deal with. It is providing a huge shift in how many customers/clients companies can deal with how they interact with their customers, and the business to consumer focus.

This additional capability will not mean, however, that old processes and practices disappear. One of the key challenges for business is how to support the increasing customer demand for all these new services and these new ways of interacting while continuing to support all the old ways.

18 How can consultants avoid getting a reputation for charging clients to tell them what they already know?

Respondent preferred not to reply.

19 Why do you think there is pressure on consultancies to merge with others?

We do not believe such pressure exists.

20 How do you think the consulting business ten years in the future will differ from the consulting business today?

Change affects us just like everybody else. We will not be the same firm in five years that we are today. Like everybody else we must change or face the consequences.

Arthur D. Little

1 Please state the full address of your head office, with telephone, fax and e-mail contact details.

Acorn Park
Cambridge
Massachusetts 02149-2390
US
Tel: 1-617 498 5000
Fax: 1-617 498 7200
e-mail: ADL.Information@adlittle.com
Web site: www.arthurdlittle.com

2 **How do you describe your activities as a consulting organization?**

Arthur D. Little is one of the world's premier consulting firms. Founded in 1886, it helps leading organizations create innovation across the full spectrum of their activities, from setting strategy and honing operations to developing cutting-edge products and technologies. The firm is distinguished from its competitors by the breadth and depth of its experience, by its technological know-how, and by its track record for successful implementation and the creation of lasting value.

3 **How many consultants did you employ throughout your organization as of September 30 1999?**

Consultants: 2030; non-consultants: 1155; total staff: 3185.

4 **What is your total annual fee income?**

Arthur D. Little's worldwide 1998 revenues were more than $600 million.

5 **What is your mission statement?**

Arthur D. Little's ambition is to become the leading consultant in helping client organizations create and implement strategic innovation for growth and exceptional financial performance. The emphasis is on innovation, and specifically on the process by which organizations achieve breakthrough outcomes across the full range of their business initiatives.

The value proposition underpinning this strategic ambition is based on two beliefs: that innovation is the fundamental source of growth, renewal, and reward, and that Arthur D. Little's spectrum of innovation capabilities – its integrated expertise in strategy, process improvement, change management, and technology and product development – can help clients establish a sustainable innovation premium, creating strong financial performance and accelerated growth.

6 **Please provide five examples of the kind of consulting work you undertake.**

Strategy and organization, process improvement, change management, technology and product development, e-commerce and e-transformation.

7 **What personal qualities do you believe a good consultant needs to have?**

Self-confidence/presence, team orientation, communication skills, collaboration skills, creativity, resilience, self-motivation, intellectual rigour, curiosity, cognitive abilities, integrity, candour, intellectual honesty.

8 **In your view, what is the secret to making your clients think you are wonderful?**

There is no great secret to it. The key is to have resourceful, innovative consultants who can understand and identify properly the real needs of the client, exploit opportunities and exceed their expectations.

9 What type of reports do your clients receive of the activity you have completed on their behalf?

We work very closely with our clients. We do not believe in the model of going away and coming back with an answer. As a result, our work is not done 'on their behalf'; the client is an integral part of any process. Our reports, developed with our clients, are a reflection of that relationship.

10 What are your most important methods of winning new business?

The best advertisement is a happy client. Our most important method of generating business is therefore continuing our relationships with our existing clients and forming new relationships with organizations to which our clients have recommended our services.

11 Most consultancies say they believe in team spirit. What do you do to encourage successful teamwork?

Arthur D. Little has a long tradition of effective teamwork. The firm invented the case team approach to client engagements, now used broadly across the consulting industry. In recruiting new employees, Arthur D. Little looks for willingness and ability to collaborate, among other capabilities. The fact that the ownership of the firm is widely distributed among its employees is also conducive to collaboration in general.

12 What procedures do you have for dealing with problems that your clients may experience with your service?

Arthur D. Little consultants work so closely with our clients, as true partners in addressing each client's challenges, that any problems tend to be clear to all parties and can be addressed immediately and resolved on the spot. We also have an extensive client feedback programme, through which we seek detailed information about the quality of our clients' experiences with us.

13 Do you believe in promoting your chief executive as a business guru?

Our CEO, Lorenzo Lamadrid, is a well-known business leader whose every minute is booked months in advance – he needs no promotional efforts from us.

14 What training do you provide for new recruits in the first year of their appointment?

Basic orientation happens at the local level; the formal professional development training for all new consultants includes nine days (issue analysis, structured communication, introduction to facilitation, interview skills, introduction to a particular industry, presentation skills, business ethics, and the ADL culture). This process continues each year throughout the consultant's career. Training is worldwide, and training groups are often carried out with colleagues from the Americas, Europe and Asia. This global training process encourages networking and the transfer of ideas.

Perhaps most important, new recruits learn prodigiously on the job, by being included immediately on case teams with seasoned colleagues.

15 Consulting work is notorious for the long hours it requires. Faced with this pressure, how do your consultants retain a sense of perspective?

We help our staff members maintain perspective by having coaches/managers who work closely with individuals, by respecting the need for work/family balance, and by maintaining an atmosphere of collegiality where people can let off steam. None of this is easy, and much depends on experienced staff staying close to their people and observing when stress is starting to reach risky levels.

16 What advice would you give to any young person (e.g. a graduate) thinking of working in consulting?

Consultants need to have drive and a desire to help people solve their problems. They need to be business-orientated and self-motivated. Working in a major consultancy offers any young person a platform to learn quickly business skills that will be invaluable to him or her throughout their career.

17 How do you think the consulting industry will change as a result of the Internet?

The Internet will have a big impact on consulting, as it is having on everything else. First of all, strategy firms, including Arthur D. Little, are starting to think like venture capitalists and looking at possibly taking financial positions in the start-up firms with which we consult. This raises some interesting questions about 'objectivity' but as long as everything is above board and visible, there should not be any major issues.

Second, in order to attract the right kind of recruits, the traditional firms are going to have to offer a number of benefits, such as the ability to invest in or to receive shares from various types of venture capital growth as well as income.

Third, the Internet is a domain in which clients are looking for 'full-service' solutions, where before they might separate strategy from implementation. The fastest-growing firms in Internet consulting are those that offer everything from strategy to implementation outsourcing. As a result, we anticipate a stream of mergers, consolidations and alliances as industry players attempt to find the right level of focus and the widest range of services.

Fourth, on the service delivery side, we are also bound to see consulting models such as pay-per-question, ask-the-expert models, and we are likely to see more and more consulting firms integrating the Internet into their service delivery and project management approaches.

Once the bandwidth is there, Internet-based presentations and Internet teleconferencing will become the norm for most consulting engagements – realizing many a consultant's dream of reaching out to the client without having to get on an aeroplane. In the end, however, the role of consultants is to move the client forward fast. The Internet cannot do that – only good consultants can.

18 How can consultants avoid getting a reputation for charging clients to tell them what they already know?

The only way to have a happy client is to deliver exceptional value by being innovative. While there is always untapped knowledge within the client itself, the skill in drawing it out, adding to it through research and analysis, and working with the client to create an innovative solution is highly valued.

19 Why do you think there is pressure on consultancies to merge with others?

Large companies are now global companies, requiring global solutions. E-commerce also reduces international boundaries for trade, increasing the number of competitors in a given market. As a result, consultancies need to have a global view and access to staff in many disciplines in different regions. Hence the pressure to merge, grow organically, or create alliances.

20 How do you think the consulting business ten years in the future will differ from the consulting business today?

The management consulting business in ten years will be essentially different from today in that the smart generalist will be supplanted by a type of individual that doesn't exist today – let's call that individual a 'knowledge engineer'. As all companies rationalize their business processes, little will be left on the 'productivity' side to differentiate one firm from another.

What will be a differentiating factor, however, will be the ability to innovate in areas such as product development, service delivery, and various sophisticated financial and organizational architectures that will involve complicated (but perhaps *ad hoc*) relationships among researchers, producers, suppliers, distributors, customers and financial institutions, all of whom may be aligned in some ways but competing in others. The whole definition of a corporation will change, and so the strategic approaches of the past will be irrelevant.

Another growth area for consultants will be 'knowledge valuation'. This will be a major concern of investors, who will be looking for increasingly sophisticated ways to differentiate one firm from another. We can call this the 'knowledge premium' or the 'innovation premium'. Right now it is a bit of a holy grail, but the savvy consultants of the future will be the ones who can really make it happen.

Finally, the next-generation consultant will be able to use technology to add content while at the same time reducing onerous travel requirements. Nothing can supplant the firm handshake and the confident look in the eye, but routine presentations and client meetings will most certainly jump on to the Net.

Caryl Varty.Co Limited

1 **Please state the full address of your head office, with telephone, fax and e-mail contact details.**

caryl varty.co Ltd
151 Holland Park Avenue
London W11 4UX
UK
Tel: +44 (0)20 7602 6160
Fax: +44 (0)20 7602 6120
e-mail: carylcvco@aol.com
Contact: Caryl Varty, managing director.

2 **How do you describe your activities as a consulting organization?**

caryl varty.co is an international strategy and marketing consultancy. Our approach is based on the belief that successful business strategies depend ultimately on clear identification and satisfaction of customer/client needs. We work for multinationals both in the UK and internationally, specializing in multi-country analysis. We cover most world markets via an extensive network of global associates, and have worked in more than 50 countries.

3 **How many consultants did you employ throughout your organization as of September 30 1999?**

We work with other independent leading consultancies as a flexible and expert network, whose composition and skill base is tailored to each specific consulting engagement.

4 What is your total annual fee income?

Respondent preferred not to reply.

5 What is your mission statement?

We don't have one. We work, act and live one: excellence and client delight in all that we do.

6 Please provide five examples of the kind of consulting work you undertake.

International market entry, brand positioning (single and multicountry), customer and stakeholder-driven strategy, corporate strategy (good corporate citizenship in non-Western environments, e.g. Islamic) and customer segmentation.

7 What personal qualities do you believe a good consultant needs to have?

Flexibility, ability to listen, quick learning, cross-cultural and client sensitivity, humility, lateral thinking, strategic thought, dedication, and willingness to work long, antisocial hours when required.

8 In your view, what is the secret to making your clients think you are wonderful?

Our total integrity, dedication and commitment to each client engagement. Our ability to listen to the client's needs rather than doing what we think the client ought to have. Our results. The fact that, as a network of individuals, our reputations stand or fall by our own performance alone and cannot shelter behind the protective facade of a large corporate structure.

9 What type of reports do your clients receive of the activity you have completed on their behalf?

Reports are tailored to the client's specific requirements. These vary from graphic presentation panels (either PowerPoint or acetate) to full-length, written reports, including executive summary, analytical content and appendices. Typically, clients prefer a formal, verbal presentation, with a follow-up hard or soft copy.

10 What are your most important methods of winning new business?

Repeat business, client referral, personal meetings, networking.

11 Most consultancies say they believe in team spirit. What do you do to encourage successful teamwork?

Choosing the right individuals is paramount: people who put the client and other team members first. Informality of working arrangements is important, encouraging the discussion of tentative and new ideas without the fear of their non-acceptance. Taking time off outside work is also important – if no more elaborate than a brief drink at the end of the evening.

12 What procedures do you have for dealing with problems that your clients may experience with your service?

We believe prevention is better than cure and we try to maintain constant dialogue and a philosophy of pre-presenting, so that the client is never surprised and is kept up to date with progress. The end result is therefore already partially accepted by the time of formal presentation, which should aim simply to formalize the findings of the engagement.

13 Do you believe in promoting your chief executive as a business guru?

Frankly, we think the business world is saturated with so-called business gurus and think their general credibility is marred by this surfeit. We believe the best means of attaining expertise and 'guru' status is through challenging and varied work with world-class clients on multifaceted (whether multicountry, multidiscipline) engagements.

14 What training do you provide for new recruits in the first year of their appointment?

None. We network with individuals who are experts in their own fields, so that we can bring to each client engagement the benefit of sector leaders. This is a different model to the traditional consultancy model of a highly qualified team leader fronting a less experienced team.

15 Consulting work is notorious for the long hours it requires. Faced with this pressure, how do your consultants retain a sense of perspective?

We emphasize the need to retain a healthy mental/physical balance and work time versus time for the self. While we encourage people to work long hours when necessary, we also encourage them to take some exercise each day, even if this is just walking outside the office. We also encourage stress-relieving 'celebration' on special occasions, such as project completion (which will not impact on quality of work the following day, but where the celebration both relieves stress and creates recognition of achievement). Finally, we expect people to be able to manage their own time so that for the most part sufficient time is allowed for personal life.

16 What advice would you give to any young person (e.g. a graduate) thinking of working in consulting.

Above all, get a reputable MBA, preferably one that offers a few months' secondment to a potential employee, which will give actual experience of the consulting environment. Second, have clear insight into your psychology and motivations to ensure you are the type of person suited to consulting – someone who is happy with uncertainty, change, new challenge, and the constant stress, as well as stimulus, of new ideas. You must combine an ability to be practical and provide excellent solutions which are not always academically purist but which are the best solutions possible, given the time-frame, resources and practicality of implementation.

17 How do you think the consulting industry will change as a result of the Internet?

'People-based' consulting businesses will become increasingly important, once the initial obsession and panic with Internet technology has become more rationally absorbed. The Internet will change the organization structure of companies and the whole competitive environment, enabling small companies to compete much more effectively alongside large ones, and in many instances making geography less important. Flexibility, the ability to change rapidly, to generate and respond to new ideas will be critical.

However, many of the core areas of strategy definition and corporate culture will continue to require the expertise of the best thinkers. Internet technology will give more opportunities, not least in providing an additional business channel, and technology will have to co-exist with other, broader, human disciplines.

18 How can consultants avoid getting a reputation for charging clients to tell them what they already know?

By proving in all that they do, throughout the consulting engagement, that they are adding value. By this we mean they should show superior skills in client handling, analysis, behaviour, and acting as ambassadors for the client. They also bring new knowledge from external and lateral engagements and industries.

19 Why do you think there is pressure on consultancies to merge with others?

To provide all consulting skills under the same umbrella via vertical and horizontal integration. This is being prompted by technology, where it is felt that technology skills must be absorbed within non-technology consultancies so that the two broad disciplines can combine to deliver technology-enabled consulting solutions. There is also pressure to merge globally, to provide physical consulting coverage of markets across the world, which the Internet brings within reach.

20 How do you think the consulting business ten years in the future will differ from the consulting business today?

Consulting companies will probably have to include or have strong relationships with external suppliers of technology know-how. There will be more and more specialist segmentation into niche consulting provision, such as specialist smart-card consultancies, alongside specialist executive coaching or organizational redesign consultancies. Consultants will be working much more flexibly from different sites, away from the corporate HQ, including home and the client site. There may be much greater movement of staff between companies, and in setting up their own Internet-based companies.

Cedar International

1 Please state the full address of your head office, with telephone, fax and e-mail contact details.

Cedar International
15 Bloomsbury Square
London
WC1A 2LJ
UK
Tel: +44 (0)20 7831 8383
Fax: +44 (0)20 7831 9571

2 How do you describe your activities as a consulting organization?

Broad-based HR consulting group.

3 How many consultants did you employ throughout your organization as of September 30 1999?

40 full-time, 37 part-time.

4 What is your total annual fee income?

Respondent preferred not to reply.

5 What is your mission statement?

Our strap line is 'Realizing Potential Through People'. Our philosophy is simple but effective. We aim to provide a high-quality, personal, cost-effective service, tailored individually to meet the needs of our clients. In so doing we hope to build long-term, mutually beneficial relationships which will enable both our clients' and our own business to develop and grow.

6 Please provide five examples of the kind of consulting work you undertake.

Management training and development, executive one-to-one coaching, career development (including outplacement and career management), strategy development and facilitation, executive recruitment.

7 What personal qualities do you believe a good consultant needs to have?

Credibility, style, charisma, energy, appropriate expertise, and the need to 'look the part' to give comfort and create trust.

8 In your view, what is the secret to making your clients think you are wonderful?

Doing what they want and more, and questioning them if the direction they want to take seems inappropriate.

9 What type of reports do your clients receive of the activity you have completed on their behalf?

Depends on the service area. In career transition, corporate clients receive written updates on the progress made by an individual outplacement client in their job search. This is in the form of a checklist but does not give specific feedback unless agreed with the individual first.

10 What are your most important methods of winning new business?

Client referral, networking, corporate hospitality events and relationship management.

11 Most consultancies say they believe in team spirit. What do you do to encourage successful teamwork?

Leading by example, frequent and honest communication, team-building events (social and business oriented), rewarding good performance as part of a team, and pairing up consultants with different abilities and experience.

12 What procedures do you have for dealing with problems that your clients may experience with your service?

Every assignment has a project director responsible for managing the overall client relationship and resolving issues pointed out by the project manager, who has day-to-day responsibility for smooth running. Any serious issues are taken to the board.

13 Do you believe in promoting your chief executive as a business guru?

Yes, through press articles, Bar Council, Institute of Directors, the speaker circuit at conferences, International Who's Who Directory.

14 **What training do you provide for new recruits in the first year of their appointment?**

Depends on the level and specific needs. Most consultants will do a two-day consulting skills course as a minimum.

15 **Consulting work is notorious for the long hours it requires. Faced with this pressure, how do your consultants retain a sense of perspective?**

We do not uphold a 'long hours' culture. It may be necessary sometimes to meet client demands, but it is the exception rather than the rule. Respect for the individual comes first.

16 **What advice would you give to any young person (e.g. a graduate) thinking of working in consulting?**

Make sure appropriate training will be given in consulting skills and business generally. Ensure secondments to clients feature in the process. Find yourself a personal coach.

17 **How do you think the consulting industry will change as a result of the Internet?**

It will become more of a commodity at one end of the spectrum but t here will still be a need for 'personal support' in areas that involve HR issues.

18 **How can consultants avoid getting a reputation for charging clients to tell them what they already know?**

By delivering value.

19 **Why do you think there is pressure on consultancies to merge with others?**

To support global clients and achieve economies of scale.

20 **How do you think the consulting business ten years in the future will differ from the consulting business today?**

Recurring issues will be the subject of online or interactive advice. One-to-one, face-to-face support will still be required for more complex projects. Expert knowledge and coaching skills will be key.

Charteris Limited

1 **Please state the full address of your head office, with telephone, fax and e-mail contact details.**

Charteris Limited
6 Kinghorn Street
London
EC1A 7HW
UK
Tel: +44 (0)20 7600 9199
Fax: +44 (0)20 7600 9212
e-mail: aw@charteris.com

2 How do you describe your activities as a consulting organization?

Charteris helps clients improve business performance and create business opportunities through the effective use of information technology. Charteris consultants offer a rare blend of business acumen, vision, and flair for technology. We act both as advisers to business and as programme and line managers. This maintains an important balance in our services, ensuring realism and a currency of knowledge that can only come from first-hand experience.

3 How many consultants did you employ throughout your organization as of September 30 1999?

There are 33 Charteris consultants at this date.

4 What is your total annual fee income?

Currently our only income is fee income and this amounts to approximately £5m per annum.

5 What is your mission statement?

Charteris provides the essential bridge between business strategy and information technology. Our key objective is to provide our clients with teams and individuals who are second to none.

6 Please provide five examples of the kind of consulting work you undertake.

Examples are:

- assisting clients to maximize the business benefit offered by e-business through formulation of realistic business strategy and information technology architectures;
- specification of business processes and systems to underpin corporate change;
- structuring the relationship between a business and its Internet service providers;
- configuration and operation of IT product and services businesses;

○ programme management of large undertakings where IT is an essential element.

7 What personal qualities do you believe a good consultant needs to have?

Charteris consultants are individuals selected on the basis of proven delivery. All members of Charteris work directly with our clients and they are focused on the success of clients' projects and on clients achieving their business objectives.

8 In your view, what is the secret to making your clients think you are wonderful?

You put forward the actual team who will undertake the assignments and you deliver what you promise. You must ensure that consultants are customer focused and that they have as their primary objective the achievement of the client's business objectives.

9 What type of reports do your clients receive of the activity you have completed on their behalf?

This varies widely between clients and is always agreed with the client at the start of each assignment. In essence, Charteris will provide as much reporting and in whatever form a client requires in order to give the client confidence in the work that Charteris is undertaking, and to reinforce the value for money that Charteris's professional fees represents.

10 What are your most important methods of winning new business?

To date our most important source of winning new business has been client referrals.

11 Most consultancies say they believe in team spirit. What do you do to encourage successful teamwork?

Charteris continues to review and invest in the infrastructure necessary to enable all members to communicate and share knowledge when working in a distributed fashion. Not surprisingly, this is heavily based on the use of IT as we seek to practise what we preach.

The Charteris team meet as a whole at least once a month to exchange experiences and to share knowledge. All members of Charteris are encouraged to attend the team meetings. In addition, the managing director sends a single report to all members of Charteris each month highlighting achievements and issues – this is timed to allow discussion of the contents of the report at each team meeting. Within specific practices there are regular meetings, e.g. the Charteris e-team meetings. At these more focused meetings, lead consultants and the business development team talk about how existing customers can be better serviced and how we might develop our services to attract new clients.

12 What procedures do you have for dealing with problems that your clients may experience with your service?

Charteris has an escalation procedure but this has never been used. Due to the seniority of the consultants that constitute the Charteris team, we expect these consultants to do all that they can to handle any concerns that the client may express. Charteris consultants take regular soundings from clients to ensure that no such concerns remain hidden until they become so large that they cannot be handled by the consultant undertaking the assignment.

In the unlikely event that Charteris ever does experience a complaint which the consultant in question cannot handle, this would be referred to one of the directors of Charteris. For every assignment a director is always assigned from the point at which Charteris makes an offer to undertake that assignment, thus providing continuity should his/her involvement ever be necessary.

13 Do you believe in promoting your chief executive as a business guru?

Charteris promotes a number of its consultants as experts in their chosen field. We do not believe in the cult of the individual as it takes a wide range of expertise to offer the services required by our clients. Consequently the chief executive is seen as no more expert than many of the other senior members of Charteris.

14 What training do you provide for new recruits in the first year of their appointment?

Charteris consultants are invited to join only if they have at least ten years of practical experience. Hence we do not have any specific professional training that recruits need to undertake. We do have a programme of familiarization where the individuals who join meet with and discuss the professional backgrounds of the other consultants in Charteris. The reverse is also true, particularly with the business development team who spend a significant amount of time understanding the exact nature of the skills that the new recruit brings to Charteris. In this way Charteris can always be sure of promising skills and experience it knows it can deliver.

15 Consulting work is notorious for the long hours it requires. Faced with this pressure, how do your consultants retain a sense of perspective?

Charteris actively encourages consultants to structure their time so that they can undertake personal development and pursue their professional interests.

Charteris supports this in a variety of ways. We also ask that consultants share any problems they may be experiencing within assignments with others in Charteris so that we can achieve a win-win for our clients and our consultants: we never want a consultant to feel that they are 'out of sight out of mind'.

16 What advice would you give to any young person (e.g. a graduate) thinking of working in consulting?

Ensure the culture of the consultancy you are joining matches your own. Gain good hands-on experience as there are too many consultancies that provide clients with staff who are effectively learning at the expense of clients. This is a situation with which clients rapidly tire and this will only add to the pressure a young person may feel. Clients want consultants who can deliver real business benefits. Consultants must expect to travel and work long hours as the jobs they inevitably undertake for their clients require objectives to be met under challenging circumstances – if it were easy, clients would not need to hire specialist experience.

17 How do you think the consulting industry will change as a result of the Internet?

We all know the Internet is changing the business landscape. In such turbulent times clients need assistance with a variety of challenges associated with managing such change. However, what clients seek more than anything else is vision combined with the elusive blend of business focus but technical understanding in order to identify ways in which the client can derive competitive advantage from the new technology.

Consultants will need to provide this essential bridge between business and technology or they will be seen as incapable of adding value. We believe the Internet will be a key factor in the business strategy of the vast majority of business from now on and so all business-focused consultancies will need to be able to add value in this new environment.

18 How can consultants avoid getting a reputation for charging clients to tell them what they already know?

You must bring skills and experience that the client does not possess. Delivering innovative business solutions that could only derive from a good understanding of business strategy and information technology is what will differentiate the good consultant from the merely competent. Charteris consultants have a further advantage in that they can point to actual experience. This comes from only recruiting senior individuals who are prominent in their field.

19 Why do you think there is pressure on consultancies to merge with others?

Charteris feels no such pressure. We believe we can differentiate ourselves on the quality of the work that we deliver and also our willingness to undertake assignments of any size. This is borne out by the way in which our client referrals have allowed us to grow. Where such quality or willingness does not exist, many consultancies seek to differentiate themselves by the sheer size of the teams they can field. However, this has the side effect that these consultancies seek only to undertake the larger assignments and that they further dilute the quality of what they can deliver.

20 How do you think the consulting business ten years in the future will differ from the consulting business today?

Clients are becoming more discriminating about how they hire consultants. In the future there will be far more pressure to show value for money. Charteris believes that clients will want to engage consultants who can show tangible experience where that experience is more than being just an adviser – we believe it will be essential to demonstrate a continued involvement in hands-on roles. In ten years one of the single most important business enablers will be the effective use of information technology, particularly the new electronic channels such as the Internet. Hence, any business consultancy that is to thrive must be active in e-business: in ten years, e-business will be business as usual.

Deloitte Consulting

1 Please state the full address of your head office, with telephone, fax and e-mail contact details.

Deloitte Consulting
Two World Financial Center
New York
NY 10281 -1414
US
Tel: 1-212 436 2000
Fax: 1-212 436 5000

2 How do you describe your activities as a consulting organization?

One of the world's top management consulting firms providing services to transform entire enterprises, from strategy, process, information technology and people. We help our clients to change, designing and implementing practical solutions that produce real, sustainable results. Already active around the globe we keep growing by increasing our penetration into key markets and developing our business internationally.

3 How many consultants did you employ throughout your organization as of September 30 1999?

Total headcount for Deloitte Consulting in 1998 was 19 560.

4 What is your total annual fee income?

Year ending September 30 1998 Deloitte Consulting had global revenues of $3.24 billion.

5 What is your mission statement?

To help our clients and our people excel. To be consistently recognized as one of the world's top three consulting firms by the year 2003.

6 Please provide examples of the kind of consulting work you undertake.

Deloitte Consulting delivers more than 20 service lines focused on people, process, strategy and technology. Some key areas of focus include:

- e-business: CRM, supply chain, outsourcing;
- change leadership;
- systems integration;
- enterprise resource.

7 What personal qualities do you believe a good consultant needs to have?

The ability to work in a team, analyze and solve business problems, listen and communicate effectively. We want people with self-confidence, initiative and flexibility.

8 In your view, what is the secret to making your clients think you are wonderful?

Our clients recognize our very different approach that delivers very different results. They choose us because our teams comprise people they can work with, people who are dedicated to achieving superior results. We have a collaborative working style and work in partnership with our clients.

9 What type of reports do your clients receive of the activity you have completed on their behalf?

Respondent preferred not to reply.

10 What are your most important methods of winning new business?

Client referrals.

11 Most consultancies say they believe in team spirit. What do you do to encourage successful teamwork?

A genuine enthusiasm for collaboration results in a collegiate spirit that encourages co-operation and teamwork. This is aided by a flat management structure in which we have developed the concept of inspired leaders.

12 What procedures do you have for dealing with problems that your clients may experience with your service?

Respondent preferred not to reply.

13 Do you believe in promoting your chief executive as a business guru?

Deloitte Consulting is proactive in its approach to the media and actively encourages comment where applicable. Our chief executive, Pat Loconco, and the Deloitte Consulting partners worldwide are regularly asked by clients and the media alike to offer industry and management expertise.

14 What training do you provide for new recruits in the first year of their appointment?

There are two structured training programmes for new graduate recruits in their first year at Deloitte Consulting. Which programme a recruit will enter is dependent on his/her competency. As a new business analyst, the recruit will complete a week's training in the US, gaining general consulting skills. This is followed by two weeks training in London learning about Deloitte Consulting and what to expect in his/her first year of work. While training in London he/she will also be taught pertinent computer skills. If he/she is joining Deloitte Consulting as a systems analyst, he/she will spend a week in London in a common programme with business analysts, followed by a week in the US dedicated to systems analysts, and will subsequently attend a technical 'boot camp' gaining specific IT training for Oracle/Peoplesoft skills, or client server skills or networking skills.

Both sets of analysts receive additional training throughout the year in skills such as business awareness, effective writing and presentation. On-the-job training complements any structured technical training they receive; this is dependent on the needs of the analyst and the project the new recruit is working on.

If a person joins Deloitte Consulting at the level of consultant or above, they attend a two-week training course called the 'Deloitte Difference'. Generally, new consultants will attend this programme 3–6 months after joining. In the first week they will be educated in generic consulting skills with a distinctive Deloitte flavour. In the second week they will learn specific technical skills dependent on their area of focus.

15 Consulting work is notorious for the long hours it requires. Faced with this pressure, how do your consultants retain a sense of perspective?

The hours an individual works will greatly depend on the project that he/she is working on and the stage the project has reached. Consultants plan their career objectives at the onset of a project. These are met through training and client engagement appointments. In this way Deloitte ensures that its consultants are constantly learning and developing new skills. Deloitte Consulting is aware that consultants may need to reduce their workload during certain stages of their career; the provision of FWA (flexible work arrangements) helps facilitate this need.

The variety of work and the changing nature of consulting ensure a challenging and stimulating working environment. Deloitte Consulting rewards its people both financially and socially for their continuous hard work. This is reflected by the fact that Deloitte Consulting was number eight in the 1999 list of the 100 best companies to work for in America published by *Fortune* magazine.

16 What advice would you give to any young person (e.g. a graduate) thinking of working in consulting?

Consulting offers a solid career path for the recent graduate. With Deloitte Consulting, employees work in a challenging and varied environment that thrives on your individuality, rather than one which stifles it. Early responsibility and the constant diversity of work ensure an interesting and rewarding job. Each project offers employees the opportunity to work with different people with a variety of transferable skills. The opportunity to travel and to work within multi-cultured project teams provides a unique insight into how a consultancy operates on a global scale. By providing career planning, mentoring and counselling for all its practitioners, Deloitte Consulting helps people to become better professionals.

17 How do you think the consulting industry will change as a result of the Internet?

The Internet is changing the economy, thus the consulting industry will no doubt be impacted. We already see significant changes in the services that clients are demanding as well as the speed with which projects must be implemented. Consulting services are becoming more varied, with an increased demand for e-business, CRM (customer relationship management), supply chain and outsourcing services. We are also seeing new entrants into the consulting industry, with traditional software and hardware firms entering the market. The future is unpredictable, but adaptability and change will be necessary to continue growth in the industry.

18 How can consultants avoid getting a reputation for charging clients to tell them what they already know?

Deloitte Consultancy provides its clients with specific knowledge, which is outside the traditional realm of the client's expertise. By working with consultants the client is guaranteed to learn of the latest technology and industry advances ahead of his competitors. By working in mixed project teams of both client and consultants, it is possible to avoid this negative reputation by providing a balance of knowledge.

19 Why do you think there is pressure on consultancies to merge with others?

The consulting industry is very competitive. Large multinational consultancies are taking over the industry by virtue of their size and scope.

20 How do you think the consulting business ten years in the future will differ from the consulting business today?

The consulting business will definitely be different in ten years from today. However, with the pace of change it is not possible to predict what it will look like in the year 2010. Change is so rapid that the future is unpredictable.

Enterprise Technology Corporation

1 Please state the full address of your head office, with telephone, fax and e-mail contact details.

305 Madison Avenue
Suite 2130
New York
NY 10165
US
Tel: 1-212 972 1860
Fax: 1-212 687 6126
e-mail address for Joseph Rosen, managing director: jrosen@etcny.com
Website: www.etcny.com

2 How do you describe your activities as a consulting organization?

ETC provides technology strategy and implementation services to the investment community.

3 How many consultants did you employ throughout your organization as of September 30 1999?

50 consultants.

4 What is your total annual fee income?

Respondent preferred not to reply.

5 What is your mission statement?

To help our clients attain a higher level of achievement in the application of technology as a strategic tool.

6 Please provide five examples of the kind of consulting work you undertake.

○ *Senior management advisory.* A mid-sized broker was concerned about the pace of change in the industry, particularly in the area of technology and alternative trading systems. The client wanted to know where they stood *vis à vis* the evolving competitive landscape. Working directly with the CEO, ETC researched and delivered a presentation to the board that articulated our vision of the trading mechanisms and securities and investments industry of the future. We recommended a number of specific actions to the client that would enhance their competitive position going forward.

○ *Strategic technology audit and planning.* Executive management of the client, a well-regarded, international equities market maker, was concerned over how well its technology capabilities measured up to the 'state of the art' on Wall Street. ETC was asked to review all business areas of the firm, with particular focus on the front office, and to recommend where the most cost-effective and competitively advantageous improvements should be made. As part of this engagement we surveyed the state of the vendor marketplace for sell-side equity trading systems.

○ *Vendor evaluation/due diligence.* The client, a leading third-market broker/dealer, had contracted to purchase a major new equities trading and order routing software system. In its contract, the client had 90 days in which to cancel the contract. ETC was engaged to conduct a technical review and evaluation of the product, as well as due diligence on the vendor firm. The study concluded that the product was inferior, the vendor could not adequately support it, and the client avoided what undoubtedly would have been a million-dollar mistake. ETC subsequently assisted the client in locating a more suitable software package.

○ *Custom software development for the 'sell side' (broker/dealers).* The client, a leading agency-only brokerage firm specializing in commission recapture and third-party research services, wanted to distinguish itself by providing outstanding client service and reporting. At the time, however, the firm's revenue and cost accounting system was a 15-year-old application running on an obsolete minicomputer at a service bureau. Each month, literally truckloads of paper were delivered to the client, and it took 30 days to get statements mailed to clients. ETC analyzed the firm's information and processing requirements, and developed a requirements document which included a comprehensive set of recommendations as to hardware and software platform, software development and software package purchases.

ETC subsequently conducted a highly successful project to implement all of the recommendations, including substantial development of customized software. As a result, the brokerage firm now completes its client statements on the third business day of the month, and every employee in the firm has instant online access to all of the information needed to provide superior client service. Within one month of the system becoming operational, the firm's clients were remarking on the obvious improvements in the service level.

○ *Software development for the 'buy side' (investment advisers/money managers).* ETC developed an integrated, multi-currency online trading, portfolio management and securities accounting system for the money-management subsidiary of one of the US's largest life insurance companies. This system includes separate online trading subsystems for equities, fixed-income and short-term (money market) traders, plus a portfolio manager's online subsystem. It includes complete investment accounting functions to support mutual funds, pooled funds, and separate accounts, as well as specialized insurance company investment accounting and statutory reporting.

7 What personal qualities do you believe a good consultant needs to have?

Integrity, intelligence, curiosity, and to be an excellent communicator and a team player.

8 In your view, what is the secret to making your clients think you are wonderful?

Put their interests above all else; have a long-term perspective; think 'out of the box' for them. For advisory projects we clearly articulate both in narrative and graphically what our recommendations are, and why. Equally important, rather than being like 'Moses coming down from the mountain' telling them what they should do, we always include in our reports a presentation of the most feasible set of alternatives together with our view of the relative trade-offs. This way the client can truly understood where we are coming from with our recommendation and then decide for themselves with the information we have provided.

For software development projects our deliverables – in addition to the functioning system we have developed and deployed – include the following set of 'documents': user manual, online context sensitive help, operations manual, programmer's guide, and database administrator's manual.

9 What type of reports do your clients receive of the activity you have completed on their behalf?

For all projects we provide the client with periodic status reports on an agreed basis. Likewise, as necessary we supplement our final written report with a formal presentation.

10 What are your most important methods of winning new business?

Client referrals are key, as most of our new business results from prospective clients calling us directly.

11 Most consultancies say they believe in team spirit. What do you do to encourage successful teamwork?

We start by ensuring that the client sees the project as a team effort and that they dedicate the appropriate resources from their end. We further facilitate this by insisting on joint participation wherever possible. Internally, we foster teamwork by hiring only those candidates that will fit in with our team-oriented corporate culture, and avoiding 'prima donnas' like the plague.

12 What procedures do you have for dealing with problems that your clients may experience with your service?

We start with the philosophy that the client is always right, and assure them that whatever is troubling them will be fixed to their satisfaction, no ifs or buts. Then we simply do whatever is necessary to make them happy.

13 Do you believe in promoting your chief executive as a business guru?

Yes, especially since he is. Our chief executive, Kevin I. Merz, publishes books and articles and speaks widely at industry conferences.

14 **What training do you provide for new recruits in the first year of their appointment?**

The most important training is on the job. New recruits are carefully teamed with heavily experienced staff in our variant of the 'master-apprentice' relationship. In our view there is just no substitute for experience, and it is critical that we enable our new talent to benefit from the 15+ years' average experience of ETC's professional staff. On-the-job training is, of course, supplemented as necessary by formal training programmes. We also have periodic in-house seminars that deal with both technical and business topics.

15 **Consulting work is notorious for the long hours it requires. Faced with this pressure, how do your consultants retain a sense of perspective?**

We actively recruit – and have been fortunate enough to attract and retain – people for whom doing an excellent job is a must. While we do pay our people very well, it is more than money that motivates our professionals but also a strong need to achieve.

16 **What advice would you give to any young person (e.g. a graduate) thinking of working in consulting?**

Get some industry experience under your belt first so you really have something to offer clients in addition to what you may have learned in school.

17 **How do you think the consulting industry will change as a result of the Internet?**

Clients may not need to spend as much time informally picking the brains of consultants because many of their questions may be easily answered through searching the web. Consultants will therefore need to be more creative in 'exhibiting' their industry knowledge and expertise to prospective clients. The Internet may also be a distribution channel for certain types of short-term engagements.

18 **How can consultants avoid getting a reputation for charging clients to tell them what they already know?**

The simple answer is to be able to provide a wider perspective than is possible from inside one single organization. Again, there is no substitute for experience.

19 **Why do you think there is pressure on consultancies to merge with others?**

Partly to serve some recruiting needs 'en masse'. Partly to supposedly achieve 'economies of scale'. One of the problems here is that if you are too big, then by definition quality will suffer since there are only so many 'top' consultants who typically cannot be hired by the thousands. In other words, this is the justification and *raison d'être* for focused boutiques.

20 How do you think the consulting business ten years in the future will differ from the consulting business today?

There will be more of an insistence on the part of clients that consultants not only be smart but also have more experience.

IBM

1 Please state the full address of your head office, with telephone, fax and e-mail contact details.

IBM Global Services
Somers
New York
10589
USA
Tel: 1-914 766 1900 (USA – information)
Fax: Please call the above telephone number to help locate the specific fax number required and obtain a direct response to your query.
e-mail: Please call the above phone number to help you locate the specific e-mail address required and obtain a direct response to your query.
Alternatively, you can contact us directly through the World Wide Web at www.ibm.com/services using the 'contact' facility.

2 How do you describe your activities as a consulting organization?

IBM Global Services is the largest information technology services company in the world and is poised to help customers use networks and the Internet to do e-business. It has 138 000 skilled professionals, consultants, project managers, architects and IT specialists in more than 160 countries. We have organized our business on a portfolio basis. The portfolio comprises Business Innovation Services, Integrated Technology Services, Strategic Outsourcing and Learning Services.

IBM Global Services Portfolio

o   Business Innovation Services
    Business Innovation Services (BIS) provides business/industry consulting thought leadership and end-to-end e-business integration of offerings like Supply Chain Management, Enterprise Resource Planning, Businesss Intelligence, Customer Relationship Management and many others. BIS

provides strong support to clients who need to address questions of the type 'what should I do?'

○ Integrated Technology Services
Integrated Technology Services (ITS) offers customers a single IT partner to manage multi-vendor IT systems complexity in today's e-business environment.

ITS creates unified value propositions that address customers' key needs for the design, deployment, testing and reliable operations of e-business environments. Our primary initiatives focus on e-business enablement, IT consolidation and optimization and continuous operations services. ITS helps clients to address questions of the type 'how should I implement?'

○ Strategic Outsourcing Services
Strategic Outsourcing Services creates business value through long-term strategic partnerships with our customers by taking on responsibility for their processes and systems.

○ Learning Services
Learning Services, which supports the three primary lines of business, helps customers design, develop and deploy curricula to educate their employees.

3 How many consultants did you employ throughout your organization as of September 30 1999?
On a global basis, we have around 138 000 professionals, operating in 160 countries.

4 What is your total annual fee income?
Our revenue in 1998 was around US$29 billion.

5 What is your mission statement?
Global Consulting Competency – Vision

We accelerate the competitive performance of our customers globally by being their preferred business and technology consulting partner and by leveraging the full power of IBM. We have a vested interest in the success of our customers.

Global Consulting Competency – Mission

Key Market:
We serve enterprises interested in using technology to change their business. We:

o identify new business/technology environment and the inherent opportunities

o align processes to technology using world's best knowledge-based assets and qualified experts.

o stay with customers through implementation

o team with customers to provide lasting value.

6 Please provide examples of the kind of consulting work you undertake.

We provide a full range of consulting and services capabilities. These vary from the formulation of an e-strategy to the implementation and programme management of highly complex systems, processes and organizational structures.

7 What personal qualities do you believe a good consultant needs to have?

Gravitas, technical competence, the ability to form client relationships at a high level, leadership, team membership, selling skills.

8 In your view, what is the secret to making your clients think you are wonderful?

Quote from the general manager, IBM Global Services Consulting Group, worldwide: 'Today, as companies ponder the transition to e-business, they are increasingly looking for a single-source provider of business, IT and systems consulting. In the e-business market, business and IT strategy are too intertwined, and the competitive pace too fast, to parcel out the job to multiple vendors. When clients go looking for that one trusted partner, they are looking for someone with a full-service, end-to-end capability. IBM has got to be top of the mind when business executives go looking for consulting expertise. That's where size works to our advantage.'

9 What type of reports do your clients receive of the activity you have completed on their behalf?

Final reports are tailored to the client's specific issues and desires. However, a typical e-commerce engagement report might cover some of the following topic areas:

o executive summary which highlights key findings, recommendations and investment requirements;

o background – a restatement of the client's key issues related to e-commerce and why the IBM Consulting Group was engaged;

o project objectives reset the engagement objectives;

○ project approach describes the unique approach that was used to study the client's specific e-commerce-related issues;

○ key findings and conclusions detail key findings, recommendations and investment requirements;

○ recommendations and benefits give precise, actionable, client-specific insights and recommendations relative to e-commerce, and also highlight benefits to the client of taking specific courses of action;

○ funding requirements – the suggested investment required to act on our recommendations;

○ describe in detail the recommended next steps and recommended approaches the client should consider.

10 What are your most important methods of winning new business?

We use all relevant methods (traditional and new) ranging from public speaking to television advertising, building on IBM's already excellent client relationships.

11 Most consultancies say they believe in team spirit. What do you do to encourage successful teamwork?

IBM has three key measures that apply to all employees, including our CEO, Lou Gerstner. They are: Commitment to Win, Execute, and Team. Our engagements invariably include people from other parts of IBM and often from other geographies. The ability to pull successful teams together is one of our competitive advantages. We also organize regular events designed so that the consulting team can get together, interact, and build team spirit.

We are a true 'e' business, and all employees have access to, and when appropriate contribute to, our comprehensive intranet environment. This includes Intellectual Capital Management (ICM) Asset Web which is IBM's knowledge and asset management collaboration system that supports the sharing of intellectual capital between consultants.

12 What procedures do you have for dealing with problems that your clients may experience with your service?

Capturing and resolving client issues is critical to us, not only to ensure that we continue to improve our processes and services, but also to ensure that we maximize our opportunities for follow-on business. If an issue arises during one of our consulting engagements, it is resolved rapidly, with appropriate management intervention, as necessary. Fortunately we find such issues are a rare occurrence.

13 Do you believe in promoting your chief executive as a business guru?

We are in the privileged position of not having to do so. Our chief executive is a business guru, and more. Lou Gerstner is business leader of one of the world's largest companies.

14 What training do you provide for new recruits in the first year of their appointment?

All newcomers to consulting within IBM, whether external recruits or internal transfers, are required to attend core competence courses within their first months of joining IBM. The courses are held at our dedicated education centres in La Hulpe, Belgium, or Palisades in the US.

15 Consulting work is notorious for the long hours it requires. Faced with this pressure, how do your consultants retain a sense of perspective?

IBM, as a company, cares a great deal about its employees. Full support mechanisms are available to any one of us who needs help with the work/life balance. We constantly reward our consultants in different ways, as we acknowledge the fact that they spend many hours/days away from home.

16 What advice would you give to any young person (e.g. a graduate) thinking of working in consulting?

The role of a consultant is a demanding one. However, we would advise any graduate with good analytical skills, the ability to solve problems, communicate, work both individually and in a team, and help people to understand how to implement changes identified, to apply for a role in consulting. While the demands are high, the rewards – for the consultant who puts into practice all the knowledge he/she acquires as a member of the IBM consulting team – are manifold.

17 How do you think the consulting industry will change as a result of the Internet?

We believe the change needed within the consulting industry to face the challenge of the Internet should have already taken place. For IBM, the Internet and the 'e' environment are becoming business as usual. It is how IBM manages its own business. A major section of www.ibm.com is devoted to the services IBM delivers, including consulting. All of which enables IBM's consultants to practise what they preach, so our clients truly experience knowledge and expertise relevant to their business issues and opportunities.

18 How can consultants avoid getting a reputation for charging clients to tell them what they already know?

By giving an impartial view and not telling clients what they already know. A consultant's role should be advisory, and as such they will apply all their expertise from previous engagements and give advice based on this knowledge. We have the added advantage in IBM of being able to fully implement any of our recommendations.

19 Why do you think there is pressure on consultancies to merge with others?

Some small consultancies may feel threatened by larger competitors, larger not only in size but also in products/capabilities. The demand for integrated consulting services has touched off some fast footwork in the marketplace, as many of the leading players hustle to line up partnerships or acquisitions that will enable them to provide a broader array of capabilities.

IBM Consulting is a global organization with the ability to mobilize a large team, quickly across borders anywhere in the world with an end-to-end capability and offering seamless integration with other IBM offerings. We do, of course, review opportunities to add even greater value to our client proposition.

20 How do you think the consulting business ten years in the future will differ from the consulting business today?

The following is a quote from the general manager, IBM Global Services Consulting Group, worldwide. 'In the consulting industry, as in most industries, e-business has changed the dynamics of competition. Before, a company might engage a management consulting firm to devise business strategy, an IT consulting firm to develop systems and architectures, and a systems integrator to handle integration and application development. While competitive dynamics may vary from one industry to another, e-business raises a set of challenges that virtually every business is facing – whether to sell direct to customers; how to deploy technology to integrate supply chains, enter new markets and leverage intellectual capital; ensuring security and privacy in electronic commerce. These are among the strategic issues that IBM's consultants are helping clients address. If it's driving the e-economy, it's driving consulting.'

PricewaterhouseCoopers

1 Please state the full address of your head office, with telephone, fax and e-mail contact details.

1 Embankment Place
London
WC2 6NN
UK
Tel. +44 (0)20 7583 5000
Fax: +44 (0)20 7822 4652
Web site: www.pwcglobal.com

2 How do you describe your activities as a consulting organization?

PricewaterhouseCoopers has over 46 500 consultants worldwide with a presence in all major cities across six continents. A global management team and organizational structure ensure that companies receive a quick response and consistent service, regardless of geography. With a worldwide pool of talent and resources, PricewaterhouseCoopers brings together the right mix of skills, experience, industry knowledge and cultural background to meet a company's specific needs and to manage large projects. Pricewaterhouse-Coopers integrates its service offerings to provide maximum value to companies in helping them meet their business objectives.

3 How many consultants did you employ throughout your organization as of September 30 1999?

In the UK, 2850 consultants (189 partners); across EMEA (Europe, Middle East and Africa), 10 180 – 9708 client-facing consultants and 474 partners.

4 What is your total annual fee income?

UK – £604 million. EMEA – $2.1 billion. Revenues at June 30 1999.

5 What is your mission statement?

Answered above.

6 Please provide examples of the kind of consulting work you undertake.

○ Strategic change:
business strategy
organizational strategy
operations strategy
information technology strategy
change strategy.

    ○ Process improvement:
      market and customer management (MCM)
      supply chain management (SCM)
      financial and cost management (FCM)
      human resources management (HRM)
      IT operations management (ITM)
      industry-specific process improvement.
    ○ Technology solutions:
      enterprise resource planning systems (ERP)
      systems integration (SI).

7 What personal qualities do you believe a good consultant needs to have?

Respondent preferred not to reply.

8 In your view, what is the secret to making your clients think you are wonderful?

Respondent preferred not to reply.

9 What type of reports do your clients receive of the activity you have completed on their behalf?

Respondent preferred not to reply.

10 What are your most important methods of winning new business?

Respondent preferred not to reply.

11 Most consultancies say they believe in team spirit. What do you do to encourage successful teamwork?

Respondent preferred not to reply.

12 What procedures do you have for dealing with problems that your clients may experience with your service?

Respondent preferred not to reply.

13 Do you believe in promoting your chief executive as a business guru?

Yes, via PR activity, conference speaking and other marketing/ communications activities.

14 What training do you provide for new recruits in the first year of their appointment?

We have an extremely detailed and rigorous training programme.

15 **Consulting work is notorious for the long hours it requires. Faced with this pressure, how do your consultants retain a sense of perspective?**

Pressures on lifestyle are an issue and we are examining ways of changing the way we work. We have a well-established training programme running for our senior people and our induction courses now include modules on survival. A further course has been designed and piloted for consultants and is being rolled out this year. The purpose of all these courses is to help our people understand how a combination of work patterns, responses to pressure, diet and exercise can affect them and what to do to safeguard their state of health and sense of well-being.

16 **What advice would you give to any young person (e.g. a graduate) thinking of working in consulting?**
Respondent preferred not to reply.

17 **How do you think the consulting industry will change as a result of the Internet?**

Respondent preferred not to reply.

18 **How can consultants avoid getting a reputation for charging clients to tell them what they already know?**

Respondent preferred not to reply.

19 **Why do you think there is pressure on consultancies to merge with others?**

Respondent preferred not to reply.

20 **How do you think the consulting business ten years in the future will differ from the consulting business today?**

Respondent preferred not to reply.

Shreeveport Management Consultancy

1 **Please state the full address of your head office, with telephone, fax and e-mail contact details.**

Shreeveport Management Consultancy
Crystal Gate
28–30 Worship Street
London
EC2A 2AH
UK
Tel: +44 (0)20 7588 8877

Fax: +44 (0)20 7256 6256

e-mail: admin@shreeveport.com

Web site: www.shreeveport.com

2 How do you describe your activities as a consulting organization?

Shreeveport's activities can best be described as strategies for growth that ensure long-term sustainable benefit, which we work with our clients to implement.

3 How many consultants did you employ throughout your organization as of August 31 1999?

25 full-time practising consultants.

4 What is your total annual fee income?

We do not disclose this.

5 What is your mission statement?

To create intelligent solutions and build structured skills transfer into every assignment so that the benefit from our input is assured and sustained. Every project is a reference.

6 Please provide five examples of the kind of consulting work you undertake.

- ❍ Transformation – business process re-engineering (including e-commerce)
- ❍ Process re-design, including e-solutions
- ❍ Strategic sourcing
- ❍ IS/IT strategy
- ❍ Public private partnerships/PFI.

7 What personal qualities do you believe a good consultant needs to have?

Enthusiasm and intellectual capacity, ability to question assumptions, pragmatic and practical approach, strong analytical skills coupled with good interpersonal skills.

8 In your view, what is the secret to making your clients think you are wonderful?

By making our clients' goals our goals. We tell our clients what we are going to deliver, then we make sure we deliver beyond their expectations. We actively involve clients in our work by facilitating strategy sessions and leading the hands-on work, from data analysis to change implementation. In this way we become a part of each client organization. Furthermore, we are